This Gift of Water

This Gift of Water

The Practice and Theology of Baptism Among Methodists in America

Gayle Carlton Felton

ABINGDON PRESS
Nashville

THIS GIFT OF WATER:
THE PRACTICE AND THEOLOGY OF BAPTISM
AMONG METHODISTS IN AMERICA

Library of Congress Cataloging-in-Publication Data

Felton, Gayle Carlton, 1942 –
This gift of water: the practice and theology of baptism among Methodists in America. / Gayle Carlton Felton.
p. cm.
Includes bibliographical references and index.
1. Baptism–Methodist Church–History. 2. Baptism–History–18th century. 3. Baptism–History–19th century. 4. Baptism–History–20th century. 5. Baptism–United Methodist Church (U.S.)–History 6. Methodist Church–United States–Doctrines–History. 7. United Methodist Church(U.S.)–Doctrines–History. I. Title.
BX8338.F45 1992 92-28386
234'.161–dc20 CIP

ISBN 0-687-33327-X

Printed in the United States of America on recycled, acid-free paper

To my mother, Kittye Phillips Carlton
and
my father, Lewis Daniel Carlton

CONTENTS

INTRODUCTION

In the early months of 1983, the *North Carolina Christian Advocate* published a series of letters from readers on the subject of baptism. These letters evinced a deep confusion expressed in contradictory opinions and not allayed by Bishop William R. Cannon's word which might customarily be accepted as authoritative. The controversy centered on the question of "rebaptism" of an adult who had received the sacrament as an infant. Writers who felt that the ceremony would be an appropriate and meaningful ritualization of their mature spiritual experiences voiced surprisingly strong support for the practice of "rebaptism."[1] In 1985, the North Carolina and Western North Carolina Annual Conferences of the United Methodist Church conducted a joint survey, through their boards of worship, which revealed that forty-five percent of their ministers were willing to rebaptize persons upon request.[2] In July of 1986, a Methodist leader speaking at an international consultation on liturgy and worship suggested that adult rather than infant baptism "might be in most cases the appropriate norm for initiation into the church."[3]

Though selective, these examples represent the perplexity and superficiality of understanding on the subject of baptism which pervades contemporary Methodism. Often, neither the persons in the pews or in the pulpits have any clear comprehension of what is going on when an infant is baptized. Parents ponder the quandary of whether to have their little one "christened" or to abdicate the decision to the child when the age of discretion arrives. After powerful spiritual experiences many individuals seek to have the sacramental water reapplied—often, a larger quantity of it, in immersion. Ministers find themselves unable to articulate a theological position which satisfies their parishioners, or even themselves. Baptismal practices are diverse and frequently divergent from the traditional norms of the faith. Where the significance of baptism as a sacrament is not understood, it is not surprising that its observance is eccentric.

American Methodists have historically engaged in a long struggle to define the significance of baptism in a way that is compatible with both their catholic-Wesleyan heritage and the other evolving elements of their theology. In the revivalistic settings typical in the nineteenth century, the emphasis upon experiential conversion obfuscated the import of the sacramental practice of infant baptism. In many ways, believer's baptism[4] appeared to be much more congenial to the American ambience. If salvation is understood to be achieved solely through the exercise of one's free decision to accept it, then a ceremony in which this commitment can be publicly professed is highly desirable. The psychological need for such an occasion had traditionally been met by the rite of confirmation, but American Methodism had no such rite and, until the latter half of the nineteenth century, lacked even a ceremony of public reception into full church membership. The conspicuous presence in many areas of Baptist churches with their dramatic practice of believer's baptism by immersion exacerbated for many Methodists the sense of need for a subjective expression of spiritual experience. For Methodists who retained much of the sectarian character of the early societies, baptism of adult believers best guaranteed a converted membership, consciously standing against the ungodly world. As some Methodists sought to ritualize these understandings, demands for "rebaptism"[5] surfaced repeatedly. In such a setting, infant baptism appears as something of an anomaly.

In spite of the lure of the siren of subjectivity, however, American Methodism has continued to affirm the sacrament of infant baptism inherited from its Anglican parentage. Even the vehemence of late eighteenth-century reaction against things English did not attenuate the disposition to the practice. Infant baptism was accepted as the historic observance of the church in its catholic tradition and, despite sectarian elements, American Methodists saw themselves as positioned firmly in that apostolic succession of authenticity. John Wesley, the founder sometimes more cited than followed, had clearly taught and practiced infant baptism as normative. If salvation is understood as a process initiated by the act of God in the life of a baby, this objective gift is best ritualized in the sacrament administered to infants. Psychologically, infant baptism commends itself powerfully to parents who want to claim their offspring as fellow members of God's family. Further, as the doctrine of original sin was vitiated, the growing perception of children as pure and innocent provided increasingly persuasive rationale for the sacrament. In actuality, American Methodists have evidently found values in infant baptism that they did not logically or theologically articulate, for they have been largely faithful in its practice and always tenacious in its defense.

My intention in this book is to delineate the development of the theology and practice of baptism in American Methodism. John Wesley's teachings will be examined for the source of both foundation and confusion. Evolution in both doctrine and observance of the sacrament will be traced from the earliest beginnings of Methodism in this country into the ongoing debates of the 1990s. A wide range of sources has been perused in this study in the attempt to ascertain not only what ecclesiastical authorities and standard authors were espousing, but also what typical preachers and lay persons were perceiving and practicing. For this purpose, church periodicals are especially revealing, and I have carefully employed several from different parts of the nation. For historical perspective, I have used denominational accounts, circuit riders' memoirs, and official church records. For theology, I have consulted a broad array of materials from systematic theologies to polemical pamphlets. Hymnals, Sunday School literature, and sermons have also been used. Sources have proven problematic for their plentitude. No limiting principle of selection has determined the sources to be used. Instead, I have attempted to cast my net as widely as possible—to discover as many and as various materials as I could, to peruse them as thoroughly as I was able, and to interpret them as fairly as I was competent to do. I began with no preconceived thesis and was, indeed, quite surprised by some of the directions into which the sources led.

Baptism has been a subject of intense interest in eighteenth-, nineteenth-, and twentieth-century American Methodism—one which has generated a prodigious quantity of literature. I have confined this study to episcopal Methodism prior to 1844, to the northern and southern branches of that church up to 1939, to The Methodist Church through 1968, and to The United Methodist Church since that time. While I have looked at some Evangelical United Brethren sources for purposes of comparison, I have not extensively investigated other Methodist denominations. Neither have I made any attempt to distinguish sharply between the Methodist Episcopal

Church and the Methodist Episcopal Church, South. Such an effort would have been unnecessary and artificial. Where there are divergences they have been noted, but the courses of development on the issue of baptism, and most other theological questions, were very similar in the two geographic branches.

My goal is simply to elucidate as thoroughly as possible the development of baptismal practice and theology in Methodism in the United States. No such study exists as far as I can ascertain.[6] In addition, I want to relate the changes in understanding of baptism to the broader theological trends which were being worked out through the period. My fundamental and motivating purpose is to illumine and enrich the understanding of the sacrament of baptism in the contemporary United Methodist Church in the hope of a fuller appreciation of this sign and means of God's saving grace.

CHAPTER I

The Practice of Baptism in the Ministry of John Wesley

The treatment of John Wesley's practice and theology of baptism here presented is from a topical rather than from a chronological perspective. It is undeniable that in the course of his long career Wesley's actions were not always consistent nor were his views static. The evidence, however, leads to the conclusion that he was not so ambivalent as some scholars have charged and that neither his practice nor his theology was so radically altered as is often averred. Rather, there appears in Wesley an evolution of thought and practice as he assimilated and correlated the truths of Scripture, tradition, reason, and experience. In his process of intellectual and spiritual maturation, some of the old ideas were left behind as they were superseded by more profound understandings. J. Ernest Rattenbury comments perceptively that many of the changes seen in Wesley are "plainly attributable to his common sense and his expanding vision through the normal experiences of life and men," not to a radical theological shift.[1] Consequent to this interpretation, in divergence from a common scholarly approach, no attempt is made to divide Wesley's career into time periods characterized theologically. The present aim is to approach the subject topically and indicate significant modifications in his practice and ideas where that information is pertinent.

The scholarly work available on Wesley is copious and burgeoning. While baptism has attracted considerably less attention than has the eucharist, there is at least peripheral treatment in virtually every historical and theological study of Wesley, as well as extended discussion in many works and several comprehensive monographs. No attempt is made here to survey the secondary sources with their spectrum of scholarly opinion, although issues especially subject to debate and a few novel interpretations are indicated. The bibliography cites the sources available for further study. The pivotal dispute among commentators on this subject is over the question of Wesley's view of baptismal regeneration and, specifically, how his Aldersgate experience may have altered his understanding. This dispute is, of course, a subset of the larger debate concerning the modifications in Wesley's theology after 1738, or the relationship between his high churchmanship and his evangelicalism.

American Methodist leaders were of independent mind from the very beginning and, while generally according Wesley considerable respect, they never subscribed unquestioningly to his doctrine. Conflicts between Wesley and the American preachers usually centered on issues of authority, but theological differences emerged as well and were augmented by the New World ethos. The Americans did not always find their starting point in the Church of England as Wesley invariably did; they had not served for decades as Anglican priests or been imbued since childhood with the subtleties of Anglican theology. Wesley's high churchmanship, as embodied in the *Sunday Service*, proved incongruous to the realities faced by the fledgling Methodist Episcopal Church and its leaders were not reticent in saying so. An example is the caveat appended by American editor John Emory to a section of Wesley's *Treatise on Baptism*:

> That Mr. Wesley, as a clergyman of the Church of England, was originally a *high-churchman*, in the fullest sense, is well known. When he wrote this treatise, in the year 1756, he seems still to have used some expressions, in relation to the doctrine of baptismal regeneration, which we at this day should not prefer.[2]

Yet in spite of their insistence on the freedom to criticize and to disagree with Wesley, American Methodists throughout the eighteenth and nineteenth centuries were deeply influenced by the works of their English patriarch. Certainly this is true on the matter of baptism and the issues subsidiary to it. Indeed, it is sometimes surprising how closely their contentions replicate Wesley's, though he is not always credited as their origin. There was divergence as well as faithfulness however, and in the course of this study both will be pointed out. Wesley will also appear as the source of some ambiguity, even confusion, on the subject. The carefully balanced synthesis of sacramentalism and evangelicalism which he maintained did not survive the Atlantic passage. Unequivocally, any attempt to analyze the baptismal practice and theology of early American Methodism must be grounded upon a firm and full exposition of Wesley's teaching.

Baptism was not, for Wesley, a subject of prime pastoral or doctrinal concern. Because it was not in the forefront of contemporary theological debate, he treated baptism much less extensively than he did many other issues. Still, there are to be found among Wesley's fulsome writings a few pieces devoted exclusively to the subject, as there are scattered, but germane, references in other works. The first, a twenty-one page tract, was published anonymously in 1751 as *Thoughts upon Infant-Baptism*, "Extracted from a Late Writer." This condensation of William Wall's massive four-volume work was republished in Wesley's name in 1780. A small piece entitled *Serious Thoughts Concerning Godfathers and Godmothers* was published in 1752. An abridged version of *Serious Thoughts . . .* was later appended by Wesley to his most comprehensive work on the subject which was published as *Treatise on Baptism*. The treatise was published in 1758 as a part of *A Preservative Against Unsettled Notions in Religion*. Not original with Wesley, it was an abridgement of his father Samuel's manual entitled *The Pious Communicant Rightly Prepared. . . .*[3] The *Explanatory Notes upon the New Testament* (1754) contains several references to baptism. Other relevant materials may be found in Wesley's sermons, his journal, his letters, and in the hymns of the Wesley brothers. The orders for administration of baptism to infants and to adults which are found in the 1784 and 1786 *Sunday Service of the Methodists in the United States of America* are also important.

As a presbyter of the Church of England, Wesley was actively involved throughout his ministry in administration of the sacrament of baptism. Most discussions of his baptismal practice focus on Wesley's months in Georgia (February 1736 to December 1737) which, with the exception of a brief service as his father's curate, was the only period during which he had pastoral responsibility for a particular parish. Wesley continued, however, to perform baptisms during the years of the Methodist Revival as he traveled and preached. Both the continuity and modifications of his views were manifested in his baptismal practice.

Wesley was always deeply concerned with the question of who could properly administer the sacrament of baptism. During his Oxford days he had become convinced, probably through the influence of the high church Non-Jurors, that baptism was invalid if administered by anyone who was not episcopally ordained—that is, ordained by a bishop in the apostolic succession. In October of 1735 while aboard the *Simmonds* waiting to sail to America, Wesley "baptized at his desire Ambrosius Tackner, aged thirty; he had received only lay baptism before."[4] Tackner was a Moravian and at this point Wesley did not recognize the validity of Moravian ordination. Later, as he became better acquainted with the group which was to be so influential on him, he accepted a probably legendary account which places them in the apostolic succession. The description of Wesley recorded in the diary of the Moravian leader August Spangenberg reveals the rigid high church views of the young Anglican:

> He has moreover several quite special principles, which he still holds strongly, since he drank them in with his mother's milk. He thinks that an ordination not performed by a bishop in the apostolic succession is invalid. Therefore he believes that neither Calvinists nor Lutherans have *legitimos doctores* and *pastores*. From this it follows that the sacraments administered by such teachers are not valid: this also he maintains. Therefore he thinks that anybody who has been baptized by a Calvinist or Lutheran pastor is not truly baptized. Further, nobody can partake of the holy meal without being first baptized: accordingly he baptizes all persons who come from other sects, although not those who have been baptized in Roman Catholicism. . . . He will therefore not share the Lord's Supper with anyone who is not baptized by a minister who has been ordained by a true bishop. All these doctrines derive from the view of the episcopacy which is held in the Papist and English churches and which rests upon the authority of the Fathers. Above all he believes that all references in Scripture of doubtful interpretation must be decided not by reason but from the writings of the first three centuries, e.g. infant baptism, footwashing, fast days, celibacy and many others.[5]

An example of Wesley's refusal to serve the Lord's Supper to those not baptized by an episcopally ordained minister was the case of Richard and Thomas Turner. This father and son were Dissenters; Wesley (re)baptized them in Savannah in June of 1737.[6] His insistence upon episcopal ordination was so stringent that he refused to accept John Martin Boltzius, Lutheran pastor of the Salzburgher community, at the Lord's Table, though he deeply admired the piety of this group.[7] One of the bills in the grand jury indictment of Wesley in Georgia referred to his refusal of the Lord's Supper to William Gough who was a Dissenter.[8] There is also some evidence, though it is not conclusive, that Wesley would not bury persons who had not received episcopal baptism. Another bill of indictment accused Wesley of refusing to read "the Office of Burial of the Dead over Nathanael

Polhill, only because the said Nathanael Polhill was not of the said John Westley's [*sic*] opinion."[9] However, a minority of the grand jury in their defense of Wesley argued that Polhill was an Anabaptist who had "desired in his life-time that he might not be interred with the Office of the Church of England."[10] The evidence is ambiguous, but Wesley's refusal would have been in accord with the rubric of the Prayer Book that stated that the Burial Service "is not to be used for any that die unbaptized."[11]

The strictness of Wesley's views on valid baptism began to abate soon after his return to England. He moved from the position of requiring Dissenters to receive episcopal baptism to simply being willing to administer to any who requested it. In an interview with the Bishop of London in 1738 he insisted in the face of the Bishop's opposition that "if a person dissatisfied with lay-baptism should desire episcopal, I should think it my duty to administer it."[12] For years thereafter, Wesley's *Journal* records instances of his baptizing persons from Dissenting groups. The evidence is not conclusive, but he may well have continued the practice all his life. Another example of moderation of Wesley's views is his *Journal* entry in September of 1749 after receiving a letter from John Martin Boltzius:

> What a truly Christian piety and simplicity breathe in these lines! And yet this very man, when I was at Savannah, did I refuse to admit to the Lord's Table, because he was not baptized—that is, not baptized by a minister who had been episcopally ordained.
>
> Can any one carry High Church zeal higher than this? And how well have I been since beaten with mine own staff![13]

Two versions of Wesley's *Treatise on Baptism* provide an indication of when he changed his mind about episcopal ordination. In his original abridgement of his father's text dated November 11, 1756, Wesley added an introductory section which stipulated that one of "the three things [which] are essential to Christian baptism [is] an episcopal administrator."[14] However when he published this work two years later, he omitted this introductory section. This evidence suggests a change in Wesley's views between 1756 and 1758.[15]

Significantly, it was Wesley's definition of valid ordination which changed and not his insistence that only one who has been properly ordained could baptize. When he revised his understanding of apostolic succession to include those within the continued tradition of apostolic truth, he broadened his acceptance of ordination to include Christian groups which did not stand in the direct apostolic and episcopal line. Hence he was able to recognize the legitimacy of ministry, with the right to administer the sacraments, as practiced in the Dissenting churches. In two works critical of Roman Catholicism, he made explicit his opposition to irregular baptisms performed by women or by non-Christians: "our Lord gave this commission only to the Apostles, and their successors in the ministry."[16]

Perhaps Wesley's most vehement controversy with his Methodist preachers in both Britain and America was over his adamant opposition to their administering the sacraments. He drew a sharp distinction between the extraordinary preaching ministry to which these laypersons were appointed and the priestly ministry of the sacraments which was to be exercised exclusively by those who were ordained. In 1772 he wrote to Joseph Thompson: "Whoever among us undertakes to baptize a child is *ipso facto* excluded from our Connexion."[17] Despite the growing pressure from both preachers and people Wesley never agreed to lay administration. In a 1784 letter he stated:

> I shall have no objection to Mr. Taylor if he does not baptize children; but this I dare not suffer. I shall shortly be obliged to drop all the preachers who will not drop this. Christ has sent them not to baptize, but to preach the gospel. I wonder any of them are so unkind as to attempt it, when they know my sentiments.[18]

Ultimately he chose to ordain men to the priestly ministry himself rather than to permit lay preachers to baptize and serve the eucharist. His doctrine of ordination proved to be less rigid than his dogma of an ordained priesthood for sacramental ministry. Wesley was unable to control completely the actions of his preachers and some of them did begin to baptize and to preside at the eucharist during his lifetime, but his opposition to the practice was consistent and intense.[19]

One point of baptismal practice on which Wesley's views changed sharply over the years was the question of the proper mode of administering the water. While he was in Georgia, Wesley insisted dogmatically on trine immersion, typical of the patristic and Eastern churches and favored by the Non-Jurors. In this practice he was following the rubric of the First Prayer Book of Edward VI (1549) rather than the later 1662 book which stipulated pouring or dipping. His *Journal* records the baptism of eleven-day-old Mary Welch "by Trine Immersion" in February of 1736.[20] Three months later Mr. and Mrs. Parker of Savannah refused to allow their child to be "dipped" nor would they certify that the child was weak, in accordance with the Prayer Book rubric. Wesley commented tersely: "This argument I could not confute. So I went home, and the child was baptized by another person."[21] One of the charges upon which Wesley was indicted in 1737 was that he introduced "novelties, such as dipping infants, etc., in the Sacrament of Baptism and [that he refused] to baptize the children of such as will not submit to his innovations."[22] Wesley was so concerned about this proper mode of baptism that he talked with the Moravian leaders about the possibility of Moravian deaconesses accompanying him on his mission to the Indians so that they might attend to the immersion of Indian women who were converted. As far as is known, the need for this ministry never arose.[23]

After his return to England, Wesley's stance began to moderate. By 1741 he apparently was allowing some option in mode to persons who came for the sacrament. He wrote to the Bishop of Bristol that year about "several persons [who] have applied to me for baptism. They choose likewise to be baptized by immersion."[24] Ten years later, his *Thoughts upon Infant Baptism* made his revised opinion explicit:

> With regard to the mode of baptizing, I would only add, Christ no where, as far as I can find, requires *dipping*, but only *baptizing*: which word, many most eminent for learning and piety have declared, signifies to *pour on*, or *sprinkle*, as well as to *dip*. As our Lord has graciously given us a word of such extensive meaning, doubtless the parent, or the person to be baptized, if he be adult, ought to choose which way he best approves. What God has left *indifferent*, it becomes not *man* to make necessary. . . .
>
> Besides, pouring or sprinkling more naturally represents most of the spiritual blessings signified by baptism, (viz.) the sprinkling the blood of Christ on the conscience, or the pouring out of the Spirit on the person baptized, or sprinkling him with clean water, as an emblem of the influence of the Spirit; all which are the things signified in baptism as different representations of the cleansing away of the guilt or defilement of sin thereby.[25]

As this passage illustrates, Wesley believed that each mode symbolized some aspect of the spiritual meaning of the sacrament. In his *Explanatory Notes on the New Testament* he argued that there is no single, fixed New Testament pattern which the church is to follow. Romans 6:4 and Colossians 2:12, for example, refer to the practice of immersion while Hebrews 10:22 and Matthew 3:6 speak of sprinkling. Wesley's comment on the latter passage is especially interesting:

> Such prodigious numbers could hardly be baptized by immerging [*sic*] their whole bodies under water: nor can we think they were provided with change of raiment for it, which was scarce practicable for such vast multitudes. And yet they could not be immerged [*sic*] naked with modesty, nor in their wearing apparel with safety. It seems, therefore, that they stood in ranks on the edge of the river; and that

> John, passing along before them, cast water on their heads or faces: by which means he might baptize many thousands in a day.[26]

In his *Treatise on Baptism*, Wesley asserted that:

> Baptism is performed by "washing," "dipping," or "sprinkling" the person. . . . [I]t is not determined in Scripture in which of these ways it shall be done, neither by any express precept nor by any such example as clearly proves it; nor by the force or meaning of the word "baptize."[27]

Frank Baker states that by 1755 Wesley was urging sprinkling as "permissible and indeed desirable" and that he was a pioneer in the advocacy of this mode.[28] Because he was convinced that there was no set New Testament pattern and that nothing essential to the gospel was at stake, Wesley was content to allow persons seeking baptism to select the mode. In March of 1759 at Colchester, for example, he "baptized seven adults, two of them by immersion."[29] His 1784 *Sunday Service* orders of baptism permitted the use of either mode.[30] Wesley's mature opinion is well-represented in a letter to Gilbert Boyce, a Baptist minister with whom he had discussed baptism:

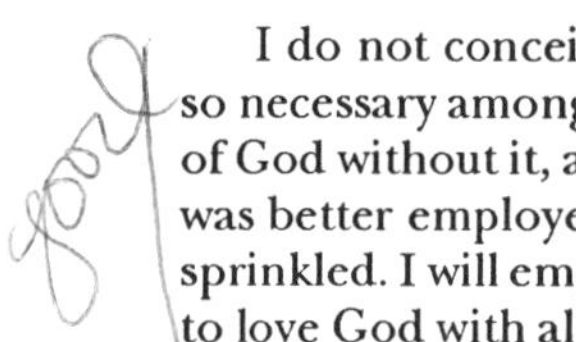

> I do not conceive that unity in the outward modes of worship is so necessary among the children of God that they cannot be children of God without it, although I once thought it was. . . . I wish your zeal was better employed than in persuading men to be either dipped or sprinkled. I will employ mine by the grace of God in persuading them to love God with all their hearts and their neighbour as themselves.[31]

Just as Wesley became much less punctilious over the years on the question of proper mode of baptism, so he similarly moderated in his opinion as to the proper place for the ceremony. During his early ministry Wesley was vigorously opposed to the general tendency in eighteenth-century Anglicanism to administer baptism to infants privately at home. In Georgia he insisted on conformity to the Prayer Book rubric which called for public administration in the church. His September 1737 Savannah journal records his displeasure with "Mr. Dison, chaplain of the independent company" who in Wesley's absence had baptized "several strong, healthy children in private houses, which was what I had entirely broke through." Though Wesley remonstrated with Dison and extracted the chaplain's promise not to repeat his offense, he "did the very same thing the next day." Wesley's comment is telling of his own attitude: "O Discipline! where art thou to be found? Not in England, nor (as yet) in America."[32] After his return to England, Wesley attempted to continue his practice of public church baptisms, but as more and more of the Anglican churches were closed to him, he was forced to accept different arrangements. By at least 1740, baptisms were often being conducted in the homes of the people. Many were also celebrated at the Foundery in London; for at least a while, a Wednesday afternoon service was the regular baptismal occasion. As he traveled about in England, Wesley apparently baptized wherever the people gathered. His diaries report ceremonies in Methodist preaching houses and at Kingswood School as well as in private homes. On occasion Wesley even baptized out of doors in a fashion more commonly associated with the Baptists.[33] An account of such a ceremony was included in a hostile publication, *The Progress of Methodism in Bristol; or the Methodist Unmasked* . . . (1743):

> In the midst of a most severe winter, (Wesley) had taken his converts, early in the morning, through frost and snow, to the river Froom, at Baptist Mills, where, on the ice being broken, he and they went into the water, where, with "limbs shuddering and teeth *hackering*," he baptized or dipped them.[34]

Wesley was determined during his Georgia ministry to conform strictly to the canons of the Church of England on the matter of godparents at baptisms. One point in the declaration which he read to his congregation at the outset was that he would "admit none who were not communicants to be sureties in Baptism."[35] This was in accord with the requirement of Anglican Canon 29.[36] It became, however, a subject of controversy in Georgia and one of the formal charges against Wesley was that he refused to accept William Aglionby as a godparent "giving no other reason than that the said William Aglionby had not been at the Communion Table with him the said John Westley [*sic*], contrary to the peace &c."[37] Another bill of indictment charged Wesley with having baptized a child "having only one Godfather and Godmother; contrary to the peace of our Sovereign Lord the King, his crown and dignity."[38] Clearly Wesley had made an exception in this case from his customary strict adherence to the Prayer Book rubric requiring three sponsors. An explanation may be surmised from his comment that this was the case of "an Indian trader's child" but Wesley berated himself for the transgression: "This, I own, was wrong; for I ought, at all hazards to have refused baptizing it till he had procured a third."[39] It is revealing that in this case the Georgia settlers were indicting Wesley for his laxity in ecclesiastical practice rather than for his rigidity as in the other charges.

Some measure of how seriously Wesley understood the responsibility of godparents may be deduced from his refusal in 1733 to sponsor his sister's child, probably because his absence would make him unable to fulfill the duties.[40] Wesley's fullest exposition on this subject is found in the tract entitled *Serious Thoughts concerning Godfathers and Godmothers* which he published in 1752 and had reprinted in 1758. His purpose plainly was to encourage the Methodist people to undertake this responsibility for each other's children. The thrust of his argument was that sponsors or sureties should be chosen with wisdom and care. He answered some objections and affirmed:

> . . . They are highly expedient. For when they are prudently chosen, they be of unspeakable use to the persons baptized, and a great relief and comfort to the parents of them. . . . I therefore earnestly exhort all who have any concern, either for their own or their children's souls, at all hazards to procure such persons to be sponsors, as truly fear God.[41]

Frank Baker refers to this work as a tract in which Wesley was "somewhat halfheartedly defending the institution of godparents,"[42] a charge of halfheartedness which is both puzzling and difficult to reconcile with the fervor of Wesley's closing exhortation:

> If then you that are parents will be so wise and kind to your children, as to wave [*sic*] every other consideration, and to choose for their sponsors those persons alone who truly fear and serve God: if some of you who love God, and love one another, agree to perform this office of love for each other's children: and if all you who undertake it perform it faithfully, with all the wisdom and power God hath given you: what a foundation of holiness and happiness may be laid, even to your late posterity! Then it may justly be hoped, that not only you and your house, but also the children that shall be born, shall serve the Lord.[43]

In his 1784 order for infant baptism prepared for the American Methodists, Wesley omitted any mention of godparents or sureties and spoke only of "friends of the child." The "friends" are, however, given no other duty than to announce the child's name in the ceremony and it is possible to interpret the term as a reference to the parents. Wesley expunged the rubric about godparents, the charge and address to them, and their answers to questions.[44] Already in *Serious Thoughts . . .* he had expressed his dissatisfaction with the responses prescribed for the godparents in the Prayer Book:

> Do not think the sponsors themselves undertake or promise, that the child shall "renounce the devil and all his works, constantly believe

> God's holy word, and obediently keep his commandments?" In truth, they neither undertake nor promise any such thing. . . . Whatever is then promised or undertaken, it is not by them, but by the child. It is *his* part, not *their's* [*sic*].

In reply to a rhetorical query as to why these questions were in the liturgy, Wesley responded:

> I answer, I did not insert them, and should not be sorry had they not been inserted at all. I believe the compilers of our liturgy inserted them because they were used in all the ancient liturgies. And their deep reverence for the primitive church made them excuse some impropriety of expression.[45]

This opinion makes understandable Wesley's omission of the questions to sponsors in his own ritual, but the resulting role for godparents was ambiguous. Evidently Wesley had changed his mind rather radically about the value of this ancient institution by 1784.

Another aspect of Anglican sacramental practice which Wesley judged to be of little value was that of confirmation. This attitude may have been engendered by the eighteenth-century spectacle of bishops confirming hundreds of persons in mass ceremonies which lacked both dignity and spiritual significance. John Bowmer suggests that Wesley himself may have been confirmed as one of eight hundred persons in a service conducted by the Bishop of London at Epworth on July 15, 1712.[46] Samuel Wesley, in accord with his view that baptism admitted one into the church, had already given communion to his son when John was eight years old (in 1711).[47] Even in Georgia during his period of most uncompromising high churchmanship, Wesley did not insist on confirmation before one received communion. That this irregularity was not motivated simply by the absence of a bishop was proven when Wesley did not revert to the normative practice on his return to England.[48] There are few references in his writings to confirmation at all; against Roman Catholic teaching he argued that it was not a sacrament.[49] In the 1784 *Sunday Service*, Wesley omitted confirmation completely. For him the rite served no purpose. Since he deleted the promises by sponsors from the baptismal order there was no need for an individual later to affirm these personally. Baptism itself constituted admission into the church and to the Lord's Table.

Something of the centrality of baptism in Wesley's early ministry is suggested by the fact that of the ten indictments against him in Georgia, five were the result of controversy on that subject. He was charged with insisting upon immersion, refusing communion to one who had only Dissenter's baptism, refusing burial rites to one who had not been validly baptized, rejecting a godparent who was not a communicant, and baptizing a child with only two sponsors.[50] Another grievance against him might evince dispute over his failure to require confirmation; he was charged with "administering the Lord's Supper to boys ignorant and unqualified."[51]

There is an interesting discrepancy between scholars on the question of how large a part baptism played in Wesley's English ministry. Paul S. Sanders writes:

> Most of his hearers had been baptized already; and in any case Wesley was not seriously concerned with baptizing them. The instances of his doing so are so rare as to exclude the notion that he considered it a normal part of his mission. Such persons as needed baptism would ordinarily have been directed to parish church or Nonconformist chapel.[52]

Similarly, Horton Davies comments: "Wesley himself rarely baptized, since most of his converts were Anglicans who had been baptized in infancy."[53] By contrast, Bernard Holland has compiled statistics on the basis of which he opines that, "We may be surprised . . . to realize just how frequently Wesley was called upon to administer baptism." Other scholars, Holland thinks, have been misled by their reliance on Wesley's *Journal* alone. He points out that Wesley's *Diaries* record frequent baptisms—at least fifty on twenty-nine occasions from July 1740 to June 1741 and at least fifty-seven on forty-seven occasions from December 1782 to February 1791, for example. "Indeed, so commonplace was it for Wesley to administer this sacrament that detailed as they are, he did not always mention such occasions in his Diaries."[54]

One other scholarly dispute about Wesley's practice of baptism deserves mention. In a comprehensive study, well-written and in general carefully documented, of Wesley's doctrine of Christian initiation,[55] John English states without equivocation that "Wesley requires baptism as a prerequisite for membership in the Methodist societies."[56] English offers no documentation for his assertion; he simply cites as example the case of a Quaker who was baptized one day and admitted to the society on the next. Similar assertion has surfaced in no other source, indeed, most writers indicate, either explicitly or implicitly, that there was no such requirement. Such a prerequisite certainly clashes with Wesley's plain statement in "The Rules of the United Societies" that "There is one only condition previously required in those who desire admission into these societies—'a desire to flee from the wrath to come, to be saved from their sins'."[57]

♦ ♦ ♦

In summary, it seems clear that the trend in Wesley's ministry was away from rigid conformity to formal ecclesiastical standards in the practice of baptism. He came to view the mode as a matter of choice and the place as a matter of convenience. Seeing no legitimate function for godparents, he ultimately eliminated them from his sacramental order. He dropped his insistence on an episcopally-ordained administrator, but remained adamant that the administrator must be one properly ordained to priestly function. Only on the question of confirmation is his opinion unchanged during his career—the rite never had a significant place in his understanding. Throughout the course of his long ministry, however, baptism was a part of his practice of Christian initiation, and he gave explicit statement of the theology which undergirded his practice.

CHAPTER II

Wesley's Theological Understanding of Baptism

Wesley's most extensive presentation of his baptismal theology was the *Treatise on Baptism.*[1] The work, published twenty years after the Aldersgate experience and intended for circulation among the Methodists, can fairly be understood as representing his mature thought. The *Treatise,* however, was written with the sacrament as administered to infants chiefly in mind and must be supplemented by references from other writings if a balanced and comprehensive delineation of his views is to emerge.

BENEFITS OF BAPTISM

The *Treatise* discusses five benefits received in baptism. The first benefit is "the washing away the guilt of original sin by the application of the merits of Christ's death." Wesley cited Scripture to prove the provision applicable to infants as well as adults. He believed strongly in the reality of original sin as the inclination to evil and the burden of guilt borne by every individual from birth. The sin of Adam has so afflicted the race that all his descendants come into the world in a condition of depravity.[2] Wesley explored details of this state of corruption at length in *The Doctrine of Original Sin, According to Scripture, Reason and Experience* in which he clearly describes the spiritual status of children: " . . . God does not look upon infants as innocent, but as involved in the guilt of Adam's sin. . . ."[3] Through

Jesus Christ, God has acted to liberate humanity from the helpless state of sin. "The virtue of this free gift—the merits of Christ's life and death," Wesley asserted, "are applied to us in baptism."[4] In this scheme, baptism is understood as the event in and through which the benefits of Christ's atonement are applied to each person so that one is then freed from inherited depravity and guilt.

This is clearly what Wesley appears to be saying in the *Treatise*, but there is a problem when one attempts to reconcile this understanding with his doctrine of prevenient grace. Wesley taught that the atoning righteousness of Christ was effectual to remove the imputed guilt of Adam's sin for all persons as soon as they are born: "Therefore no infant . . . will 'be sent to hell for the guilt of Adam's sin,' seeing it is canceled by the righteousness of Christ as soon as they are sent into the world."[5] What function then does baptism serve if the benefits of the atonement are universally and automatically operative without the sacrament? Wesley apparently did not recognize this contradiction and made no effort to relate baptism and prevenient grace. He simply went on, in the *Treatise*, to aver that baptism is "the ordinary instrument of our justification."[6] In the sacrament God's pardon is received and the baptized person is placed into a new relationship with God; the alienation of sin is removed by forgiveness. This connection between baptism and freedom from guilt is well expressed by a poem of Charles Wesley's on Mark 1:5:

Bid me step into the pool,
    By repentance I obey:
But my filthiness of soul
    Cannot thus be purged away:
Tears may wash my actual sin;
    Guilt requires a stronger flood:
Purge, and make my spirit clean
    In the fountain of Thy blood.[7]

The second benefit of baptism is its function as "the initiatory sacrament which enters us into covenant with God." F. Ernest Stoeffler has suggested that Wesley owed his understanding of infant baptism to "the tradition of Puritan covenant theology" which he inherited from both his parents.[8] Human redemption is made possible by the atoning work of Christ and apprehended by faith. God's grace has thus made it possible for persons to enter God's community of holiness which includes not only adult believers, but their children as well. Samuel Wesley interpreted infant baptism in terms of his concept of federal holiness:

> If the Children even of one believing Parent have Holiness, federal Holiness, by their Parents Charter, and may have the beginnings of real actual holiness wrought in them by the Holy Ghost, because they have had extraordinary gifts and are therefore much more capable of the ordinary. . . .

John, however, rejected his father's view of federal holiness for the offspring of covenant members; he deleted this sentence in his revision of his father's *Pious Communicant*.[9] Certainly John Wesley did not accept the implications of federal holiness which in Reformed theology were expressed in the concept of election. Robert E. Cushman's judgment is insightful:

> . . . there is, perhaps, insufficient evidence that Wesley shows direct dependence upon the elaborate covenantal theology of such representative Puritan divines as John Owen and William Strong. On the contrary, one has the impression that the covenantal theory is embraced within a composite of catholic ingredients of wider provenance.[10]

In Wesley's Arminian theology, Christ's offer of salvation was as universal as was human sinfulness. The covenant of grace was available freely to all; baptism was "a sign and seal" of the new covenant as circumcision had been of the old.[11] Wesley placed considerable stress on the analogy of circumcision because to him it provided proof that infants were included in the covenant and so were proper subjects of baptism.

"By baptism we are admitted into the Church and consequently made members of Christ its Head"[12]—this for Wesley was the third benefit of baptism and a highly significant one. Admission into the visible church was far more than a formality. It placed the baptized person within the community of faith and provided access to the means of grace. E. Dale Dunlap portrays this aspect of baptism with a meaningful image:

> Here is the door to Christian religion, a kind of double-door, if you will: entry into a new relationship to God which is the absolute priority in salvation, and entry into the nurturing community in and through which the process of salvation reaches its maturation in Christian living.[13]

Baptism for Wesley was an initiatory sacrament through which the community of God's people accepted a new member into itself and began to share with that novice the nurturing grace of God through which he or she might grow in holiness of life. As John C. Cho puts it, baptism "comes to be regarded chiefly as a corporate act of the

Church, action *pro Deo* to witness the objective givingness of the gospel of redemption . . . by setting the one to be baptized apart within the kingdom of grace, the Body of Christ."[14] It is within the Body of Christ that Christian growth is to take place, sustained and empowered through use of the means of grace. Preaching on "The Means of Grace," Wesley defined the subject as "outward signs, words, or actions, ordained of God, and appointed for this end, to be the ordinary channels whereby He might convey to men, preventing, justifying, or sanctifying grace." He specified as "the chief of these means," private and public prayer, "searching the Scriptures," and "receiving the Lord's Supper."[15] Baptism was not mentioned as a means of grace here, but it was understood as the sacrament by which one is admitted into the Christian community where these means are available:

> From which spiritual, vital union with him proceeds the influence of his grace on those that are baptized; as from our union with the Church, a share in all its privileges and in all the promises Christ has made to it.[16]

The importance of baptism for Wesley is indicated by his statement that, "In the *ordinary* way, there is no other means of entering into the Church or into heaven." Those who are baptized are then not only members of the visible church, but also "heirs of the kingdom of heaven . . . as it admits us into the Church here, so into glory hereafter."[17] As will be made clear later, Wesley must not be understood here to mean that baptism is either essential to or that it guarantees salvation; he denied both. But the fact remains that one of the benefits of the sacrament in Wesley's mind was that in God's "ordinary way" it functioned to bestow "a title to, and an earnest of" the heavenly kingdom.[18] A hymn of Charles Wesley's written for infant baptism beautifully expresses this idea in verses based on Genesis 48:16:

1. The great redeeming Angel, thee,
   O Jesus, I confess;
   Who hast through life delivered me,
   Thou wilt my offspring bless;
   Thou that hast borne my sins away,
   My children's sins remove,
   And bring them through the evil day,
   To sing thy praise above.

2. My name be on the children? No!
But mark them, Lord, with thine,
Let all the heavenly offspring know
By characters divine;
Partakers of thy nature make,
Partakers of thy Son,
And then the heirs of glory take,
To their eternal throne.[19]

These four benefits—cleansing away the guilt of original sin, entry into the covenant, admission into the church, and being made heirs of the Kingdom—are explicitly stipulated by Wesley in the *Treatise*, along with a fifth benefit—regeneration—which will be discussed later. Comments on additional effects of baptism can be gleaned from Wesley's other writings. Speaking in a sermon of the grace of baptism, Wesley quoted from the Church of England *Catechism*: " . . . which grace is 'a death unto sin, and new birth unto righteousness.'"[20] He developed this point further in explication of some of the New Testament references to baptism. One who is buried with Christ in baptism experiences the destruction of the inborn evil nature:

> . . . that entire depravity and corruption which by nature spreads itself over the whole man, leaving no part uninfected. This in a believer is crucified with Christ, mortified, gradually killed, by virtue of our union with him . . . [one who is] dead—with Christ—is freed from the guilt of past and from the power of present sin.[21]

By the power of God the baptized person rises from burial in death with Christ to a new life of holiness: " . . . our being risen with Christ, through the powerful operation of God in the soul . . . and if we do not experience this, our baptism has not answered the end of its institution."[22] One of the Wesleys' eucharistic hymns contains stanzas which speak of this baptismal experience of death and new life with Christ:

Baptized into thy death
We sink into thy grave,
Till thou the quickening Spirit breathe,
And to the utmost save.

Thou said'st "Where'er I am
There shall my servant be";
Master, the welcome word we claim
And die to live with thee.[23]

Wesley did not endorse the Lutheran concept of baptism as an experience to be lived out, returned to, and fulfilled throughout life. For Wesley, the effect of the sacrament is initiatory rather than continuing. He did, however, conceive of baptism as the beginning of the process of sanctification which encompasses the remainder of the entire Christian life. One who dies and is buried with Christ in baptism also arises with him to a new life which is characterized as a growth toward Christian perfection: "In baptism we, through faith, are ingrafted into Christ; and we draw new spiritual life from this new root, through his Spirit, who fashions us like unto him. . . ."[24] It was in his sermon "On Perfection" that Wesley most explicitly related baptismal consecration to the process of sanctification. Quoting Romans 12:1, he said: " . . . 'a living sacrifice unto God' to whom ye were consecrated many years ago in baptism. When what was then devoted is actually presented to God, then is the man of God perfect."[25] Charles Wesley's verse on Titus 3:4–7 can be employed to illustrate this:

> Our Father, moved by Jesu's prayer,
> Hath sent the indwelling Comforter,
>   The Spirit of holiness,
> To cleanse in the baptismal flood,
> Renew our spirits after God,
>   And perfect us in grace.[26]

Brian J. N. Galliers lists another effect of baptism that he says is to be found in Wesley's writings—physical healing.[27] Galliers cites the account in Wesley's *Journal* for February 1736 in which an eleven-day-old infant was immersed: "The child was ill then, but recovered from that hour."[28] This reference is not sufficiently conclusive to sustain a claim of any cause and effect linkage in Wesley's mind. Bernard Holland discounts such a claim and adds that, "This is the only occasion in all [Wesley's] writings when any connection between baptism and healing is suggested."[29] Neither of these scholars mentions a passage in the *Journal* for October 2, 1758: "In the evening I baptized a young woman, deeply convinced of sin. We all found the power of God present to heal, and she herself felt what she had not words to express."[30] While it cannot be proven that Wesley is here speaking of physical healing, there are enough references in his writings to prayer for healing to force us to leave this intriguing question open.

Since Wesley believed that all these benefits (plus others yet to be discussed) accrue to the recipient of baptismal grace, he urged that, as God's usual channel, it be conscientiously practiced in the church:

> It is true, the second Adam has found a remedy for the disease which came upon all by the offence of the first. But the benefit of this

> is to be received through means which he hath appointed: through baptism in particular, which is the *ordinary* means he hath appointed for that purpose and to which God hath tied *us*, though he may not have tied *himself*. Indeed, where it cannot be had, the case is different, but extraordinary cases do not make void a standing rule.[31]

On the other hand, the sacrament itself was never to be viewed as an absolute necessity for salvation. Wesley ridiculed the idea that children who died unbaptized were damned. He insisted that God has a way of dealing lovingly and redemptively with those who for whatever reason are unable to avail themselves of the designated means of grace. Even within the Christian community differences on this question are to be tolerated. In "Catholic Spirit" Wesley disclaimed any necessity of conformity in sacramental practice:

> Nay, I ask not of you (as clear as I am in my own mind) whether you allow baptism and the Lord's Supper at all. Let all these things stand by—we will talk of them, if need be, at a more convenient season. My only question at present is this, "Is thine heart right, as my heart is with thy heart?"[32]

Perhaps Wesley's plainest statement of the non-essential nature of the sacrament is in his letter to a Baptist minister:

> You think the mode of baptism is "necessary to salvation": I deny that even baptism itself is so; if it were, every Quaker must be damned, which I can in no wise believe. I hold nothing to be (strictly speaking) necessary to salvation but the mind which was in Christ.[33]

As truly as baptism is not essential to salvation it is surely not sufficient for it either. In his comments on Mark 16:16 Wesley affirmed that, "he that believeth not—whether baptized or unbaptized, shall perish everlastingly."[34] Charles Wesley's verses on this Scripture passage express both ideas graphically:

1. The infidel his doom shall bear,
    In endless torment cry,
   But never doth our Lord declare
    "The unbaptized shall die:"
   In education's fetters bound
    Who miss the outward way,
   Yet love their God, shall all be found
    His people in that day.

2. He winks at ignorance sincere
    In them that know His grace;
   But no unholy souls appear
    Before His glorious face:

Baptized, or unbaptized, they all
Shall die the second death
And banish'd from His presence fall
Into their place beneath.[35]

Wesley thoroughly repudiated any interpretation of baptism which implied an *ex opere operato* view. He drew a sharp distinction between two parts of the sacrament—the outward or human act and the inward or change wrought by God. In a 1758 letter Wesley argued that terms like "being regenerated [and] being born again . . . express an inward work of the Spirit, whereof baptism is the outward sign."
He emphasized the necessity of careful distinction so that it is clearly perceived that baptism:

> . . . is the outward sign of that inward and spiritual grace; but no part of it at all. It is impossible it should be. The outward sign is no more a part of the inward grace than the body is a part of the soul.[36]

Here and at numerous other points in his writings, Wesley explicitly rejects any confusion of the spiritual effects of baptism with the mechanical application of the water. There is no automatic connection between the outward and inner aspects; it is quite possible for them to be severed and they must always be understood as discrete. Herein Wesley asserted his conviction of the freedom of God who may act through the sacraments or who may transcend them. God is never restricted even to God's own ordained means. The church must never believe itself to be in possession of instruments through which God's grace is guaranteed to operate. On the other hand, while upholding God's radical freedom, Wesley also contended that the sacramental act and the spiritual effect are related in God's *ordinary* way of conveying grace. "The outward baptism is a means of the *inward*, as outward circumcision was of the circumcision of the heart."[37] Jesus' words in John 3:5—"Except a man be born of water and of the Spirit"—illustrated for Wesley the relation between the inward and outward: "Except he experience that great inward change by the Spirit, and be baptized, (wherever baptism can be had,) as the outward sign and means of it."[38] The significance of the outward act of baptism as both sign and means of the inward grace is expressed in a Charles Wesley poem on Mark 1:8:

1. What avails the outward sign,
Without the inward grace?
Lord, I want Thy Spirit Divine
The spark of love to raise.

Straiten'd through intense desire
    To feel the pure baptismal flame
Let the Holy Spirit inspire,
    And plunge me in Thy name.

2. Unbaptized, in sin I live,
    Till I Thy Spirit feel;
To Thy ransom'd servant give
    That Gift unspeakable
Witness, Pledge of joys unseen
    Thy Spirit breathe into my breast:
Partner of Thy nature then
    And one with Thee I rest.[39]

A good deal of the confusion in interpretations of Wesley's baptismal theology is the result of failure to comprehend both his distinction between the outward and inward parts of the sacrament and his insistence of their linkage in the usual operation of God's grace. Both the distinction and the linkage are illustrated in Wesley's comment in his *Journal* for February 5, 1760:

> I baptized a gentlewoman at the Foundery, and the peace she immediately found was a fresh proof that the outward sign, duly received, is always accompanied with the inward grace.[40]

BAPTISMAL REGENERATION

Wesley's conception of baptism in terms of its inward and outward aspects is foundational to a discussion of the controversial question of his views on baptismal regeneration. Much confusion results from Wesley's use of the term "baptism"—sometimes he used it to encompass both the inward and outward, other times he meant only the external act. The section on regeneration in the *Treatise on Baptism* is a good example of the dual use:

> By baptism, we who were "by nature children of wrath" are made the children of God. . . . By *water,* then, as a means (the water of baptism) we are regenerated or born again. . . . Our Church therefore ascribes no greater virtue to baptism than Christ himself has done. Nor does she ascribe it to the outward washing, but to the *inward grace* which, added thereto, makes it a sacrament.[41]

Wesley here clearly accepted the doctrine of baptismal regeneration but he carefully linked it with the inward grace of the sacrament rather than with the external mechanism. Baptism is normally the means which God employs to begin the new Christian life in a person.

Wesley had been imbued with the doctrine of baptismal regeneration by his father; while he made some changes in Samuel's work which he abridged for his own *Treatise*, these were designed to guard against any implication of *ex opere operato* and not to remove or even moderate the assumption of regeneration through the sacrament. William Wall, whose *The History of Infant Baptism* Wesley read in 1734, had as one of his major tenets that: " . . . all the ancient Christians, not one man excepted, do take the word *regeneration*, or *new birth*, to signify *baptism*; and *regenerate, baptized*."[42] Wesley condensed Wall's work to formulate his *Thoughts upon Infant Baptism* which he published in 1751 and again in 1780. Based simply upon Wesley's reliance on these two works—his use of them as the basis of his own two main publications on baptism and his failure to expunge baptismal regeneration from them—it would be difficult to argue that he repudiated the doctrine. It is important to note that when Wesley spoke analytically of baptism he was generally thinking of the sacrament for infants, since in the customary practice of the Church of England it was infants who were the prime recipients. He made this distinction explicit in his sermon "The New Birth":

> A man may possibly be "born of water," and yet not be "born of the Spirit." There may sometimes be the outward sign, where there is not the inward grace. I do not now speak with regard to infants: it is certain our Church supposes that all who are baptized in their infancy are at the same time born again; and it is allowed that the whole Office for the Baptism of Infants proceeds upon this supposition. Nor is it an objection of any weight against this, that we cannot comprehend how this work can be wrought in infants. For neither can we comprehend how it is wrought in a person of riper years. But whatever be the case with infants, it is sure all of riper years who are baptized are not at the same time born again.[43]

Based on the universal applicability of the redeeming work of Christ, an objective gift of grace occurs in the infant sacrament—"a principle of grace is infused"[44]—which effects regeneration or new spiritual life.

Scholars who emphasize the evangelical aspects of Wesley's thought, rather than the ecclesiastical, are eager to denigrate his acceptance of the doctrine of baptismal regeneration. William R. Cannon is representative of this approach:

> It must be understood, it seems to me, that Wesley's acceptance of the efficacy of infant baptism is just an acceptance, and nothing more. He affirms it as a teaching of the Church.[45]

Evidence to refute this position has already been presented. Wesley himself insisted repeatedly that he was in conformity with the teachings of the Church of England on this subject. Other scholars, following the lead of James H. Rigg,[46] suggest that while Wesley may have accepted baptismal regeneration during his early ministry, he repudiated it after his Aldersgate experience. Henry Wheeler is an example of this point of view:

> Upon this subject Wesley's views during his long life changed in a great degree. Whatever his belief was in his early years, in his later life he did not teach this doctrine.[47]

Writers of this persuasion are unable to account for Wesley's failure to repudiate or correct his two chief published works on the sacrament with their obvious acceptance of baptismal regeneration. Most arguments for Wesley's repudiation of the efficacy of infant baptism focus on his changes in the *Book of Common Prayer* when he prepared his *Sunday Service* for the American Methodists. It is not within the scope of this chapter to examine these changes in detail, as has been done by other writers,[48] but to summarize their significance. The Anglican Article on Baptism is considerably abbreviated by Wesley whose own version reads:

> Baptism is not only a sign of profession and mark of difference whereby Christians are *distinguished* from others that *are* not *baptized*; but it is also a sign of regeneration or *the* new birth. The baptism of young children is to be retained in the church.[49]

A pointed revision was Wesley's deletion of the words "regenerate and" in the *Prayer Book* sentence which reads: "Seeing now, dearly beloved brethren, that this Child is regenerate and grafted into the Body of Christ's Church." On the other hand, he retained a prayer which asks that "he coming to thy holy Baptism may receive remission of his sins by spiritual regeneration."[50] Even those scholars who insist that Wesley's intention was to purge the ritual of its implications of baptismal regeneration are forced to admit that he did a much less than thorough job of it. Some like John English attribute this simply to "hasty editing on Wesley's part."[51] Rupert Davies and Gordon Rupp suggest that Wesley was partially catering to the prejudices of American Methodists who found the doctrine of baptismal regeneration uncongenial.[52] Bernard Holland denies this, insisting that there is no evidence that either British or American Methodists disapproved of the doctrine at this time. He believes that Wesley was motivated by his desire to emphasize the need for a conversion experience rather than by a wish to expunge baptismal regeneration:

> By making these significant erasures he was not denying baptismal regeneration, but he was softening its statement in the baptismal orders—being particularly careful to remove the ambiguous word "regeneration" from this context—so that people should not be able to find here an excuse for ignoring his call for their conversion. Wesley did not exclude baptismal regeneration, as has been suggested, because the converted had come to distrust it, but because the unconverted trusted in it too greatly.[53]

Frank Baker's judgment is probably the most nearly valid:

> Although he expunged some phrases which seemed to imply that in baptism the child (or adult) was almost automatically reborn, he retained four or five others in which that spiritual blessing was requested, as in the Mozarabic prayer, "sanctify this water to the mystical washing away of sin." In other words baptismal regeneration was possible but not guaranteed.[54]

That is, Wesley's view remained the same as it had been earlier—that while the inward aspect of the sacrament was ordinarily concomitant with the outward, there was no automatic, inseparable relationship between them. Emendations in the 1786 version of the *Sunday Service* are more radical than in its predecessor but there is too much ambiguity about the motives and the source of these changes for any historian to be willing to ground a case here.[55] Many scholars, including Frank Baker, feel that the 1786 *Sunday Service* is more expressive of the views of Thomas Coke than of Wesley.[56]

Colin Williams points out that there is a distinction in Wesley between two senses of the new birth:

> First, in the preparatory sense that God enters the "dead" life of the unregenerate, bringing the grace without which it is impossible to know God or to receive him, and second, in the sense of fulfillment, in which the believer comes to conscious acceptance of Christ.[57]

In the initial sense, regeneration is definitely concomitant with baptism. Wesley affirmed this at the beginning of his sermon "The Marks of the New Birth":

> What is meant by the being born again, the being born of God, or being born of the Spirit? What is implied in the being a son or a child of God, of having the Spirit of adoption? That these privileges, by the free mercy of God, are ordinarily annexed to baptism (which is thence termed by our Lord in a preceding verse, the being "born of water and of the Spirit") we know. . . .[58]

In the second sense, baptism is not to be equated with the new birth, as is clear in this quotation from "The Great Privilege of Those That Are Born of God":

> First, we are to consider, what is the proper meaning of that expression, "Whosoever is born of God." And, in general, from all the passages of holy writ wherein this expression, "the being born of God," occurs, we may learn that it implies not barely the being baptized, or any outward change whatever; but a vast inward change, a change wrought in the soul, by the operation of the Holy Ghost; a change in the whole manner of our existence; for, from the moment we are born of God, we live in quite another manner than we did before; we are, as it were, in another world.[59]

Wesley was deeply concerned that the Anglican doctrine of baptismal regeneration, to which he subscribed, not be interpreted in such a way as to imply that spiritual rebirth was complete in the sacrament. He insisted vehemently that baptism, even understood as inward grace, was only the beginning of a spiritual process and impotent in itself to effect salvation for one who survived infancy:

> This beginning of that vast, inward change is usually termed "the new birth." Baptism is the outward sign of this inward grace which is supposed by our Church to be given with, and through that sign to all infants, and to those of riper years, if they "repent and believe the Gospel." But how extremely idle are the common disputes on this head! I tell a sinner, "You must be born again." "No," say you, "He was born again in baptism. Therefore he cannot be born again now." Alas! What trifling is this? What if he was *then* a child of God? He is *now* manifestly a "child of the devil." For the works of his father he doth. Therefore do not play upon words. He *must* go through an entire change of heart. In one not yet baptised, you yourself would call that change "the new birth." In him, call it what you will; but remember meantime that if either he or you die without it, your baptism will be so far from profiting you that it will greatly increase your damnation.[60]

Baptismal grace "is not to be understood in impersonal terms as though it were a quasi-material substance which is given in baptism and remains forever within man's soul."[61] One who has received baptism has only begun the process of spiritual development. Baptismal grace must never be presumed upon; the immediate question is always: " . . . not, what you was [*sic*] made in baptism (do not evade); but, what are you now?"[62] In "The Marks of the New Birth," Wesley ardently hammered this point:

> Say not then in your heart, "I *was once* baptized, therefore I *am now* a child of God." Alas, that consequence will by no means hold. How many are the baptized gluttons and drunkards, the baptized liars and common swearers, the baptized railers and evil-speakers, the baptized whoremongers, thieves, extortioners? . . .
>
> For ye are now dead in trespasses and sins. To say, then, that ye cannot be born again, that there is no new birth but in baptism, is to seal you all under damnation, to consign you to hell, without help, without hope. . . .
>
> Lean no more on the staff of that broken reed, that ye *were* born again in baptism. Who denies that ye were then made children of God, and heirs of the kingdom of heaven? But, notwithstanding this, ye are now children of the devil. Therefore, ye must be born again. And let not Satan put it into your heart to cavil at a word, when the thing is clear. Ye have heard what are the marks of the children of God: all ye who have them not on your souls, baptized or unbaptized, must needs receive them, or without doubt ye will perish everlastingly. And if ye have been baptized, your only hope is this,—that those who were made the children of God by baptism, but are now the children of the devil, may yet again receive "power to become the sons of God;" that they may receive again what they have lost, even the "Spirit of adoption, crying in their hearts, Abba, Father!"[63]

The objective gift of grace in baptism must be fulfilled in a subjective change of will.

The empirical evidence provided by both his personal and pastoral experience convinced Wesley that the grace of infant baptismal regeneration was insufficient to effect salvation for mature persons. As Robert Cushman puts it:

> Baptism may be the instrument of washing away of original sin and forgiveness of the same in the case of infants, yet it does not constitute more than a beginning of the process of regeneration, which requires the "new birth" and sanctification to complete. The forgiveness of original sin does not exclude the likelihood of actual sin.[64]

In his experiences as a minister, Wesley witnessed numerous instances of persons whose lives having belied their baptism were in need of saving grace:

> . . . you have already denied your baptism; and that in the most effectual manner. You have denied it a thousand and a thousand times; and you do so still, day by day. For in your baptism you renounced the devil and all his works. Whenever, therefore, you give place to him again, whenever you do any of the works of the devil, then you deny your baptism. Therefore you deny it by every wilful sin; by every act of uncleanness, drunkenness, or revenge; by every

> obscene or profane word; by every oath that comes out of your mouth. Every time you profane the day of the Lord, you thereby deny your baptism; yea, every time you do anything to another which you would not he should do to you.[65]

While a regenerate person may, in Wesley's view, commit inward sin and yet remain in a state of salvation, the commission of outward sin—"actual, voluntary transgression . . . of the revealed, written law of God . . . acknowledged to be such at the time that it is transgressed"—means that a person is no longer justified.[66] A new work of God's grace is then necessary to restore such a one to a state of salvation. In accord with his basically Arminian theology, Wesley believed that all grace may be lost, regardless of one's stage in the process toward Christian perfection, and indeed even after perfection has been attained. Baptismal grace was certainly no exception, in fact, he believed that it was almost always lost. A poem of Charles Wesley based on Mark 1:10 illustrates this contention:

1. Where'er the pure baptismal rite
    Is duly minister'd below
 The heavens are open'd in our sight,
    And God His spirit doth bestow,
 The grace infused invisible,
    Which would with man forever dwell.

2. But oh, we lost the grace bestow'd,
    Nor let the spirit on us remain,
 Made void the ordinance of God,
    By sin shut up the heavens again,
 Who would not keep our garments white,
    Or walk as children of the light.[67]

Wesley did not allow that such a loss of grace is inevitable, but his experiences taught him that it was commonplace if not quite universal. This explains why baptism could not function as a source of assurance as it did for Luther. In Wesleyan theology to "remember one's baptism" might well mean to recall what one had lost rather than to be reassured of a present state of grace.

Wesley's personal experience confirmed for him the reality of a loss of regeneration effected in baptism. In his *Journal* account for May 24, 1738, he wrote:

> I believe, till I was about ten years old I had not sinned away that "washing of the Holy Ghost" which was given me in baptism; having been strictly educated and carefully taught that I could only be saved by "universal obedience, by keeping all the commandments of God;" in the meaning of which I was diligently instructed.[68]

Wesley was here saying that the loss of baptismal grace came rather late in his own life due to the strictness of his religious training. For most children the age of reason commences between two and three years of age up to age five:[69]

> . . . the use of reason, and the abuse, generally commence and grow up together. As soon as their faculties appear at all, they appear to be disordered; the wrong state of their powers being easily inferred from their continual wrong application of them.[70]

The regenerating power of baptism and the subsequent loss of its grace are illustrated in the *Treatise on Baptism*:

> Herein a principle of grace is infused which will not be wholly taken away unless we quench the Holy Spirit of God by long-continued wickedness. . . . *Baptism doth now save us* if we live answerable thereto–if we repent, believe, and obey the gospel. . . .[71]

Because he believed that the grace of baptism was usually lost, Wesley affirmed the need for a subsequent experience of regeneration without denying the validity of the sacramental rebirth. He defined this requisite new birth in opposition to the teaching of some Anglican clergymen who distorted the doctrine of their church:

> They speak of the new birth as an outward thing–as if it were no more than baptism; or, at most, a change from outward wickedness to outward goodness, from a vicious to (what is called) a virtuous life. I believe it to be an inward thing; a change from inward wickedness to inward goodness; an entire change of our inmost nature from the image of the devil (wherein we are born) to the image of God; a change from the love of the creature to the love of the Creator; from earthly and sensual to heavenly and holy affections,–in a word, a change from the tempers of the spirits of darkness to those of the angels of God in heaven.[72]

In his insistence on both the reality of baptismal regeneration and the necessity of another experience of saving grace, Wesley was in accord with the tradition of German pietism stemming from Philip Jacob Spener:

> . . . [Spener] continued to believe that regeneration takes place at baptism in infancy; but what is significant is that he insisted also on the necessity for true Christians of a second regeneration, and it is this latter that came to be spoken of among the pietists as conversion.[73]

According to Bernard Holland, the influence of the Moravians on Wesley was decisive at this point:

> Here we have, then, the most important contribution made by the Moravians to Wesley's Christian understanding. They taught him to think of adult regeneration as conversion—a new doctrine. Yet, less noticeably, they influenced him in another way. They gave him confirmation of an already familiar doctrine—baptismal regeneration.[74]

Wesley accepted this two-fold understanding of regeneration as an experience which could be received through baptism in infancy and through conversion in adulthood. The two experiences he believed to be parts of the normal process of Christian development. Neither was necessarily dependent upon the other; actually he never clearly delineated the relationship between them. For all his stress upon the grace available through the Lord's Supper, Wesley made no reference to it as an occasion in which the baptismal covenant might be renewed, though Samuel Wesley had suggested this in his *Pious Communicant.* For son John, "the baptismal covenant is so irretrievably broken by actual sin that it requires not renewal but complete remaking: and this remaking he looked for in adult regeneration."[75] This dual quality of spiritual rebirth is clearly summarized by Bernard Holland:

> It thus seems certain that Wesley considered infant regeneration to be applicable only to the first years of life, prior to the beginning of actual sin (at about nine or ten years of age) at which stage adult re-birth becomes necessary. The two regenerations are placed in separate compartments of life, and the dividing wall between them is the onset of conscious sin. In baptism, infant regeneration restores the child to favour with God, but his first acts of conscious sin break this relationship so that a new atonement is now required, and this is effected when (and if) conversion occurs.[76]

INFANT AND ADULT BAPTISM

Wesley believed that in the ordinary course of the spiritual life, baptismal regeneration was to be received in infancy. For all his stress on the necessity of rebirth in adults, he never questioned the propriety of infant baptism. Both his major works on baptism defend the sacrament of infant baptism on theological, scriptural, and traditional grounds. "*Infants* need to be washed from original sin; therefore they are proper subjects of baptism."[77] Wesley repeatedly stressed the analogy between the covenant with Abraham and the Christian covenant:

> The *children* of Christians were never cut off from this privilege, when their fathers were received into the church, whether they were Jews or Gentiles; and therefore they are members of the Christian church also, under spiritual promises and blessings. When the Jews, the *natural branches,* were cut off from the good olive-tree, their *little buds* were cut off with them also; and when the Gentiles by a profession of faith were *grafted* in as *foreign* branches, their *little buds* were grafted in with them.[78]

He also employed an analogy with women pointing out that there is no "express command or clear example" in the Scripture for their admission to either of the sacraments; as the church has always received them, so it has and should receive infants.[79]

A major point for Wesley in upholding infant baptism was its conformity with the traditional practice of the apostolic and patristic church. He cited numerous church fathers in support and concluded "that infant-baptism was practiced in the church of Christ from the beginning, and consequently, that it is of an apostolical and divine original."[80] Indeed, "the whole Church of Christ, for seventeen hundred years together, baptized infants and were never opposed till the last century but one by some not very holy men in Germany."[81] Wesley had no concept of infant faith such as was held, at least for a time, by Luther. He argued again on the analogy of circumcision:

> Now, if infants were capable of being circumcised, notwithstanding that repentance and faith were to go before circumcision in grown persons, they are just as capable of being baptized, notwithstanding that repentance and faith are, in grown persons, to go before baptism.[82]

An insistence on prior faith as a requirement for baptism would not only disqualify infants for the sacrament, but "for want of actual faith and repentance, would equally prove them unqualified for salvation."[83] At least three functions of infant baptism are mentioned in Charles Wesley's hymn paraphrasing Matthew 19:13—dedication of the child to God, admission into the church, and prayer for future holiness:

1. Jesus, in earth and heaven the same,
    Accept a parent's vow,
To thee, baptized into thy name,
    I bring my children now;
Thy love permits, invites, commands,
    My offspring to be blessed;
Lay on them Lord, thy gracious hands,
And hide them in thy breast.

2. To each the hallowing Spirit give
   Even from their infancy;
   And pure into thy church receive,
   Whom I devote to thee;
   Committed to thy faithful care,
   Protected by thy blood,
   Preserve by thine unceasing prayer,
   And bring them all to God.[84]

The baptismal grace of regeneration is the theme of another beautiful hymn:

1. God of eternal truth and love,
   Vouchsafe the promised grace we claim,
   Thine own great ordinance approve,
   The child baptized into Thy name
   Partaker of Thy nature make,
   And give her all Thine image back.

2. Born in the dregs of sin and time,
   These darkest, last, apostate days,
   Burden'd with *Adam's* curse and crime,
   Thou in Thy mercy's arms embrace,
   And wash out all her guilty load,
   And quench the brand in Jesus' blood.

3. Father, if such Thy sovereign will,
   If Jesus *did* the rite enjoin,
   Annex thy hallowing Spirit's seal,
   And let the grace attend the sign;
   The seed of endless life impart,
   Seize for Thy own our infant's heart.

4. Answer on her Thy wisdom's end
   In present and eternal good;
   Whate'er Thou didst for man intend,
   Whate'er Thou hast on man bestow'd,
   Now to this favour'd babe be given,
   Pardon, and holiness, and heaven.

5. In presence of Thy heavenly host
   Thyself we faithfully require;
   Come, Father, Son, and Holy Ghost,
   By blood, by water, and by fire,
   And fill up all Thy human shrine,
   And seal our souls for ever Thine.[85]

There is a distinction in Wesley's thought between the grace concomitant with infant baptism and the effect of the sacrament administered to adults. Simply put, infant baptism is the ordinary vehicle of regeneration; adult baptism is accompanied by rebirth only under certain conditions and, instead, functions as a more general means of grace. The person who has been converted should receive baptism as a testimony to the faith experience and as a rite of admission into the church. Commenting on Acts 10:47, Wesley pointed out: "He does not say, they have the baptism of the Spirit; therefore they do not need baptism with water but just the contrary; If they have received the Spirit, then baptize them with water."[86] In this way baptism serves as a sign and witness of a rebirth already received. Wesley did not deny the function of the sacrament as the means of regeneration for adults: "Baptism, administered to real penitents, is both a means and seal of pardon. Nor did God ordinarily in the primitive church bestow this on any, unless through this means."[87] Unlike in the case of infants however, baptismal regeneration for adults has repentance and faith as its prerequisites:

> Infants indeed our Church supposes to be justified in baptism, although they cannot then either *believe* or *repent.* But she expressly requires both *repentance* and *faith* in those who come to be baptized when they are of riper years.[88]

Wesley's conviction that the efficacy of adult baptism is contingent upon the proper spiritual preconditions was evidenced by his skepticism on occasion:

> I baptized two Turks two or three weeks ago. They seem to be strong in faith; and their story is very probable, but I am not sure it is true. I wait for farther evidence.[89]

One of the hymns written by Charles Wesley for use at adult rites prays that regenerating grace might be conveyed through the sacrament:

1. Father, Son, and Holy Ghost,
    In solemn Power come down,
   Present with thy Heavenly Host
    Thine Ordinance to crown:
   See a Sinful Worm of Earth!
    Bless for her the Laving Flood,
   Plunge her, by a second birth
    Into the depths of God.

2. Let the Promis'd Inward Grace
    Accompany the Sign;
   On her new-born Soul impress
    The glorious Name Divine:

Father, all thy name reveal!
Jesus, all thy Mind impart!
Holy Ghost, renew, and dwell
For ever in her heart.[90]

As part of his stress on the futility of reliance on baptism to effect salvation Wesley insisted that there was no guarantee of regeneration even when repentance and faith were present. God is free in dealing with human creatures; God acts by the divine will alone and cannot be tied to any set of human expectations. Sometimes repentance is immediately followed by rebirth; in other instances, there may be a lapse of time between the two. Wesley did not mean by this to deprecate the use of sacramental means of grace, but he was underlining the sovereignty of one who is not limited to the means which God has ordained for human use. Something of the mystery and diversity of the workings of divine grace in adult baptism is suggested by this account in Wesley's *Journal* for January 1739:

> Of the adults I have known baptized lately, one only was at that time born again, in the full sense of the word; that is, found a thorough, inward change, by the love of God filling her heart. Most of them were only born again in a lower sense; that is, received the remission of their sins. And some (as it has since too plainly appeared) neither in one sense nor the other.[91]

Bernard Holland asserts that rather than limiting it to regeneration, Wesley considered adult baptism to be the vehicle of whatever grace was needed by the recipient at the critical stage of spiritual progress; it "should be regarded as a real means of grace, effectually used by God to convict, convert or sanctify." Through this interpretation, adult baptism became for Wesley "a living handmaid" to his evangelical preaching.[92] Extracts from Wesley's *Journal* evince the spiritual power which was manifested on sacramental occasions:

> I baptized Hannah C—, late a Quaker. God, as usual, bore witness to His ordinance. A solemn awe spread over the whole congregation, and many could not refrain from tears.
>
> I baptized a young woman who had been educated among the Anabaptists. God bore witness to His ordinance, and gave her such a blessing as she could not find words to express.
>
> I baptized a young woman brought up an Anabaptist; and God bore witness to His ordinance, filling her heart, at the very time, with peace and joy unspeakable.[93]

Wesley's repeated affirmation that "God bore witness to His ordinance" proves unequivocally that the sacrament as administered to adults was for him no formal, sterile ceremony. On one occasion he spoke of "a young Quaker [who] was 'baptized and filled with the Holy Ghost.'"[94] The adult sacrament, Wesley believed, functions as an assurance of salvation—an experience through which one receives "a divine consciousness that both our persons and our actions are accepted through him who died and rose again for us."[95] Such assurance was, of course, to be understood as witnessing to one's present state of salvation rather than to any guarantee of perseverance in grace. Still, such an experience as was described in the *Journal* for November 8, 1774, must have provided motive power for holy living:

> I baptized two young women, one of whom found a deep sense of the presence of God in His ordinance; the other received a full assurance of His pardoning love and was filled with joy unspeakable.[96]

Something of the emotional and spiritual intensity of the early Methodist adult baptisms is conveyed in this hymn of Charles Wesley:

1. Come, Father, Son, and Holy Ghost,
   Honour the Means Injoin'd by Thee!
   Make good our Apostolic Boast,
   And own thy Glorious Ministry.

2. We now thy Promised Presence claim,
   Sent to disciple all Mankind,
   Sent to baptize into thy Name,
   We now the promis'd presence find.

3. Father! in These reveal thy Son,
   In These, for whom we seek thy Face,
   The hidden Mystery make known,
   In Inward, Pure, Baptizing Grace.

4. Jesu, with Us thou always art,
   Effectuate now the Sacred Sign,
   The Gift Unspeakable impart,
   And bless the Ordinance Divine.

5. Eternal Spirit! descend from high,
   Baptizer of our Spirits thou!
   The Sacramental Seal apply,
   And witness with the Water Now!

6. O! that the Souls baptized therein,
   May now thy Truth and Mercy feel;
   May rise, and wash away their sin—
   Come, Holy Ghost, their Pardon seal![97]

♦ ♦ ♦

Perhaps no aspect of Wesley's thought has been the subject of more debate and confusion than has his theology of baptism. A measure of this difficulty is due to Wesley's failure to spell out his ideas clearly enough that his posterity could comprehend and utilize them. Robert Cushman is undeniably right when he speaks of:

> . . . large elements of uncertainty and, perhaps, ambiguity in the express utterances as well as exasperating silences of John Wesley himself regarding the means of baptism and its significance.[98]

In part however, this confusion has been due to the failure of students of Wesley to take some of his essential distinctions fully into account. Significant examples are his differentiation between the outward and inward aspects of a sacrament, his two-fold understanding of the nature of regeneration, and his divergent interpretations of infant and adult baptism. Any attempt to elucidate his theology of baptism must also be grounded in a Wesleyan understanding of salvation as a lifelong, dynamic process rather than a fixed, achieved state. Finally, in Wesley's comprehension of baptism, as in the other aspects of his theology, important emphases always include the grace and freedom of God, the church and sacraments, human responsibility and personal holiness of life. There is an inescapable tension in Wesley's thought between Catholic and Protestant, between objective and subjective, between ecclesiastical and evangelical. This tension results not in a conflict of elements, but in a creative synthesis.

CHAPTER III

Baptism in Eighteenth-Century American Methodism

In 1762 in Frederick County, Maryland, Robert Strawbridge, an unordained local preacher, dipped up water in his hand and poured it in the name of the Trinity upon the head of five-year-old Henry Maynard. This, the first Methodist baptism in America, probably the first in the world,[1] adumbrated many of the problematic questions that the denomination would struggle to resolve. Throughout his career Strawbridge continued to administer the sacraments, heeding neither the authority of Francis Asbury nor that of the preachers' conferences.[2]

From at least as early as 1772 to the official creation of the Methodist Episcopal Church in 1784, the issue of administration of the sacraments continued to agitate American Methodism. Since none of the preachers was ordained, Wesley was unequivocally opposed to their usurping priestly prerogatives and the 1773 conference in America clearly affirmed his position.[3] Methodists were expected to receive the sacraments from local Anglican priests—an arrangement which appeared quite logical since Methodism was still considered to be a movement within the Church of England.[4] As the years passed, however, American Methodists found themselves both less able and less willing to depend upon the Anglican clerics. Animosity between the two groups increased steadily and climaxed at the time of the Revolutionary War when many Church of England priests returned to their homeland or were otherwise dispersed. Concern for access to the sacraments exacerbated, especially in the South, until it threatened to divide American Methodism. The minutes of the conferences from 1779 to 1784 have been expurgated of references to the controversy, but the story can be gathered from other accounts. Not only did many of the preachers covet sacramental authority, but also many of the people were desirous of the privilege of receiving the ordinances from their preachers. Schism was averted in 1780 when the southern preachers—who at a conference in Fluvanna County, Virginia the previous year, had formulated a plan to ordain each other—agreed to suspend administration of the sacraments for a year in order to submit the issue to the authority of Wesley. In fact, the issue was not finally settled until Wesley's provision of ordained ministers for America at the time of the 1784 Christmas Conference.[5] When after long privation, the pent-up desire for the sacraments could finally be fulfilled, Methodists flocked to the services in large numbers. Richard Whatcoat, one of the first ordained elders, recorded in his journal occasions on which he baptized numerous adults and even more children. Thomas Coke, sent by Wesley as a superintendent of the new church, commented after five weeks in America:

> Perhaps I have in this little tour baptized more children and adults than I should in my whole life, if stationed in an English parish.[6]

This concern for access to the sacraments provides evidence that they were not without significance for eighteenth-century American Methodists. Indeed, Asbury felt that they were sometimes accorded undue importance, to the detriment of such vital matters as holy living. While Christians should avail themselves of opportunities to receive the sacraments, deprivation did not entail the loss of anything essential to salvation. His experiences made Asbury wary of the divisiveness that threatened to accompany too much stress on the need for baptism and the Lord's Supper.[7]

All of the official documents detailing the organization of the new Methodist Episcopal Church[8] contained regulations governing the administration of baptism. For the first few years these sections were brief, but in 1790 there was added a tract of more than seventy pages dealing theologically with the subject of baptism. Entitled *A Treatise on the Nature and Subjects of Christian Baptism. Extracted from a Late Author*, this work, an abridgement by John Dickins[9] of an earlier work of Moses Hemmenway (1735–1811), a Puritan preacher at Wells, Maine, had been published in Philadelphia in 1788.[10] The *Treatise* devotes fourteen pages to arguing against immersion as the sole acceptable mode of baptism and in favor of sprinkling as the mode best representative of the work of the Holy Spirit. Its remaining fifty-six pages present on several different grounds the case for baptism of infants.[11] Hemmenway's *Treatise* recurred in the *Discipline* each year until 1797; its major arguments would be repeated in perpetuity.

From the onset of their ministry in America, the Methodist preachers found themselves challenged by the Baptists on matters of baptismal practice. The intensity of this rivalry is especially clear in the writings of Freeborn Garrettson[12] and Francis Asbury. In his journal in 1782, Garrettson commented about the situation in Virginia: "I fear in these parts the anabaptists are enemies to our great Master's cause: a house built with deceit cannot stand." Speaking of a Methodist general steward who had abandoned his class,[13] Garrettson wrote: "The baptists has [*sic*] poisoned his mind with their doctrine, and into the water he has gone and out of Society we have turned him."[14] Asbury's journal contains numerous complaints about the inimical influence of the Baptists; one from 1776 is an illustrative example:[15]

> . . . the Baptists endeavor to persuade the people that they have never been baptized. Like ghosts they haunt us from place to place. O, the policy of Satan! Some he urges to neglect the ordinances altogether; others he urges to misunderstand them, or make additions to them. Christ, speaking of children, says: "Of such is the kingdom of heaven." But the practice of the Baptist says, They may be of the kingdom of glory but they cannot be of the kingdom of grace. But knowing that they who seduce souls must answer for them, I shall not break my peace about it, but leave them to God. I look on them as objects of pity, rather than objects of envy or contempt.[16]

Similar controversy existed in the western areas like Kentucky where William Burke in 1799 engaged a Baptist opponent in protracted debate on the subject[17]—one of the earliest of such confrontations which were a regular feature on the frontier during the 1800s. It was in response to the Baptist challenge that the early Methodists were forced to focus considerable attention on the subject of baptism and to articulate their own views.

Controversy with the Baptists had two foci—the correct mode of baptism and the proper subjects—with the collateral question of rebaptism. Asbury complained that the Baptists were always "preaching water" and often confusing and misleading Methodist converts.[18] While the records show clearly that the Methodist preachers did immerse those who asked for that mode, they objected strenuously to the Baptist insistence that no other mode constituted authentic baptism. At the schismatic Fluvanna conference in 1779, rules were adopted which allowed baptism by either "sprinkling or plunging." Wesley, in his *Sunday Service of the Methodists in North America* suggested dipping or pouring as alternate modes for adults, and dipping or sprinkling as the choices for infants.[19] The Methodist Episcopal Church in 1784 provided the "choice either of immersion or sprinkling" for both adults and infants and in 1786 added the additional option of pouring.[20] In the 1792 *Discipline* the order of these optional modes was changed from "dip, sprinkle, or pour" to "sprinkle, pour, or immerse."[21] Asbury realized that the issue of mode went beyond questions of ceremonial practice to concern for the very authenticity of the denomination:

> If plunging-baptism is the only true ordinance, and there can be no true Church without it, it is not quite clear that Christ ever had a Church until the Baptists plunged for it.[22]

At the request of the 1796 conference, Bishops Coke and Asbury wrote Explanatory Notes which were added to the *Discipline* in 1798. In their comments on the section on baptism, the bishops argued that while all three modes are acceptable to God, the references in the New Testament and the practice of the primitive church favor sprinkling.[23] The official position by the end of the century affirmed sprinkling as the normative mode of baptism and the option of immersion as a concession by which: " . . . we would meet the tender mind, and in matters unessential condescend as far as we conscientiously can, to the feelings and sentiments of all."[24]

American Methodists from the beginning unequivocally asserted that infants and minor children were proper subjects of baptism. In this they sought to remain faithful to their Anglican and Wesleyan heritage in the face of a powerful challenge from their Baptist competitors. Even their earliest defenses of the practice, however, reveal deviation from the grounds upon which Wesley had upheld infant baptism. Garrettson in a 1781 sermon spoke of the "propriety of infant baptism" on the grounds of "covenant holiness" as established in I Corinthians 7:14 and Acts 2:39, then went on to aver that Romans 5:18–19 proved "infant justification."[25] His quite un-Wesleyan understanding of the spiritual status of children was made plain in his journal in 1791: "I cannot conceive that infants partake of Adam's sin, neither do I suppose that it could be just in God to punish them for it."[26] The 1784 *Discipline* similarly argued for infant baptism on two grounds. In a continuation of the Abrahamic covenant, baptism was understood to replace circumcision as the sign of admission into the visible church, to which the infants of believers are eligible because they have a gracious interest in the covenant. Second, the words of Christ—Matthew 19:13–15, Mark 10:13–16, Luke 18:15–17—identify children as the heirs of heaven and so they must not be denied their place in the earthly church.[27] The Hemmenway *Treatise* on baptism, which appeared in the *Discipline* from 1790 to 1797, enjoined infant baptism in terms of the continuity of the Abrahamic covenant with the Christian church and the analogy of baptism to circumcision. Coke and Asbury in their Explanatory Notes cited the words of Christ and asserted:

> The preceding scripture evidently demonstrates, that the little children were entitled to all the privileges of the kingdom of glory, and, of necessary consequence, to all the privileges of the kingdom of grace. They must, therefore, be entitled to the benefits of that ordinance, which initiates the members of Christ's kingdom into his church below.[28]

E. F. Newell, a member of the New England conference, echoed Garrettson when, in 1800, he defined the fit subjects of baptism as, "All who are in a state of justification before God, through the all-atoning blood of the Great Redeemer—which embraces all infants and all adults who repent. . . ."[29] A sentimental poem, "On the Death of an Infant," appearing in the *Arminian Magazine* betrayed the inchoate modification in the view of children that was to characterize later nineteenth-century thought: "Blooming innocence, adieu! /Quickly ended is thy race/ . . . Lovely innocent, farewell!"[30]

Clearly two main lines of argument were emerging in support of the right of infants to baptism. One affirmed the place of children within the covenant community and, hence, their eligibility to receive its sign. The second contended that, through the benefits of the atonement, children are born into the world possessing the spiritual nature that makes them members of the heavenly kingdom and so fit subjects for entrance into the visible church through its initiatory sacrament. While these two arguments complemented each other to some degree, they led, in the nineteenth century, to different views concerning the children of parents who were not themselves considered good Christians. Apparently this distinction was not an issue in the late 1700s. Thomas Ware recorded his experience of 1787 in Tennessee:

> There were many both of those who had taken the Lord for their portion and those who as yet had not, who manifested a desire to have him the God of their children, and therefore presented them to be baptized. Of the latter class the hearts of the parents were usually

> touched when their children were dedicated to God in accordance with his own institution. Sometimes the scene was truly affecting, when the thought was impressed on the minds of the parents that their children, according to the declaration of the Savior, belonged to the kingdom of heaven, while they did not.[31]

Similarly, Asbury recorded an incident in Connecticut in 1794:

> We were called upon to baptize a child, which Mr. _______ refused to do, because the parents owned the covenant and now have broken it. This is the way to bind people to the good old Church.[32]

In these two cases, infant baptism is viewed as an instrument of outreach, at best a converting ordinance for parents.

Closely related to the controversies over the proper mode and subjects of baptism was the vexing problem of rebaptism. The disgruntled preachers at the 1779 Fluvanna conference had ruled out any repetition of the sacrament, but the Christmas Conference in 1784 proved to be more flexible. The question, "What shall be done with those who are baptized in their infancy but have now scruples concerning the validity of infant baptism?" was answered by the following directive: "Remove their scruples by argument, if you can; if not, the office may be performed by immersion or sprinkling, as the person desires." The provision was, however, omitted from the *Disciplines* after 1786.[33] The Hemmenway selection in the *Disciplines* from 1790 to 1797 labelled rebaptism as "utterly wrong." The conclusive opinion of eighteenth-century Methodism on this question was summarized by Asbury:

> One of our sisters asked me if we would not rebaptize persons that desired it. This put me to thinking and revolving the subject in my mind. I considered that there was neither precept nor example in holy writ to justify our rebaptizing one who had been baptized in the name and form which Christ commanded in Matt. xxviii, 19.[34]

The Methodist Episcopal Church established no definite relationship between baptism and church membership for the first half century of its existence. The early *Disciplines* do make it clear that baptism, for both infants and adults, was understood theologically as constituting admission to the universal church of Christ, but the ecclesiological application of this understanding remained vague. Wesley made no provision in the *Sunday Service* for either confirmation or any other ceremonial admission to membership in the Methodist Episcopal Church and this omission was not rectified by the church until the latter half of the nineteenth century. The ambiguous relationship between the initiatory sacrament and church membership is at least partly the result of the sectarian self-understanding of American Methodism—a view that was not totally dissipated by the formal creation of a churchly structure in 1784.

Prior to 1784, adults had been accepted into the Methodist societies without any requirement of baptism. Since the Methodist preachers were unordained they could not administer the sacrament and, for reasons already discussed, many persons did not receive it from the Anglican priests. Benjamin Abbott told of his conversion in the early 1770s as a result of the preaching of a Methodist itinerant who could not baptize him. Abbott became a Methodist preacher himself, but did not receive baptism until 1784.[35]

The relation of baptized children to the church was, and long remained, abstruse. American Methodism was, however, true to the Wesleyan example in its constant concern for children. As early as 1772, Asbury in formal session charged the preachers with the duty of meeting with the children.[36] His journal recorded frequent admonitions to both preachers and parents to be diligent in the religious instruction of children. The 1787 *Discipline* provided for admission into the societies of any children who are "truly awakened."[37] None of these references contain any mention of baptism in such a way as to relate it to the children's spiritual nurture or membership in society. This perplexing issue was raised but not resolved at the General Conference of 1800:

> Brother Ward moved that this conference determine what standing children are in our Church by baptism; and if it is determined that they are received into the Church, that they shall have all the privileges of the Church, (the sacrament of the Lord's Supper excepted) until their conduct is such as is sufficient to exclude them from society according to the rules, etc. Voted out.[38]

♦ ♦ ♦

A complex of problematic issues centering on the sacrament of baptism had arisen in American Methodism before the end of the eighteenth century. Much of the articulation of theological positions occurred as apologia as the new church sought to define itself. Although the process was far from complete, certain tenets were formulated, at least provisionally. While all three modes of baptism were approved and practiced, sprinkling was preferred. The propriety of infant baptism was resolutely affirmed, though its precise theological justification was less firm. After brief wavering, the church rejected the practice of rebaptism. The understanding of church membership was nebulous and its relationship to baptism tenuous.

The implied issues, plus others related to baptismal practice and theology, go with the fledgling Methodist Episcopal Church into the nineteenth century.

CHAPTER IV

Theological Articulation in the Era of Camp Meeting Revivalism: 1800–1844

In the early nineteenth century, American Methodism entered into an extraordinary period of expansion and growth. No longer handicapped by lack of ordination, Methodist preachers offered the sacraments enthusiastically to their burgeoning constituency. The large camp meetings characteristic of this period provided opportunities for mass participation in sacramental occasions. Although there were numerous variations, a common pattern was to administer baptism at 7:00 on Monday morning following a weekend meeting and then to conclude with the Lord's Supper. Baptisms of both infants and adults occurred at such services, and all three modes of applying water were utilized. A particularly exuberant description of such an occasion in Maryland was recorded by Robert W. Todd, who was impressed by the throng of children presented: "It was a baby-show that would have deprived the great American showman, Mr. Barnum, of his prestige." Todd continued in a poem which expressed not only the jocular tone of the event, but also hinted at its theological aspects:

> Babies great and babies small;
> Babies short and babies tall;
> Babies fat and babies lean;
> Babies soiled and babies clean;

> Babies romping, tumbling, falling;
> Babies crowing, babies squalling:
> Candidates for Church probation
> Full enough to stock a nation.[1]

Many baptismal ceremonies were, of course, on a much smaller scale in local churches. However, since all preachers were not ordained, baptisms were often delayed until the quarterly meetings of the circuit when the presiding elder would be present to officiate. The Methodist perception of baptism during these years will be explored from a variety of sources and angles in the attempt to assemble a theological collage.

AUTHORIZED CHURCH STATEMENTS ON BAPTISM

Moses Hemmenway's *Treatise* on baptism was omitted from the *Discipline* in 1797 and no other tract on the subject took its place until 1814.[2] In that year, a forty-five page tract entitled "A Short Method with the Baptists" became the official doctrinal statement on baptism. Its author was Peter Edwards—a native of New York who had served for several years as pastor of a Baptist church in White's Row, Portsea, Hants in England. "A Short Method" originally appeared as the fifth chapter of an eight chapter book, published in London in 1793, entitled *Candid Reasons for Renouncing the Principles of Anti-Paedobaptism*.[3] Edwards focused on the oft-repeated Baptist insistence that infant baptism could not be accepted as a legitimate practice of the church unless an explicit warrant for it were to be found in Scripture. He countered by pointing out (as Wesley had earlier) that there was no express command or example in Scripture authorizing women to participate in the Lord's Supper, yet their right to do so was unquestioned. Children were admitted into the Old Testament covenant by the rite of circumcision; their right to church membership continued, with baptism becoming the sign of the new covenant community. Baptist arguments, Edwards averred, would culminate in the conclusion that God had no earthly church for 1500 years. Edwards's tract was published in the *Collection* until 1825 when it was replaced by John Wesley's *Treatise on Baptism* and his *Thoughts on Infant Baptism*.[4] These Wesley pieces functioned as the approved statements on the subject until 1861. Also published in the *Collection* from 1825 until 1861 was a two page excerpt entitled "Remarks on Infant Baptism" by H. S. Boyd.[5] This English patristic scholar cited a passage in the works of Chrysostom referring to his having baptized the infants of the Byzantine emperor's family. This was asserted as evidence of the practice of infant baptism at least as early as the year 401. All four of these tracts concentrated on the validity of infant baptism and provided material for Methodists to justify it to themselves and to opponents. It is of interest that in these officially sanctioned documents, the question of proper mode had little place. Also worthy of comment was the fact that Wesley's works on baptism were accepted as authoritative for thirty-six years in the mid-nineteenth century.

A salient characteristic of Methodism has always been the singing of its theology. The first collection of hymns to be influential in American Methodism was Robert Spence's compilation—*A Pocket Hymn-Book.* This collection, first published in 1781, was based on John Wesley's 1780 *A Collection of Hymns for the Use of the People Called Methodists.* The Spence *Pocket Hymn-Book* went through various editions and was widely used until 1821.[6] The 1790 edition contained nine eucharistic hymns but none suggested for use in baptisms.[7] In 1802, Ezekiel Cooper published a revised edition which included three hymns under the heading of "Sacramental—Baptism." These hymns, the first to be recommended for use on baptismal occasions in American Methodism, were "Celestial dove, descend from high," "My Saviour's pierced side," and "Come, Father, Son, and Holy Ghost":

1. Celestial dove, descend from high,
   And on the water brood:
Come, with thy quick'ning power apply
   The water and the blood.

2. I love the Lord, that stoops so low
   To give his word a seal;
But the rich grace his hands bestow
   Exceeds the figure still.

3. Almighty God, for thee we call,
   And our request renew;
Accept in Christ, and bless withal,
   The work we have to do.

1. My Saviour's pierced side
   Pour'd out a double flood:
By water we are purified,
   And pardon'd by his blood.

2. Call'd from above, I rise,
   And wash away my sin;
The stream to which my spirit flies
   Can make the foulest clean.

3. It runs divinely clear,
   A fountain deep and wide;
'Twas open'd by the soldier's spear,
   In my Redeemer's side![8]

The first was characterized by its reference to baptism as a "seal" or "figure" of the workings of divine grace. The second, based on John 19:34, portrayed water as symbolic of the cleansing from sin made available by the death of Christ. Inspired by Matthew 28:19–20, the third evoked the presence of the Triune God in the sacrament. The next major hymnal of the Methodist Episcopal Church was published in 1821; it retained these three baptismal hymns.[9] In 1836, Nathan Bangs prepared a collection of ninety hymns to supplement the 1821 book. This supplement contained the first hymns specifically designated for use at the baptism of children:

1. How large the promise, how divine,
   To Abr'am and his seed!
"I am a God to thee and thine,
   Supplying all their need."

2. The words of his extensive love
   From age to age endure;
The angel of the covenant proves,
   And seals the blessing sure.

3. Jesus the ancient faith confirms,
   To our great father given;
He takes our children to his arms,
   And calls them heirs of heaven.

4. O God, how faithful are thy ways!
   Thy love endures the same;
Nor from the promise of thy grace
   Blots out our children's name.

1. Lord of all, with pure intent,
   From their tend'rest infancy,
In thy temple we present
   Whom we first received from thee;
Through thy well-beloved Son,
Ours acknowledged for thine own.

2. Seal'd with the baptismal seal,
   Purchased by th' atoning blood,
Jesus, in our children dwell,
   Make their heart the house of God;
Fill thy consecrated shrine,
Father, Son, and Spirit divine.

1. See Israel's gentle shepherd stand
   With all-engaging charms:
Hark how he calls the tender lambs,
   And folds them in his arms!

2. "Permit them to approach," he cries,
   "Nor scorn their humble name:
For 'twas to bless such souls as these,
   The Lord of angels came."

3. We bring them, Lord, in thankful hands,
   And yield them up to thee;
Joyful that we ourselves are thine,
   Thine let our offspring be.[10]

In "God of eternal truth and love," God was implored to return to the child the divine nature and image. There was prayer that "grace attend the sign" and that the child receive "pardon, and holiness, and heaven." "How large the promise, how divine" asserted the perpetuity of the Abrahamic covenant which included infants and was reaffirmed by Christ who explicitly identified children as "heirs of heaven." Baptism was understood more as a service of dedication in "Lord of all, with pure intent," with the child's heart described as a "consecrated shrine" to be filled by the Divine. The last hymn in this group portrayed Christ as "Israel's gentle shepherd" welcoming the children; it was clearly based on Matthew 19:13–15 and its parallel pericopes. These hymns accentuated many of the motifs that were developing as the Methodist Episcopal Church sought to define and defend its baptismal theology.

DIALECTICAL DEFINING OF BAPTISMAL THEOLOGY

Unlike Wesley, whose writings on baptism are largely commentaries on the well-accepted position of his church, American Methodists were forced to formulate their baptismal theology in the context of denominational controversy. As Methodism spread beyond its earliest centers in the mid-Atlantic states, it encountered virile competitors in the Campbellites and Baptists of the West, as well as in the entrenched Calvinists of New England. It was in struggling to define itself over against these traditions that Methodism developed and articulated its theological understanding of its inherited baptismal practices.

The Campbellites

Those persons who accepted the teaching and leadership of Alexander Campbell emerged as an identifiable group in the American religious spectrum in the early decades of the nineteenth century. The Campbellites were at first centered in western Pennsylvania and Virginia; their strength grew with the westward moving frontier. Accounts of debates between Campbellite and other Protestant preachers appeared in the periodical literature as early as the 1820s, and such events apparently became a regular and popular feature of frontier religious strife throughout the century. The *Western Christian Advocate*, published in Cincinnati by the Methodist Episcopal Church, avidly reported these debates. Especially detailed and protracted attention was focused on "the greatest theological dispute the world has ever witnessed"—the great debate in Lexington, Kentucky lasting from November 15 to December 2, 1843.[11] The protagonists were Alexander Campbell himself and Nathan Lewis Rice—a Presbyterian preacher who championed the views that Methodists also espoused. Methodists were urged to purchase copies of the book-length account of this debate from the Methodist Book Concern and to utilize its arguments in defending their views. Peripheral issues in such debates included the questions of proper mode and subjects of baptism and the validity of the Campbellite practice of baptizing in the name of Christ. Methodists consistently derided the Campbellites' stress on exclusive immersion,[12] but reserved much of their vehemence on this subject, and on infant baptism, for clashes with the Baptists. Methodists also insisted that baptism was not valid unless administered in the name of the Trinity. The central issue in almost all of the Campbellite-Methodist debates was that of the relationship between baptism and the remission of sins. Methodist spokespersons accused Campbell of teaching that water baptism really did wash away one's sins, that it was the only means through which pardon was to be received, and that it was the sole prerequisite for justification. In the pages of the *Western Christian Advocate* furious attacks were launched on this pernicious doctrine of "water regeneration." Especially noteworthy was a series of twenty-six substantial articles on the subject by William

Phillips of Newport, Kentucky, printed in the *Advocate* during 1835 and 1836.

This dispute with Campbellite theology forced the Methodists to become more precise about their own understanding and practice of baptism. A significant exemplar of the development was published in 1835 by F. E. Pitts, a member of the Tennessee annual conference, entitled *A Book on Baptism: Chiefly Designed as a Refutation of the Errors and Infidelity of Campbellism.*[13] Pitts charged that Campbellites destroyed the meaning of baptism as emblematic of the work of the Holy Spirit when they made it instead representative of the death, burial, and resurrection of Christ in order to justify immersion. He presented a long argument replete with scriptural citations to prove that water baptism could not remit sins and that faith was the only essential condition for salvation. Immersion, Pitts contended, was not expressly authorized in Scripture and pouring or sprinkling were more likely to have been the modes used in biblical times. Children were constituted members of the church by divine authority in both the Old and New Testaments and so are entitled to baptism which is the door into the visible church. Pitts could not resist a jab at the Baptists who were themselves somewhat discomfited by Campbellite views. He commented that some have called Campbellism "a judgment from God upon the old-side Baptist church;" at the least it must be seen as "an exuberant production of the rigid views of immersionists."[14] Pitts hoped that the specter of Campbellism would motivate the Baptists to moderate their practice of close communion.

Pitts included in his book the report of the committee on baptism of the Kentucky annual conference of 1833 as expressive of a defensible Methodist position in the face of Campbellite influence. The report stipulated that baptism should not be administered in any of three cases: (1) when an adult applicant "does not give satisfactory evidence of true repentance and faith," (2) when a person has been baptized previously, (3) when an adult applicant "has grossly erroneous views of the design and use of baptism"—as that it is representative of the death, burial and resurrection of Christ. The report continued, saying that Methodist ministers have the option to refuse to administer baptism in four additional situations: (1) when the parents seek the sacrament for themselves, but do not believe in infant baptism and so decline to offer their children, (2) when it "cannot be administered without great indecency, as is frequently the case in immersion," (3) when life or health would be endangered, and (4) where the only available water is impure.[15] Disputation with the Campbellites continued for decades and provided an important context in which Methodists attempted to refine their own doctrinal stance.

The Baptists

The perennial and foremost rivals of the early American Methodists were always the Baptists. Controversy between the two denominations centered on the Baptist insistence upon immersion as the only acceptable mode and its corollary, close communion; on the eligibility of children to receive baptism; and on the precipitate of these two questions—the issue of rebaptism. The official, and generally accepted, Methodist position was that either of the three modes of administering water—sprinkling, pouring, and immersion—was valid and that the quantity of water used was of no significance. The pivot of contention was the Baptist claim that only immersion was true baptism. Methodists recognized that such an exclusive claim represented the Baptists as the only authentic Christian church. Methodists were insulted by the Baptist refusal to accept at the Lord's Supper those who had been baptized by sprinkling or pouring. In the periodicals of the Methodist Episcopal Church—the various *Christian Advocates*, *Zion's Herald* and the *Methodist Quarterly Review*—articles and letters on the subject proliferated.[16] J. Porter of the New England Conference expressed Methodist sentiment succinctly when he stated that exclusive insistence on immersion:

> . . . is an impeachment of the wisdom of God, and an infraction of religious rights. [Further,] . . . making the mode of baptism the condition of church fellowship and communion is contrary to Scripture, and degrading to the principles of Christian union.[17]

When Baptist missionary Adoniram Judson translated the Bible into the Burmese language using "immerse" instead of "baptize," many Methodists were incensed at what they took to be tampering with God's Word for partisan motives.[18] The weapon of ridicule was often employed against the Baptists by describing occasions on which immersion was administered when it was unhealthy, indecorous, or impractical.[19]

The Methodist Episcopal *Discipline* had, since 1786, stipulated that adults who were seeking baptism or the parents of children brought for the sacrament had the privilege of choosing either of the three accepted modes. Records from the early 1800s—especially those of camp meetings, revivals, and quarterly meetings where large numbers of baptisms were performed—make it clear that this option was exercised. Results of the meetings were commonly reported in terms of numbers sprinkled and numbers immersed. (Sprinkling and pouring tended to be thought and spoken of as variations of a single mode). An account from Peter Cartwright may be taken as typical:

> On Sunday I preached on baptism, and opened the doors, and received one hundred and nineteen into the Church, and baptized forty-seven adults and thirty children in the altar, and then marched off to the creek and immersed twenty-seven, making in all one hundred and nineteen accessions on trial, and one hundred and four baptized; this was the fruit of a prayer-meeting.[20]

In accordance with church law, most Methodist ministers were willing to perform baptisms by immersion and did so when requested. There is, though, considerable evidence that immersion was frequently looked upon as a practice to be reluctantly tolerated if the applicant could not be talked out of it, rather than as an equally desirable option. Immersion was stigmatized as "a very clumsy mode . . . a human invention which has crept into the Church since the apostles' day."[21] Robert Boyd of Pennsylvania made this disparaging view explicit, calling immersion, "turning aside from the ordinary and most proper course, . . . a provision for well meaning persons whose hearts are supposed to be much better than their heads."[22]

In spite of the status of immersion as an authorized option for Methodists, an attitude of genuine antipathy was not uncommon among preachers. In his report to Bishop Asbury about a camp meeting in the Richmond district, Stith Mead exulted, that of one hundred adults baptized, none had chosen immersion.[23] Jacob Gruber, a famous itinerant in Pennsylvania, was known to be strongly opposed to immersion.[24] Robert Finley was a controversial figure in Indiana for his frequently preached sermon on baptism in which he opined: "I will not say that any man who baptizes by immersion is an indecent man; but I will say, he has been guilty of an indecent act."[25] Such opposition was justified theologically on the grounds that insistence upon immersion was evidence of a view of baptism so distorted as to render the act invalid when so understood. In one of the earliest commentaries on the beliefs and practices of American Methodism, William Phoebus, who had been present at the Christmas Conference, argued that baptismal water was to be applied to the subject, not the subject to the water—"baptism is *with*, not *in* water."[26] Several commentators contended that in Scripture immersion is associated with destruction—as in the Flood and the annihilation of the Egyptians at the Red Sea—rather than with salvation.[27] In a sermon published in

Greensboro, North Carolina, S. S. Bryant summed up the misconceptions which made immersion more superstition than sacrament:

> It is far from certain that all who have been immersed with religious intent have indeed received the sacrament of baptism. If when immersed, the object of the rite in the mind of the subject is to set forth the resurrection and burial of the Lord Jesus Christ–if it is done to imitate Christ's personal baptism–if the intention is by going down into the water to express humility, it is not Christian baptism; and though this be done religiously, by a minister and in good faith, though immersed you are not baptized.[28]

These views of immersion were, of course, associated with the Baptists whose baptismal practice was being declared inauthentic, just as the Baptists had so labelled the "baby sprinkling" of the Methodists.

Although such extreme aversion to immersion was not typical, preachers and theologians were able to marshal a substantial list of justifications for their preference for sprinkling or pouring.[29] Many arguments focused on matters of practicality. Immersion was demeaned as usable only under optimal conditions of water supply and weather. It was pointed out that immersion was frequently inconvenient and uncomfortable, dangerous to health–especially in cases of age or infirmity, and shockingly "indecent"–meaning immodest–especially for women. These drawbacks were not viewed as simply matters of expediency; God would not have ordained the use of a mode beset with such improprieties. Interminable debates went on about the meaning of the New Testament word for "baptize," with Methodist students of Greek obdurate that it was not equivalent to "dip." Even if the meaning of the term was conceded to carry connotations of submersion, it was denied that this was to be followed literally, any more than the Lord's Supper was meant to be a full meal just because of its name. Old Testament scholars averred that Jewish purification rites employed sprinkling of water and that this understanding carried over into Christian baptism. New Testament scholars argued that the apostolic mode of baptism, as described in Acts, was sprinkling or pouring. John probably baptized by sprinkling, but even if not, his practice was no paradigm for the church since it was not Christian baptism. Jesus was most likely sprinkled by John since his baptism was actually a ceremony of priestly consecration. Theologians were adamant that baptism represented cleansing, not death-burial-resurrection, and that pouring was the mode most appropriately symbolic of the work of the Holy Spirit. Historians cited authorities from the patristic period to the Reformation who upheld sprinkling and pouring.[30] All of these arguments would be extensively refined and elaborated in the coming decades.

The Baptist practice of immersing converts who had previously received baptism by another mode—usually as infants—was the target of much complaint by Methodists. In general, Methodist spokespersons expressed firm opposition to the practice. At the very least it was pointless—"a seal, though applied a thousand times, leaves but one impression."[31] Worse, it was "a profanation of this sacrament."[32] Any flexibility on the issue of repeating baptism was seen as an aspersion of the sacrament as administered to infants and hence, for pedobaptists, an act "inconsistent and destructive."[33] In actuality, no Christian denomination practiced rebaptism as such; Baptists repeated the rite only because they considered infant baptism invalid.

A motif which was emerging in this period—especially in *Zion's Herald* and the *Western Christian Advocate*—was the responsibility of the church to provide to its people proper teaching on the subject of baptism so that they would not be prey to immersionists' arguments. In an attempt to meet that need, the 1836 General Conference directed the Sunday schools to provide instruction on "the nature, design, privileges and obligations" of Christian baptism.[34] Some interesting equivocation appeared, however, when the persons seeking Methodist baptism had been previously baptized as Roman Catholics. Such persons often claimed that the priests from whom they received the sacrament were themselves unregenerate, even immoral. Peter Cartwright was one who in such circumstances took a Donatist stance and agreed to repeat the sacrament.[35] Another hint that the question was not completely resolved came at the General Conference of 1844 when J. B. McFerrin proposed an inquiry into the expediency of introducing a rule in the *Discipline* explicitly prohibiting rebaptism. The motion was referred to committee and no further action taken at that time, but the issue would resurface in the future.[36]

A major focus of the ongoing debate with the Baptists was the eligibility of infants to receive baptism. Extensive discussion in the various *Christian Advocates* provided evidence that this issue augmented in importance as it functioned as a badge of identification for Methodists over against their anti-pedobaptist rivals. Many Methodist leaders were outspoken on the subject. As a presiding elder, William McKendree insisted that his preachers take an unyielding stand on infant baptism and set them an example by preaching on it at every quarterly meeting.[37] Heman Bangs wondered "how any parent can keep his children from Christ" which, he said, was the effect of denying them baptism.[38] Church periodicals urged readers to buy and study the writings on the issue by John Wesley and Richard Watson which were available from the Methodist Publishing House in tract form.[39] The pastoral address of the 1840 General Conference urged infant baptism and the Christian nurture of children.[40] Still, the very abundance of statements in support of infant baptism suggested that Methodist response was not universally positive.[41] An 1840 article in *Zion's Herald* presented what was probably the most accurate assessment. The writer complained that Methodist parents were neglecting to have their children baptized because of sectarian influences: "There is a vague prejudice against it which, if it should not be dissipated, would at least be enlightened and confirmed by investigation." Even when the sacrament was observed, it was too often simply a beautiful ceremony conducted with no real understanding of its import:

> It is scarcely understood that the child is inducted by this ordinance into a nominal but important relationship to the church. . . . It cannot be disguised that our church needs a universal revision of this subject. The usage had better be entirely repudiated than retained in its present indefinite form. We would respectfully suggest the thorough consideration of this subject to our ministry, both in the study and in the pulpit.[42]

Most of the arguments in favor of infant baptism had been enunciated in the eighteenth century and were reaffirmed and elaborated throughout the nineteenth. Children were asserted to have been part of the covenant between God and humanity since at least the time of Abraham; baptism had simply replaced circumcision as the covenant sign in the Christian dispensation. In the Jewish context within which Christianity originated, children would have been included in the covenant community and entitled to its token unless clearly barred, since such had been the practice in Old Testament times and in proselyte baptism. Jesus himself had explicitly affirmed the place of children in the Kingdom which included the visible church. Baptism initiates children into the church which will function as a school to teach them their relationship and obligation to God. Baptism of children was the typical practice of the New Testament church as evidenced by the household baptisms in Acts and as alluded to in many Scripture references—Matthew 28:19, I Corinthians 10:11, Ephesians 6:1, and I John 2:12–13, as examples.

Evidence for infant baptism did not cease with the Bible, but continued in the testimony of the fathers and in archaeological and artistic remains. Methodists insisted that the Baptist claim that faith and repentance were prerequisites for baptism substantiated the repulsive doctrine of infant damnation which even Baptists refused to accept, for the Scripture also said that those qualities were essential for salvation. Baptism also served as a comfort to bereaved parents (an important consideration in an age of high infant mortality) by providing assurance of heavenly reunions. The conclusions were summarized in a popular refrain which cited four places in which infants were found–in the church before Christ, in pedobaptist churches, "in the Savior's arms," and in heaven–in contrast to two places where infants were not to be found–in the "land of despair" (hell) and in the Baptist church.[43]

The Calvinists

One of the most significant arguments in favor of infant baptism was based on an understanding of the moral status or spiritual nature of young children. While it came to be widely agreed that there were properties characteristic of infants which gave them an affinity for the heavenly kingdom, and hence eligibility for the sign of entrance into the earthly church, the specifics of these spiritual qualities were the subject of extensive and prolonged debate. Any optimistic view of the spiritual nature of infants was a point of particular antagonism in areas where Calvinism was regnant, so controversy on the subject burgeoned as Methodism strengthened in New England in the early 1800s. Richard Watson, the English Methodist theologian so influential in America,[44] had stated the dichotomy clearly when he asserted that Calvinism implied the eternal punishment of infants who die, while Methodism was:

> . . . assured of the salvation of infants, also, because "the free gift has come upon all men" to [in order to] justification of life and because children are not capable of rejecting that blessing, and must, therefore, derive benefit from it.[45]

Methodism's most stalwart champion in the theological struggle with Calvinism was Wilbur Fisk who enunciated his position thusly:

> . . . the merits of the atonement are so available for and in behalf of the whole human family, that the guilt of depravity is not imputed to the subject of it, until by intelligent volition he makes the guilt his own by resisting and rejecting the grace of the gospel; . . . [the dying infant] being thus by grace in a justified state . . . is entitled to all the promised blessings of the new covenant [including baptism, the sign].[46]

Timothy Merritt suggested that the doctrines of election and reprobation were inconsistent with the practice of infant baptism.[47] Calvinists, of course, denied this, for their justification for baptizing infants was based upon the place of the offspring of believers in the covenant community. Methodists, too, had used variations of this argument as far back as Wesley himself, but in the context of controversy with the Calvinists a problem arose—what about the baptism of the children of unbelievers? If the right to the sacrament was a correlate of membership in the covenant community of which baptism was the initiatory sign, then surely it should be administered only to the children of Christian parents. But, if eligibility for baptism was a function of the spiritual nature of the child and a sign of God's universal grace made available through the atonement, then the sacrament could rightly be offered to every child. A protracted debate within Methodism ensued, fanned by Calvinist criticism of baptizing children of "vicious and profane" parents.[48]

Prior to the emergence of this question as a point of controversy, Methodist authors appeared to assume that children who were presented for baptism would be of families within the covenant community. Richard Watson was not speaking to this debate when he stated that the "infant children of believing parents are entitled to be made parties to the covenant of grace, by the act of their parents, and the administration of baptism."[49] Similarly, when early American Methodists declared that baptism should "be administered to all infants whose fathers or mothers are true Christians," they were defending the practice of infant baptism in general rather than defining which infants were entitled to it.[50] It was the dialectic with New England Calvinism that forced Methodists to address the specific problem of which children were to be baptized. Peter Sandford acknowledged in a 1829 sermon that a difference of opinion existed as to which children were eligible. He argued that the children and foster children of a person baptized into any branch of the Church of Christ were proper recipients. Interestingly, the 1832 editor of this sermon added a note in which he contended, against Sandford, that all infants who were presented by their parents should be granted the sacrament.[51] In 1839, the *Western Christian Advocate* reprinted a letter from the *Vermont Chronicle* in which the writer argued explicitly that the children of unbelievers were not to be baptized since the promises of the covenant extended only to the offspring of believers.[52]

Articles in the periodical literature as early as 1828 claimed that all children were the proper subjects of baptism since their right to it comes not from the faith of their parents but from Christ's atonement.[53] Timothy Merritt summarized this pole of the argument succinctly:

> We have a much better ground for baptizing infants than the piety of their parents; even their belonging to Christ, and their interest in him. . . . [T]he right of infants is wholly independent of the piety of their parents.[54]

In 1842 Orange Scott, a New England Methodist itinerant and presiding elder,[55] triggered a lengthy exchange in *Zion's Herald* when he submitted an article entitled "Children of Unbelievers" and asked for responses to it. Scott acknowledged that most writers with whom he was familiar did confine baptism to the children of believers, but he questioned the theological soundness of such a view:

> . . . are all infants members of the spiritual church of Christ? Are they equal in every respect, as to moral qualities? If these questions be answered in the affirmative, and it be admitted that all children are equally members of Christ's mystical body, then I ask, on what authority we deny infant baptism to the children of unbelievers? . . . If baptism be the sign of any inward grace, why refuse it to any who have that inward grace?

A response from a correspondent using the pseudonym "Consistency" failed to address the issue of spiritual qualities of infants, but did introduce a line of argument that would continue to be developed in the following decades:

> . . . while in such families and subject to the dictation and control of unbelieving parents, they can sustain no other relation to the visible church than the parents do, until they are capable of assuming a different relation voluntarily, and consequently have no right to any of its ordinances; nor would they derive any advantage, if admitted to that of baptism, for this plain reason, that the church has no control over them more than others, and the child has no instruction in relation to its duties and obligations more than others.

A correspondent from Maine argued against "Consistency" that children were not baptized because of the relationship that they have to the church, but because of the relationship that they sustain to God. If their relation is dependent upon that of the parent, it would be altered by the parent's apostasy. Another contributor to the debate agreed with Scott that all infants have the same moral qualities, but denied that this meant that all were entitled to baptism:

> . . . children have always sustained the same visible relation to the divine covenant which their parents have. . . . The peculiar holiness of those children belonging to the visible church is of a relative or

> federal character. A mere fitness in moral character, therefore, does not fix the relation to the visible church.[56]

This exchange defined the parameters of a debate which would continue throughout the century. In 1844 the question of baptizing the children of non-members was raised at the General Conference, but no action was taken. The records suggest a consensus of unwillingness to discuss the matter, with some delegates contending that because baptism was covered in the doctrines protected by the Restrictive Rules, it was not constitutionally open for debate.[57]

The question of the spiritual or moral nature of infants agitated the Methodist Episcopal Church throughout the nineteenth century, especially as it related to the theological justification of infant baptism. Opinions were widely divergent; Allen Wiley spoke of "a fierce and unpleasant controversy . . . among Methodist preachers, concerning infant purity on one hand, and innate depravity on the other. . . ."[58] The Anglican priest and early supporter of Methodism, Devereaux Jarratt simplified the question by insisting that children were either "in a gracious state" or they were damned and, if in a state of grace they were entitled to baptism.[59] Francis Asbury spoke of infants as "the present subjects of salvation" but vehemently denied "infant purity" saying that such a doctrine was "directly opposed to Watts, Wesley, Fletcher and all gospel divines." In a letter to McKendree, he averred:

> . . . to suppose that infants have no sinful nature or anything to do with sin, until they know the law and willfully commit sin, is like Baptist logic [that if] infants cannot repent and believe, infants are not fit subjects of baptism. . . . that infants are justified, regenerated and sanctified as adults, I doubt if Scripture will bear us out.[60]

The dominant position expressed by Methodist theologians in the first half of the nineteenth century was that infants were born with a corruption of nature—a propensity to sin—but not with any imputed guilt, since that had been canceled by Christ's atonement. Infants were, then, in a state of justification but not of purification or holiness. Only actual, personal sin committed after accountability brought guilt. Infants were morally fitted for the state of probation which earthly life provided. They were included in both original sin and the covenant of grace.[61]

The Anglicans and Episcopalians

Another denominational dialectic within which Methodists formulated their understanding of baptism was that with the Church of England and Protestant Episcopal Church, or at least the high sacramental theology with which Methodists identified them. The issue here was the meaning of baptismal regeneration for infants. Most Methodist writers agreed with Devereaux Jarratt that baptism was referred to as regeneration "because it is natural to call the sign by the name of the thing signified."[62] The *Methodist Magazine* in 1818 affirmed that the doctrine of regeneration was to be sharply distinguished from that of baptismal regeneration, which it denied had been taught by either the apostles, the reformers, or Wesley.[63] The *New York Christian Advocate* contained more material on the issue than other periodicals and often the dispute centered on the views of Wesley. Daniel Curry, influential editor of several church periodicals, did not attempt to deny that the founding patriarch had taught baptismal regeneration, but did deny that his views were authoritative for American Methodists: "Wesley's *Treatise on Baptism* has never been received as any part of Methodist doctrine; and therefore his American editor (Bishop Emory) has annexed to it a note of dissent."[64] John Hersey contended that baptism effected a forensic rather than a spiritual change in the child's character: baptism "legally introduces our children into Christ's Kingdom on earth; consequently they are in that act legally brought to life; so that baptism may be called a new birth."[65] In general, Methodists were adamantly opposed to any understanding of baptism which failed clearly to differentiate the outward sign—"the act of man"—from the inward grace—"the operation of the Holy Ghost."[66]

Along with these efforts at theological definition and defense, an understanding of infant baptism was beginning to develop which would grow stronger during the nineteenth century and finally become regnant in the twentieth—baptism as the act of dedicating one's children to God. Thomas Ware was one of the few writers to employ this terminology in the eighteenth century.[67] In the early 1800s, several articles spoke of dedication in baptism as did Peter Cartwright in accounts in both of his books.[68] Memoirs also reflected this conception of baptism. E. F. Newell of the New England conference described the baptism of his infant son as "confirming publicly what we had before done privately." John Stewart wrote similarly of the baptism of his first-born: "we gave him to God, promising that we would try to bring him up in the nurture and admonition of the

Lord."[69] The 1840 *Discipline* directed pastors to "diligently instruct and exhort all parents to dedicate their children to the Lord in baptism as early as convenient. . . ."—the first official use of this phrase. "Instructions for Baptized Children" in the Children's Department of the *Western Christian Advocate* admonished its readers to pious living since your "parents have dedicated you to God because you owe all the blessings of life to Him."[70] S. S. Bryant's 1843 "Sermon on Infant Baptism" presented a cogent statement of the theology of the sacrament which had evolved:

> God has given to your children, as fully as to you, the promises connected with the covenant of grace. The sign and seal of the covenant is baptism. The spiritual influences and the grace of the covenant are with God, to be bestowed according to the rules which he has revealed in his word: the external, visible sign is left with you; and if you would heed the commandment to "train them up in the way they should go;" or "suffer the little children" as he tells you he desires they should "to come unto him," the obligation is imperative that you make the first step in the training, a solemn consecration to the service of the Almighty, and bring them in the only way they can be brought to him, through the holy sacrament of baptism. . . . The baptism of a child sets forth the faith of the parents in God's covenant promise; by this dedication they declare to the Church and the world, their faith in the efficiency of his blood to cleanse them and their children from all unrighteousness. . . . The parent acts in obedience to the command of Christ, "suffer the little children to come unto me." He carries them to him. . . . There can be no error, for Christ has declared his fitness, "of such is the kingdom of heaven."[71]

ISSUES OF BAPTISM AND CHURCH MEMBERSHIP

American Methodists evinced little doubt about the propriety of infant baptism, but considerable confusion as to its theological significance. Especially problematic was the issue of the ecclesiastical import of baptism—what was the relationship of baptized children to the church and how should the church care for such children? Freeborn Garrettson posed the situation in his 1826 semi-centennial sermon to the New York Conference:

> Can we answer to God for our conduct towards the rising generation? We baptize thousands of little children, and what becomes of them? The primitive ministers and Christians held them as members of Christ's mystical body, saluted them with the church's kiss of peace, gave them the eucharist, and had great patience with their childish

> inadvertencies, giving them instructions and admonitions, as their tender minds could have hold of Christ in the promises, and actually to feel themselves put into possession of their promised inheritance, by a living, active faith in the Son of God. When any of them proved stubborn and rebellious, refusing to accept their covenanted blessings, the bread that did not prove salutary, was withheld under suspension; or after long forbearance, when necessity compelled, they were excommunicated. Till thus prohibited, as far as they were capable, they were entitled to all the immunities of the Christian church. Our children should be put in classes, and as soon as they are able to receive religious instruction, they should be met weekly by the minister, or some other suitable person appointed for the occasion. I am well satisfied, that if parents, or guardians, and the church generally, were to take due pains in training the rising generation, instead of running wild, and fashioning themselves after the world as they grow up, their minds would be drawn to God, and most of them would embrace religion.[72]

Church law continued to manifest the Methodist concern for children which had been characteristic since Wesley. The 1824 *Discipline* required pastors to form the children into regular classes for religious instruction and to have a leader to conduct such classes in the preacher's absence. In 1836 the content of this instruction was broadened to include "the nature, design, privileges and obligations" of baptism, as well as "the nature of experimental religion." Dealing more explicitly with the question of membership, the 1840 *Discipline* stipulated that baptized children "who are well disposed may be admitted to our class meetings and love feasts, and such as are truly serious, and manifest a desire to flee the wrath to come, shall be advised to join society as probationers." In spite of these provisions, the periodical literature witnessed to a continuing dilemma:

> If baptized infants should have a place in the visible church and the Methodist Episcopal Church acknowledge no specific relation, does not infant baptism become nearly an unmeaning ceremony?[73]

S. S. Bryant was one of many commentators who pointed out that, because of the failure of parents and church, children who had received baptism often "grow up in a disregard of its obligations, live in sin and are far from God as if they had never been presented at the altar, and it does them no good."[74]

A concomitant of the discussion about the place of baptized children in the church was the question of their participation in the sacrament of the Lord's Supper. The *Treatise* by Moses Hemmenway which had appeared in the *Discipline* in the 1790s had directed that children had both a right and a duty to participate:

> . . . when they can so far understand the nature and design of [it] and have such a measure of knowledge and faith, that they can discern the Lord's body, and examine themselves. . . .

The issue became a point of controversy when anti-pedobaptist critics argued that if children were to be admitted to one sacrament, they had an equal right to the other. Benjamin Lakin, an itinerant in Kentucky and Ohio in the early years of the century, delineated a distinction which was often repeated when he called baptism "a passive ordinance" to which children were eligible, but the Lord's Supper an "active" one of which children were not capable.[75] Henry Slicer contributed other elements to the debate, arguing that infant communion was nothing more than "an act of superstition" since infants "cannot discern the Lord's body" and "partake in a remembrance of Him." All baptized children were not to be admitted to the Lord's Supper, just as Jewish children were barred from eating the Passover meal until they were twelve years old.[76]

When the subject was adults, the questions of the relationships between baptism, conversion, church membership, and participation in the Lord's Supper were even more complex. In the sectarian ethos of early American Methodism, baptism was not prerequisite to membership.[77] The sacrament was often postponed because of the scarcity of ordained preachers and, even into the first decades of the nineteenth century, it was not unusual to find unbaptized persons holding official positions in local congregations.[78] An exchange of correspondence in the *Western Christian Advocate* in 1835 made clear that there was some opposition to a requirement of baptism for membership. One writer insisted that, "baptism is not the door of admittance into our church" and that ministers could not expel members for neglecting it.[79] The General Conference of 1836 clarifed this issue by amending the *Discipline* to state that none might be received into the church until they had been baptized. Editors Thomas Morris and Leonidas Hamline spoke what they understood to be the last word on the question:

> The sacrament of baptism is to be retained in our church. All children of her members are to be baptized; and it is the duty of parents to present them for baptism, and those who neglect it, or do not believe in it, are unfit members of the Methodist Episcopal Church, whatever their qualifications may be in other respects. Those who refuse to be baptized themselves, when they have the privilege of choosing between baptism by affusion and baptism by immersion, after sufficient time is given them for consideration and the commu-

> nication of instruction, had better choose another branch of Christ's church for their home than the Methodist Episcopal.[80]

Even then all controversy was not squelched. In debate during the General Conference of 1844, at least two speakers contended that the requirement of baptism for membership was an unconstitutional violation of the Restrictive Rules.[81] However, no serious effort to remove the requirement was undertaken.

Many who accepted baptism as a necessary condition for membership did not consider it, however, as a sufficient condition for denominational affiliation. The sacrament was widely viewed as introducing a person into the general church of Christ, but not into a particular branch of it.[82] Membership in the Methodist Episcopal Church had from the beginning been contingent upon satisfactory completion of a period of probation which in 1788 was set at six months.[83] There was little controversy during the first half of the century about this probationary stipulation. Discussion centered, instead, on the relationship between baptism, conversion, and church membership. John Wesley had specified "one only condition" for those desiring admission to the Methodist societies: "a desire to flee from the wrath to come, and to be saved from their sins."[84] American Methodists following this provision administered baptism to persons who were deemed to be "true penitents," as well as to those judged to be converted believers, and admitted both groups into the church as probationary members. Baptism could as acceptably precede spiritual regeneration as follow or be simultaneous with it. This practice was justified repeatedly by references to the baptism of the Samaritans in the eighth chapter of Acts.[85] Persons who sincerely desired to embrace the gospel should be brought into the church—the best place to get and keep religion.[86] Such persons should be incorporated into classes and baptized as quickly as possible to guard against the danger of their being wooed away by Baptists or other rival groups.[87]

The Methodist practice of baptizing and admitting into membership penitents who could not yet claim conversion was a focus of criticism by persons of other denominations. Methodists defended themselves by asserting that their church's requirements were in reality stricter than those of its competitors, since persons were admitted first into the six months period of probation who in other denominations would be immediately inducted into full membership. Peter Cartwright summarized this position:

> The Methodist Church, in our humble opinion, stands, in this respect, on preeminently Scriptural ground. They give every sinner

> a chance, and take them on probation for six months, not as members, but under the care of the Church, on trial for membership; and surely, if they do not in that time give satisfactory evidence that they are in good earnest in seeking their salvation, what then? Expel then? No; for they are not members to expel. What then? We simply drop them and consider them no longer probationers for membership; leave them where we found them; we have at least tried to do them good, and have done them no harm. This is the safety-valve of the Methodist Episcopal Church; six months on trial for membership. How dreadfully have other sister churches been troubled in their mode of operation! They generally believe that a Christian can never fall away so as to be finally lost, and that it is wrong to receive any into the Church who are not Christians. Well, in order to get people into the Church, they are often found hurrying them into a profession of religion when they have none; and then, when such fall away, with what astonishing mortification they have to confess they were mistaken; that these souls were deceived; that they never had any religion! And yet they hurl their anathemas at Methodist preachers for taking persons as probationers for membership without religion, while they have actually done infinitely worse, for they have taken them into the Church as full members, and as Christians too, when they were not. Now if our economy is wrong, what must theirs be?[88]

Clearly the prime goal of the probationary period was that persons be assisted in coming to an experience of saving faith; the trial period was sometimes extended beyond six months if that had not occurred. Ultimately though, the absence of a salvation experience did not function as a barrier to full church membership:

> In the Methodist Church, it is not required as a condition of membership, that the person must have a knowledge of salvation by the remission of his sins. But it is required that he be resolved to forsake all sin, do all the good in his power, and use all the means of grace. . . .[89]

The name of every person listed in both class and church records was supposed to be prefixed with either an *S* or a *B*–indicating whether the person was a seeker or a believer. "And when a person professes to receive the witness of adoption, the *S* is changed for the *B*, when, in the judgment of charity, the change is real. . . ."[90] Questions of the requisite spiritual status of church members would grow increasingly problematic with a greater emphasis on conversion later in the century.[91]

The final issue in the complex surrounding baptism and church membership was that of eligibility to partake of the Lord's Supper. Attention was concentrated upon this question at least partially because of the Baptist practice of close communion—refusing the sacrament to all who had not been immersed.[92] This Baptist usage was the target of sustained polemical discussion and it may be logically assumed that Methodist reluctance to be too dogmatic in their own requirements was motivated by their antipathy to close communion. The practice was attacked as destructive to Christian unity and as delegitimizing the faith of proponents of other denominations. Methodists perceived themselves as irenic and tolerant, while viewing Baptists as rigid and arrogant. Periodicals in the opening decades of the century contained occasional queries about the propriety of allowing unbaptized persons to commune; obviously such a practice was fairly common.[93] In the absence of a clear position in either Scripture or church law, no definitive opinion was articulated.

♦ ♦ ♦

By 1844, the Methodist Episcopal Church had evolved its theological understandings of baptism in the contexts of dialectical contacts with other denominational groups. The modes of sprinkling and pouring were identified as preferable to that of immersion. Baptism for infants was affirmed as the sacrament which recognized their membership in the church of Christ. Disagreements continued over the precise grounds for their eligibility and over the pragmatic connection between infant baptism and denominational membership. Even greater ambiguity existed in the areas of adult conversion, membership and access to the sacraments. An article from the Congregationalist paper *The Puritan* raised embarrassing questions for the Methodists whom it criticized: "But how a person can join a class which is part of a church, and be admitted to the most holy ordinances of the church, and still not be a member of the church, is hard to be understood."[94] Obviously, further evolution and refinement were needed and these processes continued in both the northern and southern branches of the divided church.[95]

CHAPTER V

Salient Issues in the First Decades of the Divided Church: 1845–1866

The 1844 General Conference of the Methodist Episcopal Church outlined a plan of separation by which the denomination divided itself into northern and southern branches. The Methodist Episcopal Church, South was organized in 1845–46. Competition between the two churches was intense in the antebellum years and grew into antipathy during the Civil War and Reconstruction periods. The points of conflict were not, however, theological, and no significant divergence on issues related to baptism can be descried. Congruent currents of thought existed in the two churches on this subject, although the majority of the written material was produced by and for the northern branch.

AUTHORIZED CHURCH STATEMENTS ON BAPTISM

From 1825 to 1861, Wesley's two treatises comprised the major portion of the material on baptism in the *Collection of Interesting Tracts* published by the Methodist Episcopal Church. When the Wesley pieces were dropped, they were replaced with a sixty-page tract by a contemporary, but anonymous, author which remained an official doctrinal statement on baptism until the *Collection* ceased to be published after 1892. Approximately half of this tract was devoted to a defense of infant baptism, chiefly as a scriptural and historical practice. The latter half of the piece argued for sprinkling or pouring as the preferable mode of baptism.

As early as the 1820s attempts had been made at General Conference to revise the ritual for infant baptism. Concern was focused on this portion of the prayer: " . . . by the baptism of thy well-beloved Son Jesus Christ in the river Jordan did sanctify water for this holy sacrament." Critics objected not only to the idea of sanctified water, but also to the implication that the baptism of Christ was to be viewed as paradigmatic. The southern church omitted this section in 1854, and the northern, a decade later. Other modifications in the ritual were subtle attempts to tone down suggestions of baptismal regeneration and of original depravity. For example, in 1864 the Methodist Episcopal Church removed that portion of the prayer which beseeched God to grant to the infant "that thing which by nature he cannot have" and the portion of the Mozarabic Sentences which asked that "the old Adam may be so buried." Also significant were the additions—in 1864 in the Methodist Episcopal Church and 1866 in the Methodist Episcopal Church, South—of an address to and vows for the parents.

The Methodist Episcopal Church, South issued its first hymnal in 1847—*A Collection of Hymns for Public, Social, and Domestic Worship*. It contained four hymns listed for use at the baptism of adults and four for infant baptism. Charles Wesley's "Come, Father, Son, and Holy Ghost" was retained from the 1802 hymnal, but the other three adult baptism hymns had not previously appeared in an official American Methodist hymnal:

1. 'Twas the commission of our Lord,
 "Go, teach the nations, and baptize:"
The nations have received the word
 Since he ascended to the skies.

2. "Repent, and be baptized," he saith,
 "For the remission of your sins;"
And thus our sense assists our faith,
 And shows us what his gospel means.

3. Our souls he washes in his blood,
 As water makes the body clean;
And the good Spirit from our God
 Descends, like purifying rain.

4. Thus we engage ourselves to thee,
 And seal our cov'nant with the Lord;
O may the great Eternal Three
 In heaven our solemn vows record!

1. Rites change not, Lord, the heart,—
   Undo the evil done,—
   Or, with the utter'd name, impart
   The nature of thy Son.

2. To meet our desp'rate want,
   There gush'd a mystic flood;
   O from His heart's o'erflowing font
   Baptize this soul with blood!

3. Be grace from Christ our Lord,
   And love from God supreme,
   By the communing Spirit pour'd
   In a perpetual stream.

1. Baptized into thy name,
   Mysterious One in Three
   Our souls and bodies claim
   A sacrifice to thee:
   We only live our faith to prove,
   The faith which works by humble love.

2. O that our light may shine,
   And all our lives express
   The character divine,
   The *real* holiness!
   Then, then receive us up t' adore
   The triune God for evermore.[1]

" 'Twas the commission of our Lord" described the sacrament in terms strongly reflective of the views of John Calvin. "Rites change not, Lord, the heart" repudiated the doctrine of baptismal regeneration, while "Baptized into thy name" emphasized that faith must be proven in living. Three of the infant baptism hymns were holdovers from the 1836 hymnal—"How large the promise," "God of eternal truth and love," and "See Israel's gentle Shepherd stand." Added was "Thus Lydia sanctified her house" which portrayed infant baptism as a practice of the New Testament church:

1. Thus Lydia sanctified her house
   When she received the word;
   Thus the believing jailer gave
   His household to the Lord.

2. Thus later saints, eternal King,
   Thine ancient truth embrace;
   To thee their infant offspring bring,
   And humbly claim the grace.[2]

In response to action of the General Conference, the Methodist Episcopal Church published a substantially enlarged official hymnal in 1849.[3] Three previously used baptismal hymns were omitted, but ten selections were included under this rubric, with no distinction as to use with the adult or infant ceremonies. Four of these hymns were carried over from the 1836 book—"Come, Father, Son, and Holy Ghost," "How large the promise, how divine," "See Israel's gentle Shepherd stand," and "God of eternal truth and love," while another—"Baptized into thy name"—appeared in the southern hymnal of 1847. The five new hymns were designed for use at infant baptisms:

1. Our children thou dost claim,
O Lord Our God, as thine:
Ten thousand blessings to thy Name,
For goodness so divine.

2. Thee let the fathers own,
Thee let the sons adore;
Join'd to the Lord in solemn vows,
To be forgot no more.

3. How great thy mercies, Lord!
How plenteous is thy grace,
Which, in the promise of thy love,
Includes our rising race.

4. Our offspring, still thy care,
Shall own their fathers' God;
To latest times thy blessings share,
And sound thy praise abroad.

1. Jesus, kind, inviting Lord,
We with joy obey thy word,
And in earliest infancy
Bring our little ones to thee.

2. Born they are, as we, in sin;
Make the' unconscious lepers clean;
Purchase of thy blood they are,—
Let them in thy glory share.

1. Great God, now condescend
To bless our rising race;
Soon may their willing spirits bend,
The subjects of thy grace.

2. O what a pure delight
Their happiness to see;
Our warmest wishes all unite,
To lead their souls to thee.

3. Now bless, thou God of love,
This ordinance divine;
Send thy good Spirit from above,
And make these children thine.

1. Behold what condescending love
Jesus on earth displays!—
To babes and sucklings he extends
The riches of his grace.

2. He still the ancient promise keeps,
To our forefathers given;
Young children in his arms he takes,
And calls them heirs of heaven.

3. Forbid them not, whom Jesus calls,
Nor dare the claim resist,
Since his own lips to us declare
Of such will heaven consist.

4. With flowing tears, and thankful hearts,
We give them up to thee;
Receive them, Lord, into thine arms;
Thine may they ever be.

1. Jesus, we lift our souls to thee;
Thy Holy Spirit breathe,
And let this little infant be
Baptized into thy death.

2. O let thine unction on *him* rest,
Thy grace *his* soul renew,
And write within *his* tender breast
Thy name and nature too.

3. If thou shouldst quickly end *his* days,
His place with thee prepare;
And if thou lengthen out *his* race,
Continue still thy care.

4. Thy faithful servant let *him* prove,
Begirt with truth divine;
A sharer in thy dying love,
A follower of thine.[4]

In "Our children thou dost claim" and "Behold what condescending love," gratitude was expressed to God for extending the blessings of the covenant to children. Two of the hymns—"Great God, now condescend" and "Jesus, we lift our souls to thee"—were prayers evoking God's spiritual blessings on children. "Jesus, kind, inviting Lord" contained the reference to infants as "unconscious lepers" born in sin. Clearly some diverse understandings of the sacrament were being expressed concurrently.

DEFINING OF DOCTRINE AND PRACTICE

Much of the articulation of Methodist doctrine and practice in this period was accomplished in a dialectical, even polemical, context. Although American Methodism was becoming more self-confident, it still defended and defined itself against other denominational traditions. Salient questions of the mid-nineteenth century relating to baptism included baptismal regeneration, propriety of modes, rebaptism, and justification for infant baptism.

Baptismal Regeneration

Methodist spokespersons continued to condemn the Campbellites for their "God-dishonoring and soul-destroying" linkage of water baptism and remission of sins.[5] But at the same time, the Methodists themselves were vulnerable in this area, at least to the minds of their Baptist critics. James R. Graves, editor of the *Tennessee Baptist* in his vitriolic attack, *The Great Iron Wheel*, charged that Methodism clearly taught that in baptism "all infants and children are actually cleansed from original sin, and regenerated. . . ." Graves quoted from the Methodist ritual for infant baptism and from Wesley's *Treatise on Baptism* to substantiate his contention.[6] While they vehemently denied such charges, Methodists themselves evinced concern about Wesley's views on baptismal regeneration. His *Treatise* was a source of embarrassment which was exacerbated by the fact that it continued to be published under the auspices of the General Conference. Some writers attempted to deny that Wesley had actually accepted baptismal regeneration, but this position proved difficult to sustain in the face of the explicit evidence in his writings. More commonly, American Methodists tried to argue that Wesley changed his views later in life and that the *Treatise* represented an early, transient phase of his thought.[7] Perhaps it was this discomfiture with Wesley's position that motivated his American followers to deprecate so frequently what they saw as erroneous doctrine in Anglican and Episcopalian tradition.[8]

Writers in both northern and southern branches of the church asserted repeatedly that baptism was not to be understood as synonymous with spiritual regeneration. Baptism was neither the agent of regeneration nor its essential antecedent. Baptism was rather to be understood as the sign, seal, and promise of regeneration—which work must be done by the Holy Spirit, in the Spirit's chosen way and time.[9] Methodists condemned as a "dangerous heresy" any teaching which made baptism an essential condition for salvation.[10] They argued that no Methodist minister believed in baptismal regeneration and that the use of the word "regeneration" in reference to infants meant only a change in covenant condition—of relation to God and the church—and not a change in moral status.[11] Incessant were the calls for revision in the baptismal rituals in order to expunge any hint of baptismal regeneration. Concern focused on the use of John 3:5 which many insisted had no reference to baptism and, hence, no place in the rituals.[12] There was real apprehension that baptism might be understood in such a way as to vitiate the role of repentance and faith in the salvation process. In their enthusiasm for personal, experiential conversion and their determination to avoid too high a view of the sacraments, American Methodists often tended to denigrate the significance of baptism and exposed themselves to the danger of what S. M. Merrill called "semi-Quakerism."[13]

Mode

Continual dispute with the exclusive immersionists was a Methodist preoccupation throughout the nineteenth century; the theological and periodical literature of 1845–66 contained much material on the subject.[14] In general, the Methodist position was that there was no scriptural warrant for insisting upon any particular mode of baptism to the exclusion of others. Neither lexicographical study of New Testament Greek nor historical analysis of New Testament practice identified immersion as the original mode of the Christian sacrament.[15] Many Methodist writers averred that sprinkling or pouring was the preferable mode, not only for its practicality, but also because it best represented the operation of the Holy Spirit in regeneration.[16]

Historical records provide evidence that Methodist preachers usually were willing to adhere to the *Discipline* and allow converts to choose their mode of baptism.[17] Immersion was most commonly practiced on the frontier and in other areas where competition with Baptists and Campbellites was keen. Emphasis was usually placed on the inconsequential nature of the choice of mode as long as the spiritual significance of the sacrament was perceived.[18] In seeking to underline this point, R. Abbey asserted, "It is known that in the early Church not less than probably twenty different modes of baptizing were practiced."[19] Few writers were quite so liberal, but standard Methodist opinion was well expressed by Thomas A. Morris: "We are opposed, not so much to immersion, as to that sort of bigotry, which says, you shall receive the ordinance of baptism in this way, or you shall not receive it at all."[20]

Concurrent with these irenic expressions toward immersionists, there was a common Methodist attitude of condescension, sometimes edging toward contempt. After explaining the superiority of sprinkling or pouring and tracing how immersion had developed as a result of superstition about the effects of the water, Thomas Summers allowed:

> . . . we are disposed to make any concession to the immersionists which will not involve a surrender of principle, or a sanction of error. We are ready to recognize their mode of performing baptism as valid, though a departure from the primitive mode, and a clumsy way of performing an otherwise simple, beautiful, and impressive ordinance. We may, indeed, in special cases and in condescension to weak consciences, administer the ordinance by plunging—though, in such cases, affusion ought not to be omitted. . . .[21]

In his discussion of John the Baptist, Summers could not resist a sarcastic, anti-immersionist footnote:

> They certainly had not any contrivances like those described in an advertisement before us: "Baptismal pants, expressly designed for baptizing purposes—manufactured from Vulcanized Metallic Rubber McIntosh cloth, warranted perfectly water-proof." These, we discover, are offered to "the reverend clergy": we are not informed whether it would be lawful for the subject, as well as the administrator, to be encased in India-Rubber, or whether there be any similar invention for those who stand most in need of it.[22]

Methodists often claimed that persons who sought immersion were motivated by the dramatic appeal of the ceremony and by a prideful desire to be the center of popular attention.[23] Another line of attack was exemplified by Orceneth Fisher, who traced the history of immersion from the Anabaptists to the Campbellites, spicing his account with caustically unflattering descriptions of the performance of the rite. Fisher insisted that immersion had been invented by the Jews—an example of "their moral degeneration"—and had crept into the early church as a perversion. Such immersion required the subjects to be naked and such an "indecent rite," Fisher declared, could not possibly be from God.[24] A more scholarly, but equally incisive, impeachment of immersion was presented in two sermons by Daniel D. Whedon entitled "The Double Baptism—Real and Symbolical." Because Whedon was so influential in nineteenth-century American Methodism—as a theologian and editor of the *Methodist Quarterly Review*, 1856–84—his views were significant. Whedon contended that immersion could not be baptism because the Scripture always represented the baptizing element as descending upon the subject: "Pouring alone (or sprinkling, which is merely moderate pouring) . . . is the only adequate symbol . . . of the Spirit's operation." Immersion was seen by Whedon as a form of "self-conversionism" since "all comes from man, and nothing from heaven." He insisted that, in spite of the option allowed in the *Discipline*, Methodists should always employ sprinkling or pouring:

> Immersion, then, is not baptism; for he is an illogical reasoner, who first declares that immersion is not authorized by Scripture, that it does not express the idea which the divine mind intended it to symbolize, and then declares that the form is indifferent. . . . Affusion alone meets the divine purpose, and fulfills, formally, the divine command.[25]

Specimens of intense anti-immersion sentiment were common in the periodicals of the church where the practice was repeatedly labelled as "anti-scriptural," "a device of disordered human imagination," "utterly derogatory to human dignity," and "a sacrifice of self-respect."[26]

The stimulus for much anti-immersion adamancy on the part of Methodists was the development of Landmarkism among the Southern Baptists in the middle of the century. Originated by the influential editor James R. Graves, this movement insisted that the only true church was the Baptist, which could trace its history back to the time of Christ. The evidence of authentic historical succession was that each minister had to have been immersed by an administrator who had himself been so baptized.[27] Methodists took vehement exception to such a claim, calling it "childish and ridiculous"—"Baptist humbug." They scornfully pointed out that Roger Williams, colonial minister from whom most American Baptists traced their origin, was not himself immersed by a properly immersed administrator.[28]

Methodists spun elaborate denials that immersion was a practice of New Testament times. Much of this argument centered on the activities of John the Baptist. To Baptist calls to "follow your Lord into the water," Methodists asserted that Jesus' baptism was an act of consecration inducting Him into the priesthood, thus in no way an example for His followers. Although John's baptism was not a Christian rite and not paradigmatic for Christians, it was almost surely administered by sprinkling or pouring rather than immersion, in accordance with Exodus 29:1–4 and Leviticus 8:6.[29] Long and complex expositions by Methodist authors detailed the evidence for these contentions. Many claimed that John's baptism was a Jewish ceremony of purification and these were always acts of sprinkling or pouring.[30] Some cited the testimony of travellers that the current of the Jordan River was too swift to allow immersions; others, that John did not baptize at the river at all, but at a place far south in Canaan.[31] There were, for decades, numerous variants of the argument that John did not baptize by immersion, since that would have been a "literal and physical impossibility." Hiram Shaffer's intricate hypothesis was based on the numbers of persons involved: the total population of Judea in John's time must have been around five million of whom some three million may be assumed to have come for baptism. In his eight-month ministry, it would have been necessary for John to have stood "in the water up to his waist, and baptized for six hours every day" at the rate of thirty-four baptisms every minute. Obviously this could not have been done by immersion, but would have been possible by sprinkling.[32] Similar arguments were developed to prove that the three thousand converts on the Day of Pentecost could not have been immersed since there were no pools of water in Jerusalem which could have accommodated them.[33]

Rebaptism

Since 1786 Methodist church law had made no provision for rebaptism, but questions on the subject continued to surface. One focus of uncertainty was the validity of the initial administration of the rite. During this period, Campbellite and Mormon immersions were frequently cited as being such perversions as to disqualify them as legitimate baptisms.[34] The question of the validity of lay administration arose occasionally, although this was never a widespread concern. Since Wesley, Methodism had insisted that the sacraments were to be performed only by ordained ministers. Since baptism was not understood as essential for salvation, there was no justification for "emergency" lay administration. Still, with many unordained preachers active in ministry, lay administration did sometimes occur.[35] Thomas Summers's conclusions were representative of majority opinion on the subject: Lay persons are not to baptize since this is a function of the ministerial office. However, there was no Scripture forbidding lay baptism:

> . . . if they should at any time administer the ordinance, and it should appear that it was seriously done—the subject, matter, and form were according to the institution—and the party baptized, or if an infant, his natural representatives, endorsed the act by assuming the obligations of baptism, there ought to be no rebaptization.[36]

Summers recognized a significant role for the opinion of the recipient of baptism, saying that his or her satisfaction with the rite was a major factor in deciding whether or not it should be repeated.[37] An even stronger subjective emphasis was expressed by a *New York Christian Advocate* correspondent who insisted that any persons dissatisfied with their childhood sprinkling should be allowed rebaptism by whatever mode they preferred. Great loss of membership in the Methodist church, he argued, resulted from refusal to sanction the repetition of the sacrament.[38] Perhaps the extreme of this position was expressed by Tennessee itinerant Green Jackson who told in his autobiography about persuading the minister to immerse him when he sought church membership in 1855, even though he had been baptized in infancy: "And while he [Jackson himself] does not now see any reason whatever for the necessity of his rebaptism, yet he does not at all regret it." Jackson went on to explain that he understood the sacrament not only as initiatory, but also as symbolic:

> So it becomes evident that the particular mode of baptism which any one may select on coming into the Church depends altogether upon the peculiar fact in his Christian experience which he wishes to make most prominent by that sacred ceremony. If he should desire to emphasize his resurrection from the death of sin into the spiritual and eternal life, he will be immersed; but if he should have in view the precious truth that he has been saved from sin and ruin by the baptism of the Holy Spirit, he will by all means prefer pouring; and in case he should attempt to place special stress upon his purification from all unrighteousness by the blood of Jesus, he will be sure to ask baptism by aspersion.
>
> Now the writer has already given symbolic expression to his spiritual resurrection and baptism of the Holy Spirit by the two modes of the sacred ordinance which he has received, *immersion* and *pouring*, and he has often felt that he would like to be baptized also by *sprinkling*, that he might thereby declare the conscious fact that he

> has been washed, cleansed, and sanctified by the blood of Jesus his Saviour, and he can see no good reason why this should not be done.[39]

Such views as Jackson's, while not rare, were not typical of nineteenth-century Methodism. Most writers expressed strong opposition to rebaptism, chiefly on the grounds that it denied the validity of infant baptism. The analogy of baptism to circumcision and its function as a rite of initiation underlined its unrepeatable quality.[40] The famous Congregationalist minister Henry Ward Beecher stirred up controversy in the 1850s when he accepted the idea of "free rebaptism." Methodists argued that baptized persons who backslid and forfeited their salvation did not need rebaptism when they repented any more than persons who travelled in a foreign land would have to be readmitted to citizenship when they returned home.[41] As for baptized infants who as adults requested rebaptism: "we should refuse; for we make a mockery of the ordinance in reapplying it when we believe it is invalid. . . . If we are sincere in the act, we unbaptize the rest of our Church."[42]

Infant Baptism

Strong emphasis on the validity of infant baptism was a perduring characteristic of episcopal Methodism; arguments in its defense were prolix, and exhortations to its observation incessant. There is no evidence in the eighteenth- and nineteenth-century sources of any equivocation on the subject. Alongside this comprehensive support for infant baptism were, however, recurring complaints about its neglect. Presbyterian writer Henry Brown opined in 1856 that "no Church which holds the ordinances of infant baptism neglects it so much [as the Methodist]."[43] Methodist commentators agreed, pointing out particular areas of the country where the problem was most acute.[44] Apologia was plainly addressed to Methodist people themselves as well as to their anti-pedobaptist rivals.

Most of the typical justifications for infant baptism were expanded recapitulations of earlier contentions. The place of infants in the Old Testament covenant and their eligibility for its initiatory sign continued to be a major point of emphasis as did the actions and words of Christ in receiving children.[45] It was repeatedly affirmed that infant baptism was the common practice of the New Testament church,[46] the patristic era, and, indeed, the universal and perpetual observance of Christendom, with only a few aberrant exceptions.[47] A significant addition to the arguments in favor of infant baptism was

the emerging emphasis upon subjective, even psychological, benefits for both children and parents:

> . . . such as the fact that the child is no longer a heathen, that the laws of God are upon the parents, that they acquire a power over the child, that a divine pledge of covenant favor is given to the infant, and that a salutary restraint will thus be imposed upon the child in later life.[48]

Baptized children who were taught, as they became able to understand, that their lives had been committed to God by their parents, would grow up with a sense of spiritual and ecclesiastical responsibility. Parents whose children had been baptized would be stimulated to more conscientious efforts of Christian training.[49] In his membership manual for the Methodist Episcopal Church, South, Josephus Anderson averred that "to have our children in the same religious covenant as ourselves . . . meets a want of our nature."[50] This increasing stress on the role of the parents and on the importance of Christian nurture was expressed in the addition to the ritual—in the north in 1864 and the south in 1866—of an address to the parents or guardians:

> Dearly beloved: Forasmuch as this child is now presented by you for Christian baptism, *you* must remember that it is your part and duty to see that *he* be taught, as soon as *he* shall be able to learn, the nature and end of this holy sacrament. And that *he* may know these things the better, *you* shall call upon *him* to give reverent attendance upon the appointed means of grace, such as the ministry of the word and the public and private worship of God; and further, ye shall provide that *he* shall read the Holy Scriptures, and learn the Lord's Prayer, the Ten Commandments, the Apostles' Creed, the Catechism, and all other things which a Christian ought to know and believe to *his* soul's health, in order that *he* may be brought up to lead a virtuous and holy life, remembering always that baptism doth represent unto us that inward purity which disposeth us to follow the example of our Saviour Christ; that as he died and rose again for us, so should we, who are baptized, die unto sin and rise again unto righteousness, continually mortifying all corrupt affections, and daily proceeding in all virtue and godliness.

This address concluded with a parental vow to fulfill these duties.[51] This focus on the responsibilities of parents exacerbated the long-standing debate over which children were eligible to receive the sacrament.

THE NATURE AND NURTURE OF CHILDREN

Among nineteenth-century Methodists, infant baptism was almost universally understood as a token of the divine covenant and described as a sign of covenant relationship and blessings. Indeed, once expurgated of all traces of the idea that the rite effectuated some objective change in spiritual status, no other conception was viable: "In every infant baptism there is either a solemn mockery, or the performance of a regenerating rite, or an acknowledgement of the child's covenant relation to Christ."[52] Specific interpretation of the covenant and of its membership was quite problematic and opinions were diverse. The chief point of concord among Methodists was that infants were included in the covenant and were entitled to its emblem. But, as pointed out in an exchange of letters in the *New York Christian Advocate* in early 1845, the crucial question was whether baptism was to be restricted to the offspring of believing Christians or offered to all infants as eligible to receive it. What were the requisite grounds of baptism—upon what criteria did children qualify? Samuel Gregg, through his widely read book *Infant Church Membership*, became the best known proponent of the view that the children of unbelieving parents should not be baptized, since parents who are not themselves in the covenant could not ratify a covenant role for their children nor properly train them in its responsibilities.[53] Gilbert Haven represented an only slightly more moderate position when he conceded that the right to baptism "inheres in all children," but concluded that the sacrament "is properly conferred, except in extraordinary cases, only on those of believers, because they alone can experimentally bring them up in the obligations it imposes. . . ."[54] A very similar view was enunciated as the official position of the Methodist Episcopal Church in the 1856 *Discipline*:

> *Question 1* Are all young children entitled to Baptism?
> *Answer* We hold that all children, by virtue of the unconditional benefits of the atonement, are members of the kingdom of God, and therefore, graciously entitled to baptism; but as infant baptism contemplates a course of religious instruction and discipline, it is expected of all parents or guardians who present their children for baptism, that they use all diligence in bringing them up in conformity to the word of God, and they should be solemnly admonished of this obligation, and earnestly exhorted to faithfulness therein.

The theological confusion of this position is apparent. Children are declared to be spiritually fit subjects for baptism through the saving act of Christ, yet in practice disqualified because of shortcomings of the parents. This ambivalent stance was vigorously assailed by numerous Methodist writers. The words of William McKaig in the *Western Christian Advocate* were exemplary:

> Is there any moral fitness belonging to the [infants of believing parents] that is not possessed by the innocent children [of unprofessing parents]? They are all equal participants in the provision of salvation or they are not. To deny the right of all to the provision of the atonement, would be equivalent to admitting the doctrine of infant damnation. . . . If all are in a savable state, why not let them all have the badge of salvation? . . . To say they are not entitled to salvation until their parents believe, would be to make their eternal destiny depend upon the caprice of the parents—an absurdity.[55]

Perhaps the two most influential spokespersons who espoused such views were Leonidas Rosser and Thomas Summers, both of whom wrote copious, popular works on baptism. Rosser insisted that "all children indiscriminately are entitled to baptism, in their own right . . . independent of natural relations" and that the "only barrier to baptism is moral unfitness" from which no child suffers.[56] Summers rejected what he called "the Calvinistic theory, that only the children of believing parents are to be baptized" and argued that it was "their personal connection with the Second Adam" that entitled them to the privilege.[57] Some went even further, insisting that "if wicked parents should desire their children dedicated to God, it is the Minister's duty to do it."[58] In 1865, Professor B. H. Nadal of Drew University stated flatly that Methodists administered infant baptism "regardless of moral character and church relations of parents."[59] The continuance of ambiguity was evinced by William Brownlow when he listed the proper subjects of baptism as "penitent adults, adult believers, and the infant children of all baptized parents" plus servants with whose training they are charged, then immediately appended this footnote:

> We of course hold the doctrine that all infant children, whether of believing parents or not, are entitled to baptism on account of their own relation to Christ and to his kingdom, and not that of their parents.[60]

Perhaps the closest approximation to a consensus, despite its lack of theological coherence, was posited by Editor Stevens of the *New York Christian Advocate* when he asserted that although all children were entitled to baptism "by virtue of their redemption by Christ," still a minister might "properly hesitate in cases where the child might not be properly nurtured."[61]

The complex of issues relating to the moral condition or spiritual nature of children was the subject of extensive discussion. The periodical literature of 1845–66 featured innumerable articles and letters contributing to debate. Some elements in the church were fearful of what they perceived to be an increasingly optimistic view of human nature that threatened to attenuate the traditional understanding of original sin. The Address of the Bishops at the 1860 General Conference of the northern church contained this warning:

> We confess also to some slight apprehension of error on the subject of infant regeneration creeping in among us. We know not that it can be said to really exist in the Church. But we fear that our just zeal for the spiritual welfare of childhood, and our inspiring views of the great benefits to the atonement, may divert our attention from the seventh article of religion in our Discipline. . . .[62]

In deference to the classical and Wesleyan insistence on original sin, most commentators began their treatments of the moral condition of infants with an affirmation like that of J. B. McFerrin: "In a word the infant is a child of nature, born in sin, inheriting corrupt passions and affections that lead him astray from God and virtue. . . ."[63] Even in a funeral sermon for a child in Vermont, preached explicitly to counter Calvinist dogma, Volney Simons commenced with the obligatory concession, describing infants as "morally depraved"—"blackened and deformed . . . by hereditary pollution."[64] Despite such reiterations of traditional theology, mid-nineteenth-century Methodists were developing a position on the moral nature of infants that was quite at variance from that of Wesley. The crucial distinction was made by asserting that infants, though born depraved—with original sin—were nevertheless born under a dispensation of grace that freed them from the burden of original guilt. Infants, having committed no personal sin, bore no responsibility and merited no punishment. The consequences of Adamic sin had been removed by the atonement of Christ. Although children had depraved natures they could not properly be defined as sinners: "the heritage of depravity is met by the heritage of grace."[65]

Some difficulties arose when this theological understanding of the spiritual nature of children was related to the practice of infant baptism. In classical and Wesleyan Christianity, the sacrament had been understood as the means by which the curse of original sin was removed. Although American Methodists repudiated any regenerating potency of the rite itself, some tried to retain the traditional linkage. Thomas Summers touted infant baptism as a refutation of

Pelagianism because it "assumes the depravity of our nature, and symbolizes the means by which that depravity is removed."[66] Increasingly through the century however, Methodists were grounding the practice of infant baptism on the heritage of grace rather than that of depravity. Infants were deemed to be justified, members of the divine kingdom, and proper recipients of its initiatory emblem. Their eligibility for the sacrament was based on the positive aspects of their spiritual nature, rather than on the negative. When a correspondent to a church paper asked, "If infants are impure or unholy, on what grounds are they baptized?" his assumption was clear.[67] The inherent contradictions lurking here were brutally exposed by Baptist editor J. R. Graves, the caustic critic of all things Methodist. Graves charged that Methodists contradicted themselves in practicing infant baptism:

> . . . just as soon as they have come to years of discretion and accountability—even before—the world hears these very ministers who baptized them, and thus pronounced them regenerate and sanctified in heart by the Holy Spirit, declaring that these very "elect children" are the children of wrath, even as others, exposed to the wrath of God, and calling them to repentance and regeneration. . . . How is it, I ask, that the whole mass of your baptized children without a single exception, are found unregenerated the very first day of their accountability?[68]

Methodists would struggle with these, and many related, questions throughout the century.

There was substantial agreement among Methodist spokespersons by the mid 1800s that infants were born in a state of grace made possible by the benefits of Christ's atonement and that this gracious provision was the basis for the practice of infant baptism. Sharp debate continued over exactly what this state of grace was, what nomenclature was appropriate for it, and what was its relationship to later spiritual experiences. Some were unwilling to describe infants as justified—at least without careful definition of the term. It was argued that infants, while in "a state of safety," had not received forgiveness. They were proper recipients of baptism because they were potential or provisional subjects of salvation.[69] Daniel Curry, who asserted this position, contended that even to say that infants were justified implied no moral fitness on their part, since justification rested only on the favor of God.[70]

While rarely using the term "prevenient grace," many writers enunciated the Wesleyan view that, through the agency of divine redemption, all persons had received gracious ability to participate in the working out of their own salvation. Infants were understood as having been restored to a free moral state: "all children are born innocent, born redeemed, born into a condition of trial as favorable as was that of Adam and Eve." Every individual was thus placed "upon a platform of freedom to choose good or evil for himself."[71] The majority of the writers of the period were willing to state unequivocally that infants were born in a state of justification.[72] Samuel Gregg's comments were representative:

> We do not claim for infants a state of holiness in the highest sense, either natural or evangelical. But we do claim, in their behalf, a state of evangelical innocence or justification, such as adults must be made to enjoy by being converted, or pardoned, through the medium of faith in Christ. . . .[73]

There was considerably more disagreement over use of the term "regeneration" to denote the spiritual status of infants. All concurred that through the grace of divine providence, dying infants were regenerated to fit them for heaven, but what about those who lived? Rosser was representative of the preponderance of opinion expressed prior to 1858 when he insisted that children, though born justified, have "the necessity still of regeneration by the Spirit, which is to be obtained by repentance and faith. . . ."[74] Much discussion centered on the meaning of regeneration as applied to infants. The consensus was that no change in moral condition was implied, only a change in legal status—"a change in covenant conditions, that is, a change in relation to God and to the Church."[75] In that carefully limited sense, regeneration of infants could be linked to baptism.

The debate over the spiritual status of infants intensified sharply in 1858, triggered by the publication of T. F. Randolph Mercein's *Childhood and the Church.*[76] Mercein maintained a quite elevated view of the spiritual state of childhood, reminiscent of that expressed by the Romantic poets. While acknowledging the existence of "a heritage of sin," he argued that children were through the grace of the atonement, born in a moral condition from which they could only descend. Childhood was the crucial period for "the development of a nature already in the soul." Mercein was not reluctant to characterize the spiritual state of infants in theological terms: "the unconscious babe is a Christian babe, justified and regenerate . . . "; the experiences of physical and spiritual birth were "distinguished in character, rather than in order of time." The purpose of the Christian Church was to care for children in such a way as to enable them to maintain and mature in their spiritual development: "infant nurture is not a preparation for an experience to come, but a cultivation of an experience that is. . . ." Children were proper subjects of baptism because of their personal state of grace and were thus initiated into the influence of the church. It was only because of the failure to nurture them properly in the faith that any children ever needed to experience conversion later in life. Because Christian nurture in home and church was absolutely essential, Mercein would deny baptism to the children of irreligious parents:

> How can God, through his Church, assume a formal and visible charge over a child when the only officer through whom that charge can be exercised is not found in the Church–when the conducting chain of the sanctifying power is wanting?[77]

These views of Mercein, who died soon after his controversial book was published, became the focus of extensive debate within the church–especially in the periodical literature. Those who supported Mercein defended him, and themselves, against charges of Pelagianism by pointing out that he acknowledged inherited depravity. They contended that Methodist authorities as far back as Wesley and Watson had deemed it impossible to separate justification and regeneration. Many argued that infant baptism was to be understood as the sign of regeneration and that there was no basis for the sacrament if infants were not regenerate.[78] Perhaps the best known and most influential proponent of these views was Gilbert Haven[79] who praised and echoed Mercein:

> Heaven does, indeed, lie about us in our infancy, heaven in its purest and most powerful forms. Whatever be the faith of the parent, the undeveloped faith of the child is Christian. . . . Our connection with Adam corrupts and ruins us at our conception; our connection with the second Adam restores us to as fair a condition at the same point as it would have been had the first parents kept their first estate.[80]

The position articulated by Mercein, Haven, and their supporters was widely and vehemently challenged. Opponents labelled it "novel," "startling," "unScriptural," "a dangerous error." They asserted that the church baptized infants because they were in a state of gracious acceptance with God, despite their possession of an unholy nature, and not because they were considered to be truly regenerate. Many commentators insisted that both Scripture and Methodist standards had always distinguished clearly between justification as the forgiveness of sins and regeneration as the change in spiritual nature. Infants were born justified in that they were freed by the grace of the atonement from guilt or responsibility for original sin–they were redeemed, innocent. Infants were not born regenerate or pure or with a holy nature. The most compelling evidence of this was to be found in the lives of children and the behavior manifested as they grew up. Children did not spontaneously love God or live in holiness; instead they exemplified selfishness and inclination toward all manner of evil. Such obvious expressions of sin proved that the moral nature of children was essentially corrupt and must be changed by another act of divine grace. This change or rebirth could not occur until a child was old enough to respond and accept. The commentators who expressed these views accused Mercein and his supporters of confusing prevenient grace, which is present in every life from birth, with sanctifying grace, which enables real holiness of life as one matures in the faith.[81] There was much concern that regeneration was being misunderstood and depreciated: "regeneration is either a very small blessing, or else it is not congenital."[82]

In a review of Mercein's *Childhood and the Church*, Thomas Summers attempted to articulate a median position. Summers insisted that he was reaffirming the beliefs of traditional Methodism:

> All Arminians believe that children are born in sin—in total depravity. . . . But they all, moreover, believe that all children, as soon as they are born, sustain a gracious relationship to God, through the atonement of Christ, and are all brought under the influence of the Holy Spirit. . . . These two great principles distinguish Arminians on the one hand from Pelagians, and on the other from Calvinists; and both together constitute the only rational, scriptural basis for the baptism, church membership, and Christian culture of children.

While acknowledging that, "according to the Arminian scheme, regeneration is a concomitant of justification; so that if infants be justified, they are also regenerate," he tried to squelch debates over terminology:

> There is little advantage in using the figurative terms of justification and regeneration—borrowed from jurisprudence and physiology—to set forth the moral condition of irresponsible infants. . . . Our ignorance of the psychological character of infancy, and of the mode of the Spirit's operation on the infantile nature, suggests the impropriety of refining on the subject. . . .[83]

Summers' mediating effort was not successful nor was his irenic attitude typical. For most Methodists, questions of the precise spiritual condition of children were of fundamental importance. This was the case not because of any taste for arcane speculation, but because such issues underlay the more immediate question of how the church was to produce Christians. If it were conceded that infants were both justified and regenerated at birth, then there was no ground or need for conversion. Was the training of children at home and church to be geared to making or to maintaining Christians? Sharp and protracted debate on these and related issues was a continued feature of the periodical literature during the mid-nineteenth century.[84] There were few if any who blatantly claimed that there was no need for anything in a person's life approximating conversion. Controversy usually centered on the timing of such an experience, specifically whether or not it had to be preceded by a period of living in sin. Could children be so brought up that as the first accountable act of their lives they accepted the saving grace of Christ, or must they for a time, experience personal sin so as to become aware of their need for salvation?

Daniel Curry used his potent position as editor of the *New York Christian Advocate* to promote his more traditional views: "The condition of the infant is that of a sinner needing to be converted and not that of a saint only requiring to be kept and confirmed in a state of grace and salvation."[85] Similar opinions were widely expressed in other periodicals: "I have no sympathy with the notion that the child is born a Christian or that he may be so educated as to grow up to be experimentally a Christian without the work of regeneration;" "Our children do not grow up pious without they are first converted."[86] Exponents of this position argued that while infants were redeemed by the grace of the atonement, when they grew to the age of accountability they inevitably fell into patterns of sinful living—manifesting the inherited depraved nature. Persons capable of making rational moral decisions made wrong ones and became increasingly sinful until they eventually were convicted and repented. God graciously pardoned their sins and they were regenerated—spiritually reborn. The goal of those responsible for the Christian training of children should be to have them come to this experience of conversion as early in their life as possible. Curry opined that a "very large proportion of our Sunday School children should be soundly and thoroughly converted before they are twelve years old."[87]

Commentators on the other side of the debate argued that there was no need for the child to experience any period of sin: "The child is able to believe by so far as he is able to sin, then he may be saved at the very moment he is competent to sin."[88] At the precise point in the process of maturity where unconditional salvation was superseded by moral responsibility, children could voluntarily retain their state of grace by exercising personal faith. To hold any other position was to concede that there must be a time in a person's life when dying, he or she would be damned.[89] It was only because of the lack of proper training that most children were not converted as soon as they were accountable:

> . . . in the case of the child whose Christian education has been duly attended to, that work may advance by degrees as the powers of the soul are unfolded, and the elements of character made susceptible of the Spirit's impress.[90]

In accord with this understanding of the spiritual development of children, Methodism began in the late 1840s to manifest deep concern for proper Christian nurture. While the continued need for adult conversions in the revivalistic modes of the past was not denied, a distinct shift in emphasis was discernible. The periodical literature was replete with exhortations to parents and church leaders to fulfill their duties to children. The opinion was expressed repeatedly that if the church would devote a fraction of the effort that it expended on converting sinners to the training of its children, its state would be much improved. An exchange of letters between John McClintock and Stephen Olin[91] exemplified this modified emphasis. Olin wrote of the wide response to his sermon "The Religious Training of Children." He had received numerous requests for copies: "the subject itself seems to interest everybody." In that sermon Olin criticized parents and the church as derelict in their duty to children and averred that, with proper nurture, children "grow up Christians. They are sanctified from the womb." McClintock expressed his similar concern about the practices of the church:

> . . . the naughtiness of baptizing infants and then treating them as if they were heathen, until the breath of a revival comes over to convert them, instead of holding them as initiated into the Church, as our standards do, and training them up for her service and God's. . . . On the matter of the relation of baptized infants to the Church, my mind and heart are constantly at work. I think that I have written or spoken to you before about it and that you agree with me in whole or in part; but I should like to hear from you more definitely. I have just received Bushnell's "Christian Nurture," and I really must go great part of the way with him.

Olin's reply expressed his concurrence and his desire to see Methodism define itself in a position between revivalism and sacramentalism:

> You ask my opinion of Dr. Bushnell's book on "Christian Nurture." Most favorable, I assure you. The book ought to create a sensation. . . . I might not concur with each of his opinions or

> statements, but I now think of no exceptions, and I regard his work with high admiration. I can truly say that I have been on his opinion in regard to this subject for twenty years, though I, of course, was incompetent to state or argue it as he has done. Such doctrines need to be proclaimed from the housetops. No part of the world needs them as do the American Churches. We [the Methodists] are the worst off, excepting always the Baptists, who are principled to the wrong. The Episcopalians are, perhaps, the best. They would unquestionably be, but for baptismal regeneration, which pledges them to the opposite pole of error, the Baptists having the other.[92]

The positions which were being delineated in these letters became increasingly characteristic of American Methodism as the century progressed.

The regnant understandings of the nature and nurture of children which had evolved in the antebellum period can be encapsulated by summarizing the views of Freeborn G. Hibbard.[93] Hibbard's book on baptism was the standard work on the subject in the Methodist Episcopal Church course of study from 1848 until 1876. This authoritative position made his periodical articles and his later book, *The Religion of Childhood*, subjects of serious attention, wide debate and significant influence.[94] Hibbard posited that, while all infants were by nature under condemnation, they were born in a state of grace: "The date of redemptive power and grace to each individual of our race is coincident with the date of existence."[95] In that sense, all children may be assumed to be and spoken of as regenerate:

> All I mean by it is, that infants are, whether baptized or not, in a state of grace; that they are embraced in the provisions of the atonement; that, if they die in infancy, they will be saved, and if they live, they will come under the gracious economy of Heaven, and receive the free offer of life.

This spiritual condition of children was the basis for infant baptism and relations with the church. Yet, not all infants should be baptized, even though they were in a moral condition of eligibility. The determinative question was that of how the child would be raised:

> If it have unbelieving parents, it is irrelevant to baptize the child . . . because there is no adequate pledge that the ends of baptism, so far as relates to early education, will be answered in the child.[96]

Hibbard became more and more convinced that improper understanding of the nature of children was resulting in their being improperly trained. The purpose of his 1864 book was "to encourage the early consecration of children to God, and their faithful Christian nurture." He urged that the church recognize that God's work of grace for children meant "a moral effect wrought in them, the impartation of a positive 'gift', a principle of life, a meetness for heaven, or quickening of their nature."[97] Children, thus, had a real claim to membership in the church: "The idea that the Church is made up only of believers, is as rational and Scriptural as that a family, or commonwealth, is made up only of adults."[98] Both parents and the church are charged with the crucial duty of treating children as present members of the visible and invisible kingdoms of Christ. They should be nurtured in such a way as to come early in life to accept saving grace by their own act of volition. Daniel Curry, who did not fully agree with Hibbard's views, did concur on the importance of the issues:

> The most important problem now offered to evangelical Protestantism relates to the relation of young children to the Gospel, together with their capabilities to receive and retain saving grace, and the consequent duties of the Church and the family as to their religious nurture . . . [this problem] involves nearly every chief point in theology.[99]

ISSUES OF BAPTISM AND CHURCH MEMBERSHIP

Closely related to the questions concerning conversion or nurture in the making of Christians was the issue of church membership of baptized children. There were some who continued to insist that baptism made one a member of the catholic church of Christ but not of any particular denomination or local body.[100] Such a limited view was usually predicated upon the fear of an uncommitted constituency which would vitiate the church:

> If we are as a Church to adopt the mode . . . of recognizing baptized children as regular probationers in the Church, and at a certain age to ask them a few catechetical questions, and then admit them to the sacramental table with all the rights and privileges of full membership in the Church, we will soon have a Church composed of formalists, not only without the power, but like those churches that have adopted this policy, absolutely denying the power and laughing to scorn the idea of experimental religion, the glory of our beloved Methodism.[101]

By mid-century such a position was espoused only by a diminishing minority. Increasingly, there was explicit recognition that all children baptized in the Methodist Episcopal Church—north or south—were members of it and deserved to be so treated:

> The idea of admitting a person into the Church visible, and yet not making him a member of any visible section of that Church, is absurd. . . . If every member of the visible Church is to receive his nurturing grace through connection with the body of Christ, some section must hold him in living unity, and be the particular channel of his grace.[102]

The focus of concern was the "glaring want of consistency between our ecclesiastical theory and our universal practice."[103] There were repeated calls for the church to reform its practice, to develop a structured program of training for its children, to delineate a careful procedure for bringing children into full membership. Such a plan would recognize that baptized children did not need to "join the church," but only to ratify the membership they had been initiated into through the sacrament. It would also have provisions for the formal expulsion of those who, though baptized as infants, grew up apostate. Gradually a consensus emerged that the official practice of the church in dealing with children should include at least three elements: insistence that parents have their offspring baptized, requirement that children receive catechesis and nurture, public reception into full membership.[104]

In the 1850s and 60s both branches of Methodism acted to clarify and formalize the place of children in the church. The 1856 General Conference of the northern church devoted "more attention to the interest of the children of the church than any other session in our history."[105] A section entitled "Of Baptized Children" inserted into the *Discipline* attempted to delineate the theological basis of infant baptism, the ecclesiastical status of the baptized child and the practical course of action for the church in dealing with baptized children. In answer to the question, "Are all young children entitled to Baptism?" the *Discipline* stated:

> We hold that all children, by virtue of the unconditional benefits of the atonement, are members of the kingdom of God, and, therefore, graciously entitled to baptism; but as infant baptism contemplates a course of religious instruction and discipline, it is expected of all parents or guardians who present their children for baptism, that they use all diligence in bringing them up in conformity to the word of God, and they should be solemnly admonished to this obligation, and earnestly exhorted to faithfulness therein.

All baptized children were to be regarded as "placed in visible covenant relation to God, and under the special care and supervision of the Church." The actions of the church on behalf of such children were to include the maintaining of a register with "the dates of their birth, baptism, their parentage, and places of residence." Their progress into full church membership was detailed as follows:

> *Answer. 2.* As early as they shall be able to understand, let them be taught the nature, design, and obligations of their baptism, and the truths of religion necessary to make them wise unto salvation; let them be encouraged to attend class, and to give regular attendance upon all the means of grace, according to their age, capacity, and religious experience.
>
> *Answer. 3.* Whenever they shall have attained an age sufficient to understand the obligations of religion, and shall give evidence of a desire to flee from the wrath to come, and to be saved from their sins, their names shall be enrolled in the list of probationers; and if they shall continue to give evidence of a principle and habit of piety, they may be admitted into full membership in our Church, on the recommendation of a leader with whom they have met at least six months in class, by publicly assenting before the Church to the baptismal covenant, and also the usual questions on doctrines and discipline.[106]

Three further changes occurred by action of the 1864 General Conference. Answer 2, quoted above, was amended to read:

> *Answer 2.* At the age of ten years, or earlier, the preacher in charge shall organize the baptized children of the Church into classes, and appoint suitable leaders (male or female) whose duty it shall be to meet them in class once a week, and instruct them in the nature, design, and obligations of baptism, and the truths of religion necessary to make them wise unto salvation; urge them "to give regular attendance upon the means of grace;" advise, exhort and encourage them to an immediate consecration of their hearts and lives to God, and inquire into the state of their religious experience; *Provided,* that children unbaptized are not to be excluded from these classes.[107]

Answer 3 was modified to say that the names of children "may, with their assent," be placed on the list of probationers. An unequivocal statement was added requiring that "persons baptized in infancy must publicly assent, before the Church, to the baptismal covenant;" for the first time, a ritual for reception of probationers into full membership was brought into use.[108] In the southern church, a similar process of specification was going on. The 1856 *Discipline* required preachers "diligently to instruct and exhort all parents to dedicate their children to the Lord in baptism as early as convenient." These baptized children were to be "faithfully instructed in the nature, design, privileges, and obligations of their baptism." Their progress toward membership was outlined thusly:

> Those of them who are well-disposed, may be admitted to our class-meetings and love feasts; and such of them as are truly serious, and manifest a desire to flee the wrath to come, shall be advised to join the Church as probationers.[109]

The revised statement in the *Discipline* two years later implicitly recognized baptized children as probationary members and outlined their progression toward full membership:

> . . . and as soon as they comprehend the responsibilities involved in a public profession of faith in Christ, and give evidence of a sincere and earnest determination to discharge the same, see that they be duly recognized as members of the Church.[110]

In 1866, the southern church added a ritual for reception into full membership.[111]

These new rituals for receiving baptized persons into full church membership were not understood or spoken of as rites of confirmation.[112] Wesley had prescribed no ceremony of confirmation and had considered baptism as sufficient initiation into the church. Nineteenth-century Methodists often inveighed against confirmation as it was practiced by Roman Catholics and Anglicans.[113] An exceptional view was expressed by influential editor and historian Nathan Bangs who asserted that in apostolic times, confirmation involving the laying on of hands was considered an essential component of the baptismal rite:

> Indeed, I consider baptism but half performed, unless the application of water to the body be followed by the imposition of hands and prayer, that the blessing of the Holy Spirit may descend upon the subject of this holy ordinance.[114]

Clearly Bangs understood confirmation as an appendage of the sacrament of baptism and not as a separate later rite. Majority opinion in Methodism came to stress the need for a public ceremony when a child had matured to the capability of personal affirmation of vows.

A few commentators proposed to make children's first participation in the Lord's Supper "the symbol of their confirmation," at the end of their probation and beginning of full membership.[115] This pattern does not appear to have had wide support. More writers were concerned to defend Methodist practice against the charge that infant baptism required infant communion. While acknowledging that baptized infants had communed in the church from the third to the twelfth centuries, Methodists found the practice of Judaism more congenial. It was argued that "... as under the former [dispensation] infants were circumcised, but not required to offer sacrifices, so under the latter they are baptized, but not required to commune."[116] Frequent contentions were made that Jewish boys were not admitted to participation in Passover until they were twelve years of age even though they had been circumcised to initiate them into the covenant.[117] Emphasis was placed upon the cognitive aspect of the Lord's Supper and the necessity of careful instruction of children in preparation. Communion was described as "an eminently intellectual act" to be celebrated only by those capable of understanding it."[118] Some argued, though, that children could be taught very early the significance of the bread and wine. Gilbert Haven asserted that children could comprehend Eucharist much easier and earlier than they could prayer: "The child knows the meaning of food before he does of conversation."[119] Others predicated a child's participation in the sacrament upon his or her spiritual experience: "Right to the holy eucharist is founded upon faith and a new creature. . . ."[120] In general, receiving of the elements of the Lord's Supper was understood as a privilege of baptized children only after they benefitted from some nurture in the faith.

The controversy about the place and privileges of baptized children in the church was theologically a conjunct of the debate over the requisites for adult membership. Baptism as a requirement for church membership had been formalized in 1836 and dissension was negligible thereafter. It was explicitly and frequently reaffirmed, however, that the sacrament effected no change in spiritual condition:

> And although none are members of the visible church who are not baptized by water, yet this lamentable defect will not prevent their entrance into the kingdom of glory, as it does not prevent their entrance into the kingdom of grace, if they do not willfully and contumaciously slight the holy ordinance.[121]

Since baptism was understood as the rite of admission into the visible church, there was a strong consensus that it should be available to all who were truly penitent: "Baptism is one of the means of grace, and, therefore, suitable for penitents, who need all the help they can get."[122] It was recognized that the practice of infant baptism was incompatible with any insistence upon a prior experience of spiritual rebirth for adults. New Testament examples, especially from the book of Acts, were cited to substantiate this position.[123]

The chief focus of debate was the question of what spiritual condition was to be prerequisite for church membership of adults. On this point there emerged one of the few theological differences to be found between the northern and southern branches of episcopal Methodism. Periodical literature in the southern church contained numerous articles arguing that the church was to function as the "school of Christ," into which penitent persons were to be admitted and there find salvation. Southern spokespersons emphasized the qualifications of repentance and desire to receive saving grace. They insisted that many degrees of faith must be recognized, not simply a sharp distinction between lost and regenerate.[124] Moses Henkle's views were representative:

> [The problem is that] many seem to recognize no middle ground between being under Divine displeasure and being assured of pardon. . . . [When a person] possesses the qualities required in our General Rules, he is within the range and provision of gospel promises; and in that state is not a child of wrath, nor can, without losing that state be lost; and yet he may not have that trusting faith that saves from doubt, and assures him of pardon and acceptance. . . . The only safe and scriptural mode of proceeding seems to be, to receive him who appears to be earnestly desirous to flee from the wrath to come and be saved from his sins, not as a son, but a servant; not because he has already attained assurance, but because he ardently desires it. . . .[125]

These positions, which their proponents justified as authentically Wesleyan,[126] were embodied in the *Discipline* of the Methodist Episcopal Church, South in 1866. The General Conference that year abolished the legal probationary period for full church membership—a requirement of American Methodism since 1785 and one retained by the northern branch until 1908. The ritual for receiving members into the church, first adopted in 1866, included no question asking for a profession of an experience of grace or of saving faith. Only a statement of desire was elicited: "Do you earnestly desire to flee from the wrath to come, and to be saved from your sins?"[127]

The Methodist Episcopal Church apparently experienced considerable dispute in the 1840s and 50s on the subject of requirements for membership. Some of the debate was internal, but much of it, particularly in the western areas, was in response to criticism from persons of other denominations. Methodists defended their church's practice of admitting to membership persons who were convicted and repentant, though not yet regenerate. There was no confusion in discerning spiritual condition. Persons were designated in class roll-books as either "S" for seeker or "B" for believer, with the sign changed when appropriate. To admit only the regenerate was not only unscriptural and un-Wesleyan, but also would require a superhuman ability to judge human hearts.[128] The 1840 *Discipline* required candidates for membership to "give satisfactory assurances, both of the correctness of their faith and of their willingness to observe and keep the rules of the Church."[129] This provision was generally understood not as a test of spiritual experience, but as a guard against heretical doctrine. It was asserted repeatedly, especially in the *Western Christian Advocate* where the debate was most copious, that the difference between Methodist membership practices and those of other denominations was one of definitions rather than of standards.[130] All churches admitted unconverted persons to membership; Methodists designated such as seekers and urged them toward saving grace, while others simply equated repentance with regeneration: "He that is Methodistically a believing penitent, is Calvinistically a converted person."[131] Clearly, the prevailing sentiment in the west, as in the south, favored the admission of penitent persons to full church membership.

This position must, however, have represented only a minority in the northern branch of the church for it was contrary to the direction in which the Methodist Episcopal Church moved. As early as 1847, articles in *Zion's Herald* were arguing strenuously that unconverted persons should not be admitted to full membership. Such a practice would tend "towards the establishment of a worldly church," would "chill us at the heart," and would be fatal "for the true vitality of Methodism." One writer, while admitting that "the evil" existed in the west, asserted that "in all New England, the instance has never occurred, of admission to full membership, except on profession of evangelical faith."[132] Serious, repentant persons might be accepted as probationers, but if they had not been justified and regenerated by the end of their six months' trial they were to be continued in that status. Countering the claim for "desire" as the sole requirement for membership as stated in the General Rules, these writers averred that the character and lifestyle required by these Rules was impossible for anyone who lacked saving faith. There were numerous requests that the General Conference clarify the issue "by making the new birth an invariable condition of membership among us."[133] In 1864 when a ritual for reception of members was adopted, it required an affirmative answer to the question, "Have you saving faith in the Lord Jesus Christ?"[134] Both the northern and southern churches, then, required baptism for admission to church membership. Neither, however, linked the sacrament directly to the requisite spiritual condition—the point upon which debate and difference were concentrated.

Both branches of Methodism continued to be reluctant to stipulate that baptism was to be a precondition of participation in the Lord's Supper. While most commentators acknowledged that such an order was normal and appropriate, any requirement was disdained as uncomfortably reminiscent of Baptist close communion.[135] There were hints discernible at mid-century of a tendency to view an experience of saving faith and conversion as the qualifying factor, with little appreciation of Wesley's understanding of the converting function of the ordinance.[136] There were also glimpses of a more highly developed ecclesiastical attitude toward the sacraments. Orceneth Fisher opined that the Lord's Supper was to be understood as the Christian Passover and that just as no uncircumcised Jew was allowed to eat, no unbaptized person could commune.[137] Freeborn Hibbard used the same analogy, arguing that "previously to baptism, the individual has no rights in the visible church. . . . The eucharist from its very nature, is a church ordinance, and as such can be properly participated in only by church members."[138] This position continued to be that of a minority.

♦ ♦ ♦

As the two branches of episcopal Methodism entered the post-Civil War years, many theological and ecclesiastical questions related to baptism remained unresolved. This absence of conclusiveness was not the result of any lack of discussion; perhaps it was, indeed, exacerbated by the very abundance of dialogue. C. W. Miller concluded in 1861 that, "The subject of Christian baptism has received more attention during the last half century than any other subject of Christian theology."[139]

CHAPTER VI

Late Nineteenth-Century Controversies: 1867–1900

The post-Civil War decades were a time when the two branches of American episcopal Methodism experienced contrasting conditions. For the northern church, it was a period characterized by expansion and triumphalism. For the Methodist Episcopal Church, South, it was an era during which the ecclesiastical body shared in the struggles of southern society endeavoring to recuperate from devastation and defeat. Neither section, however, experienced a hiatus in theological interest or expression. The complex of issues related to baptism continued to elicit profuse dialogue.

AUTHORIZED CHURCH STATEMENTS ON BAPTISM

The General Conference of the Methodist Episcopal Church continued to publish the *Collection of Interesting Tracts* through 1892. After Wesley's works on the subject were dropped in 1861, the sole piece on baptism included in the *Collection* was the anonymous treatise previously mentioned.[1]

Both branches of Methodism produced hymnals in which clues to the prevalent theology might be found. The first authorized hymnal since 1849 was published by the northern church in 1878; it would remain the official collection until 1905. Only three of the ten baptismal hymns were retained from the 1849 edition—"Come, Father, Son, and Holy Ghost" had been a standard since 1802; "See

Israel's gentle Shepherd stand" had first appeared in 1836; and "Behold what condescending love," in 1849.[2] Five new baptismal hymns were added. One of them—"Rites cannot change the heart"—had first appeared in the southern church's hymnal of 1847.[3] Charles Wesley's "Captain of our salvation, take," with its images of training soldiers of Christ, was appropriate for adult baptism:

1. Captain of our salvation, take
   The souls we here present to thee,
   And fit for thy great service make
   These heirs of immortality;
   And let them in thine image rise,
   And then transplant to paradise.

2. Unspotted from the world, and pure,
   Preserve them for thy glorious cause,
   Accustomed daily to endure
   The welcome burden of thy cross;
   Inured to toil and patient pain,
   Till all thy perfect mind they gain.

3. Train up thy hardy soldiers, Lord,
   In all their Captain's steps to tread;
   Or send them to proclaim the word,
   The gospel through the world to spread;
   Freely as they receive to give,
   And preach the death by which we live.[4]

Also intended for adult rites were "I am baptized into thy name" and "O Lord, while we confess the worth"; both emphasized the living of consecrated lives:

1. I am baptized into thy name,
   O Father, Son, and Holy Ghost!
   Among thy seed a place I claim,
   Among thy consecrated host;
   Buried with Christ and dead to sin,
   Thy Spirit now shall live within.

2. My loving Father, here dost thou
   Proclaim me as thy child and heir;
   Thou, faithful Saviour, bidd'st me now
   The fruit of all thy sorrows share;
   Thou, Holy Ghost, wilt comfort me
   When darkest clouds around I see.

3. Hence, Prince of darkness! hence, my foe!
   Another Lord hath purchased me;
   My conscience tells of sin, yet know,
   Baptized in Christ, I fear not thee:
   Away, vain world! sin, leave me now!
   I turn from you; God hears my vow.

4. And never let me waver more,
   O Father, Son, and Holy Ghost;
   Till at thy will this life is o'er,
   Still keep me in thy faithful host,
   So unto thee I live and die,
   And praise thee evermore on high.

1. O Lord, while we confess the worth
   Of this the outward seal,
   Do thou the truths herein set forth
   To every heart reveal.

2. Death to the world we here avow,
   Death to each fleshly lust;
   Newness of life our calling now,
   A risen Lord our trust.

3. And we, O Lord, who now partake
   Of resurrection life,
   With every sin, for thy dear sake,
   Would be at constant strife.

4. Baptized into thy Father's name,
   We'd walk as sons of God;
   Baptized in thine, we own thy claim
   As ransomed by thy blood.

5. Baptized into the Holy Ghost,
   We'd keep his temple pure,
   And make thy grace our only boast,
   And by thy strength endure.[5]

"This child we dedicate to thee"—translated from German by a Unitarian minister—evinced the increasingly popular view of infant baptism:

1. This Child we dedicate to thee,
   O God of grace and purity!
   Shield it from sin and threatening wrong,
   And let thy love its life prolong.

2. O may thy Spirit gently draw
Its willing soul to keep thy law;
May virtue, piety, and truth,
Dawn even with its dawning youth.

3. We, too, before thy gracious sight,
Once shared the blest baptismal rite,
And would renew its solemn vow
With love, and thanks, and praises, now.

4. Grant that, with true and faithful heart,
We still may act the Christian's part,
Cheered by each promise thou hast given,
And laboring for the prize in heaven.[6]

The Methodist Episcopal Church, South published *The New Hymnbook* in 1880. It contained no new hymns for use at baptism and dropped "Rites cannot change the heart" and "Baptized into thy name" (not to be confused with "I am baptized into thy name"). Retained from 1847 were "Twas the commission of our Lord," "Come, Father, Son, and Holy Ghost," "See Israel's gentle Shepherd stand," "Thus Lydia sanctified her house," and "How large the promise."[7] The *Hymnbook of the Methodist Episcopal Church, South*, published in 1889, included all of these hymns except "Twas the commission of our Lord." Added in 1889 was "God of eternal truth and love"—which had been in the Methodist hymnal of 1836—and "Baptized into thy name"—which had appeared in 1847 but not in 1880.[8]

No significant alterations were made in the baptismal rituals of either church after the mid 1860s until the twentieth century. The consensus was expressed by Thomas Summers: "Our ritual is a standing protest against Pelagianism on the one hand, and Romish baptismal regeneration on the other, as well as so-called Zwinglianism, the undervaluation of the sacraments."[9]

DELINEATION OF THEOLOGY AND PRACTICE

The issues of prime concern during the last third of the century remained consistent with those of the earlier periods. Many still felt it necessary to deprecate putative remnants of baptismal regeneration. The debate about modes, and the correlate—rebaptism—was interminable. Modifications in the understanding of infant baptism occasioned much discussion.

Baptismal Regeneration

A substantial number of Methodist spokespersons agreed with George Hughey that, "The most wide-spread and dangerous heresy that afflicts Christendom today is the doctrine of baptismal remission and sacramental salvation."[10] The Campbellites continued to be a target for trenchant criticism of their linkage of water baptism and remission of sins.[11] Also the object of polemics was the view attributed to the Roman Catholic, Orthodox, Anglican, and Episcopal traditions in which salvation was understood to be effectuated by or through the sacrament.[12] There was repeated agitation in both churches–in the press and in General Conference sessions–to modify the baptismal rituals to purge any residual taint of such theology. The adult ritual was censured for its use of John 3:1–8, which some insisted had no reference to water baptism. The order was said to "squint smartly at baptismal regeneration" by implying that those who had not received the sacrament were not regenerate.[13] The infant baptism ritual was excoriated for its opening sentence which after stating that "all men are conceived and born in sin," continued "none can enter into the kingdom of God, except he be regenerate and born anew of water and of the Holy Ghost. . . ." These phrases were seen by some as "relics of Popery" and as errors deriving from the "false doctrine of the guilty impurity of children because of Adam's sin."[14] Others contended that "born of water" had always been interpreted in the Methodist tradition to mean being baptized in water symbolizing, not effectuating, spiritual birth.[15] Virtually all commentators concurred with an essential distinction between the inward experience and the outward rite:

> Except a man be born externally by water he cannot enter into the external kingdom; except he be born internally by the Spirit he cannot enter into the internal and eternal kingdom. Baptism is the condition of induction into the kingdom: external baptism for the kingdom external, internal for the internal.[16]

Mode and Rebaptism

Logomachy with the Baptists continued throughout the century especially in the South and West. Thomas Summers justified the perennial treatment of baptismal issues in Methodist periodicals by charging that, immersionists "are perpetually annoying our members in some parts of the Connection."[17] Methodists were particularly incensed by Baptist claims of an authentic historical succession of immersionists who constituted the true church. Keen delight was expressed at the consternation of Baptists over an article written by W. H. Whitsitt in the 1890s. Dr. Whitsitt, president of Southern Baptist Theological Seminary, contended that his denomination should not define itself by its practice of immersion. He argued that Baptists had baptized by sprinkling until 1641. Controversy over his work, fanned by Methodist gibes, forced Whitsitt's eventual resignation.[18]

Methodist periodical literature in all parts of the country featured an incessant flow of articles on the subject of baptismal modes. No original lines of argument emerged, but the old points were rehashed and elaborated at great length. Writers complained bitterly about the "New Version movement" through which immersionists were attempting to disguise their sectarian purpose in producing a Bible with "immerse" and its cognates substituted in all references to baptism.[19] In addition to material in the periodicals, an unusual quantity of books and pamphlets on the subject of baptism was published by Methodist authors during the post-war decades. Many were stridently anti-immersionist and characterized by an acerbic tone.[20] These works reiterated the familiar arguments against immersion on scriptural, historical, and pragmatic grounds concluding that it was a superstitious innovation, hazardous to health, and offensive to decency. The chief purely theological caveat was that immersion understood with reference to death, burial, and resurrection was "a grotesque perversion of symbols" which seriously compromised the validity of the rite.[21] Much less caustic in style were the writings of other authors who accepted the option of immersion while strongly asserting the superiority of sprinkling or pouring. Many of these writers were careful to stipulate that sprinkling and pouring were not to be perceived as distinct but as essentially one mode, varying only in the minor detail of the copiousness of the water.[22] Their objection was to the claims of Baptists and others that immersion was the exclusive or even the superior mode of baptism. Typically they insisted that the questions of how and how much water was applied were secondary and undeserving of so much divisive debate.

While affirming the validity of all three modes, however, few Methodist spokespersons failed to express a preference for sprinkling or pouring.[23] This was the stance taken by the two writers whose works of theology occupied influential positions on the course of study in the last two decades of the century—William Burt Pope and John Miley.[24] At least two prominent Methodists were proponents of greater tolerance. Miner Raymond, an influential seminary theologian, argued that there was no discernible relationship between the manner of applying the water and the work of the Spirit; the apostles probably "varied their mode of applying the baptismal water as convenience required."[25] Occupying a more popular, potent rostrum was James Buckley, editor of the *New York Christian Advocate* from 1880 to 1912. He editorialized frequently about the equal validity and acceptability of all three modes and, hence, the unimpeded right of choice enjoyed by every individual.[26] Although mode continued to be a subject of disputation throughout the century, the emerging majority position was that articulated in 1880 at the General Conference of the Methodist Episcopal Church. That Conference declined to accept a proposal to eliminate immersion as an option, but did change the order of words in the *Discipline* so as to list immersion as the last choice.[27]

The question of rebaptism was correlated with disputes over mode and over the validity of infant baptism, since the persons involved were most commonly ones who had been sprinkled as babies. Methodist church law had contained no allowance for rebaptism since 1786 and the preponderance of scholarly opinion was unequivocally opposed to it. Still, rebaptism continued to be practiced in limited degree, and debate went on. Opponents asserted that if baptism were properly understood, there were simply no legitimate grounds for its repetition, which therefore denied the validity of infant baptism, dishonored the sacrament and the God who ordained it.[28] Agitation increased in favor of an explicit prohibition and the General Conference (MEC) of 1868 added a footnote to the section in the *Discipline* on reception of members: "Rebaptism, whether of those baptized in infancy or in adult age, is utterly inconsistent with the nature and design of baptism as set forth in the New Testament."[29]

Controversy was not squelched even in the face of this clear statement. Supporters of rebaptism contended that the footnote, "amounts to an expression of opinion, not a law."[30] Editor Buckley wrote in 1881 that, although the footnote stated that rebaptism was inconsistent with the New Testament, there is "no direct prohibition of rebaptizing persons in the *Discipline*." In response to a reader's query concerning a person baptized in infancy but not nurtured in the faith, Buckley advised: "We think we would now rebaptize a person who had been left without religious instruction, and afterward preferred to be immersed."[31] Other writers agreed with Buckley that converts from Mormonism and other deviant sects should be baptized, but insisted that this was not true repetition of the sacrament if the validity of the rites of these groups was denied. There was greater uncertainty about persons who had been sprinkled as infants in Roman Catholicism and later asked for Methodist immersion.

Buckley had no qualms: "We certainly would without hesitation, and with great delight."[32] Other writers contended that an appropriate cognitive understanding of the symbolism of the sacrament was essential to its validity and used the "rebaptization" at Ephesus in Acts 19 as a paradigm.[33]

More practical concerns were enunciated by those who lauded the Methodist tradition of free individual decision and warned of the dangers from Baptist competition. James Porter insisted that "tens of thousands of our children and converts have been driven into Baptist churches" by the refusal of some Methodist preachers to rebaptize and that he had himself "satisfied all consciences, and relieved the Baptists of the trouble of looking after our converts and lending us their robes."[34] Finally, after several earlier attempts had failed, the General Conference of 1896 excised the footnote opposing rebaptism. This action did not, however, result in clarification of the issue for differences in interpretation remained. Buckley averred that the General Conference had recognized the right of every minister to exercise his discretion in each case:

> All persons who were sprinkled in childhood applying for admission to the Methodist Episcopal Church can be immersed; and there is no law against the immersion by a Methodist pastor of any person who, having been sprinkled in infancy, later in life, as a result of Bible study, concludes that sprinkling is not a proper mode.[35]

Stephen Merrill, in contrast, opined that the General Conference removed the footnote,

> . . . evidently intending to make it lawful for our ministers, in extreme and doubtful cases, to administer the rite where applicants were uncertain as to their baptism, and conscientiously believed it their duty to be baptized.[36]

The southern branch of the church experienced debate on the subject also, although no official action forbidding rebaptism was taken. Thomas Summers presented the standard view opposing repetition of the sacrament for one who had validly received it at any age or by whatever mode.[37] The source of the most relentless agitation for General Conference action to enunciate official approval for rebaptism was a Columbia, South Carolina paper, *The Christian Neighbor.* Editor Sidi Browne campaigned ardently for the right of rebaptism for anyone dissatisfied with the mode or with having received it as an infant. Especially, Browne argued, should persons who had been converted be able to profess their faith by being baptized:

> When a person has by wickedness of life, so invalidated the baptismal covenant as to separate himself from the church. May not such on resumption of vows and restoration to Church membership, be rebaptized if he desire it.[38]

Obviously debate would carry over into the twentieth century. Perhaps the closest to a majority opinion in both branches of the church was expressed in a comment by O. P. Fitzgerald, editor of the *Nashville Christian Advocate* and later bishop: "There is no law on the subject but the drift of opinion is against the practice of rebaptizing anyone."[39]

Infant Baptism

Probably the greatest problem that infant baptism posed for late nineteenth-century Methodists was the disparity between theology and practice. Writers in both the northern and southern parts of the church complained frequently about its neglect. Thomas Summers asserted that, there "ought to be no more baptisms of adults in Christendom than there were circumcisions of adults among the Jews."[40] Yet, statistics indicated consistently that many more adult than infant baptisms occurred.[41] There was disagreement over how much the paucity of infant baptisms was simply the result of neglect and how much it evinced that many Methodists remained "thorough antipedobaptists—except [in the matter of] close communion."[42] Leaders agreed that more teaching and preaching on the subject were needed, and elaborate vindications continued to be published.[43] One of the chief points of emphasis during this period was the covenant standing of children:

> If the Abrahamic covenant is in force today, as it surely is, unless it can be shown to have been repealed, there is no power on earth to disprove the right of our infant offspring to recognition in the Church by Christian baptism.[44]

There was also great stress on historicity of the practice of infant baptism since apostolic times and the unanimous testimony of patristic authorities.[45] Although infant baptism had only occasionally been spoken of in terms of dedication throughout the century, this interpretation became more prominent in the latter decades:

> The deep meaning, the significant character, the essential idea, in infant baptism, is this—the solemn obligation that parents, in the sight of the church, and in the sight of God and the holy angels, freely and voluntarily recognize and assume to do the right and true part by their children, and, above all, to teach them their duty to God, the

> Author of their existence and the One before Whom they must eventually appear.[46]

This view was closely associated with the escalating emphasis on proper religious training and nurture of children.[47] The most pervasive understanding of infant baptism at the end of the century was that expressed by James Buckley:

> Infant baptism is of immense importance, in our view, as indicating the relation of children to the atonement of Christ, and as a solemn act of consecration on the part of the parents to whom God has given these children.[48]

THE NATURE AND NURTURE OF CHILDREN

As had been the case for several decades, a major focus of discussion was the question of the spiritual status of infants and, hence, their moral fitness for baptism. It was not that Methodists doubted that moral fitness–indeed, they universally affirmed it–but that they interpreted it in various and conflicting ways. The subject received expansive treatment in books and church periodicals in the 1867–1900 period. Disagreements were sharp and debates eloquent, but the basic issues remained the same as in earlier years. Some modifications in position can, however, be detected, notably a more optimistic assessment of human nature and, consequently, less dwelling on depravity and sin. In general, a state of depravity was assumed as the basic human condition and infant baptism justified on that ground–not that the sacrament was a remedy for depravity, but that it symbolized the need for and availability of atonement. Methodists continually asserted that one "must believe either the horrid doctrine of infant damnation or the doctrine of infant baptism."[49]

Thomas Ralston and Miner Raymond were two prominent theologians of the period who articulated quite conservative views on the moral nature of children. Ralston argued that infants are born unholy and legally guilty, though not personally accountable to God in judgment. Raymond wrote in terms of this corrupted nature having received through Christ's atonement the *potential* to be justified and regenerated.[50] John Miley was slightly more optimistic saying that, "Infants are born into the covenant of redemption, and are all *in some measure* recipients of its grace [italics mine]." Still he insisted that, "The doctrine of infant regeneration, or that all infants are born in a regenerate state, is openly contrary . . . to the truth of native depravity."[51] Other writers were more positive, affirming that the guilt of original sin had been "fully offset" by Christ's atonement. Thus, "infants are depraved beings in a state of justification, or acceptance with God by virtue of the relation of the human race to Christ."[52] Another group of commentators, arguing that justification and regeneration were inseparable, contended that both terms described the moral state of infants. Daniel Whedon pointed out that children could be both depraved and regenerate. He saw infant baptism as symbolic of the spiritual regeneration already inherited from Christ.[53] This position was buttressed by proponents who understood it as authentically Methodist:

> Arminian theology as taught by Wesley, Fletcher, Fisk, Hibbard, Whedon, and others regards all infants as being in a justified and regenerated state.[54]

This interpretation endeavored to maintain appropriate balance between the doctrine of original sin and the positive spiritual state of the child:

> It is of course not to be denied that we inherit from Adam a depraved nature, but while this is offensive to God and therefore condemnable, we are not guilty and punishable until by our own act we make choice of our depravity. . . . Through the atonement, justification is unconditionally bestowed and the child brought into acceptance with God. . . . The work wrought in him is of the same nature as that in the adult regeneration. He is born under a system of grace, and by grace is God's child and entitled to all that grace has purchased.[55]

Stephen Merrill represented a school of thought which emphasized the duality of the moral nature of infants:

> . . . the gracious influence upon them [does not] destroy or eradicate from their being the germs of inherited evil. . . . The germ of spiritual life . . . can coexist in the heart with the primal bias to evil [in a] state of coincident occupancy.[56]

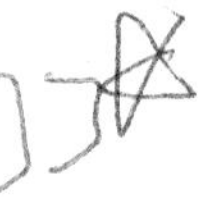

The perceptible shift that was occurring—from emphasis on the corrupted nature to stress on the gracious condition—had its extreme expression in the emerging doctrine of infant purity. Several of the major church papers ran extended series of articles and letters debating these points at great length and with sharp controversy. The use of terms like "model of innocence" and "moral purity" rekindled the dispute which had centered on Mercein's work in the late 1850s.[57] The regnant theological position by the end of the century was well expressed in Cooke's *Christianity and Childhood*:

> American Methodist Arminianism rejects this theory of inherited guilt, placing itself upon the axiom that if personal volition is necessary to personal sin, then personal sin is necessary to personal guilt. . . . All infants, whether in a dying state or not, are, through the Atonement, in that state of salvation, however named, which corresponds to acceptance in the adult believer.[58]

Concomitant with the ebbing significance of inherited depravity and guilt, was an attenuated view of conversion and an appreciated role for Christian nurture. While usually reticent to deny the necessity of conversion, many writers pushed the timetable for spiritual rebirth ever earlier in a child's life until eventually it coincided with the beginning of moral accountability. This change in Methodist doctrine did not occur without vehement resistance from those who insisted that any person who lived to attain an age of responsibility would inevitably commit sin.[59] Due to the inherited tainted nature and to the influences of the social environment, it was impossible to bring up a child who did not fall into sin. A major purpose of the Sunday school was to be the arena wherein children learned of their sin and need for salvation, and of the saving work of Christ in their behalf. Any failure to inculcate these truths in children would result in their falling away.[60]

> There must come a time in the history of every child where there shall be a public and formal recognition of the claims of God, a conscious acceptance of the work of grace previously accomplished, and a deliberate surrender to the Lord Christ as a personal Redeemer.[61]

Rather than conceding that this personal acceptance of saving grace would be preceded by a period of sinful living into adolescence or adulthood, Methodist leaders urged the church and the home to facilitate conversions early in a child's life. The consensus was that this should occur by the time that the child was ten years of age if not earlier.[62] Others insisted that no period of actual sin was necessary prior to conversion. Bishop O. P. Fitzgerald stated:

> The saving grace of God meets every child at the line of moral accountability and helps us to the making of that choice of Christ as a Savior which is the essence of saving faith. In other words, as soon as a child can sin knowingly, it can believe savingly.[63]

Bishop Enoch Marvin agreed, but added that this was only possible if the child had been trained in a sense of sin since, "The Savior can be consciously received only by the conscious sinner."[64] There was clearly a very short step remaining between this position and denial of the necessity for conversion at all. Gradually the common parlance was moving toward speaking of children "maintaining" or "continuing" in the gracious state into which they had been born:

> Children are born into the kingdom of God, and here they should be kept by moral culture and Christian training, to grow up in the beauty of holiness. It is our duty to bring up children so that they should be Christians from the beginning.[65]

Children should be considered, and taught to consider themselves, as the children of God rather than of the devil. They should perceive themselves as regenerate rather than as supplicants for salvation.[66] This theological stance was linked to infant baptism:

> Our children belong to God from the start [and] . . . if all available means are faithfully used they need never depart from Him. This is the chief significance of infant baptism—a formal recognition in the most solemn manner that the little ones are in the kingdom, and that it will be somebody's fault if they are suffered to slip out of it. . . . [Infant baptism] is a protest of the most vigorous kind against the idea so prevalent in the world that in the normal course of things the evil one must have the young people for a considerable period. . . .[67]

Any expectation that children grow up in a continual state of grace was firmly predicated on the necessity of appropriate Christian training. With proper nurture at home and church, "children would pass from their natural state into spiritual union with Christ by such easy gradations as not to be conscious of the time of the transition." This process would not, however, occur automatically. It would require an understanding on the part of the church of the spiritual potential of children and a commitment to reify it:

> The idea which the Church must embody in her articles of faith, which she must distinctly and unequivocally enunciate, and illustrate in her practice . . . is that the child is to grow up in the Church as a Christian.[68]

The periodical literature of these decades was replete with expressions of concern for religious training and with advice to parents and pastors on the subject; many books on the topic were published.[69] In the minds of many Methodists, emphasis was clearly shifting from evangelistic efforts in the larger society to cultivation programs within the church constituency:

> One reason the church has failed in the world . . . is that they let the children go wild, and then try to tame them, and about one-half of them never get back. If there had been as many prayers prayed, and as many tears shed to have kept them in the fold, they never

> would have been prodigal; but would have commenced labor in the Father's field.[70]

The symbiotic relationship between this view and the practice of infant baptism was well illustrated in Editor Buckley's popular question and answer column in the *New York Christian Advocate*. Buckley argued frequently that children should not be baptized after they had reached an age capable of making any moral distinctions and decisions–usually around four or five years of age. Since such children had not been dedicated to God as infants and raised up with Christian nurture, they must wait and be converted and baptized as adults when they attained an age of accountability. The extreme expression of the conjunction between infant baptism and adequate nurture was Buckley's reply to a query about baptizing mentally deficient persons or "idiots":

> Certainly not. They cannot be baptized as adults, because they cannot make a profession of faith. They cannot be baptized as infants because they are not capable of being subjected to training; neither is there any hope that they will develop into rational beings in this life.[71]

The escalating understanding of infant baptism as the dedicatory commencement of a childhood of religious tutelage would appear necessarily to limit the sacrament to the offspring of Christian believers. Some in Methodism vigorously subscribed to that view arguing that, "Baptism is a church ordinance, and implies Church membership." Parents who were not church members were not qualified to present their children for baptism.[72] Others moderated this stance slightly, saying that while parents did not absolutely have to be members, they must be "Christians in faith."[73] Yet, there was significant reluctance in both the northern and southern churches to taking that logical position and, indeed, vehement exhortations to the contrary. An editorial in the *Christian Neighbor* was representative:

> Let baptismal regeneration, infant condemnation and unregeneration, and the notion that only the children of Christian parents have the right to be baptized, all be buried to the same depth and in the same grave; they belong together. . . . It seems clear that justification is the birthright of every child of Adam and Eve; every one of them belongs to the family which links heaven and earth together; and every one of them has a right to membership in the visible Church on earth, and consequently a right to baptism; and all this because of their relation to Christ.[74]

The pages of the *Nashville Christian Advocate* were the site of battle, especially during 1871. Lovick Pierce expostulated: "How supremely ridiculous to baptize a child outside of the Church!" The right of parents to bring their offspring for baptism was contingent upon their membership in the covenant community. "Sinners must be made to feel that they are unfit to have children. . . ."[75] Another prominent leader J. B. McFerrin insisted that, although he had been a Methodist for fifty years and read all the standard authorities and participated in the organization of the southern church, " . . . I never read, or heard till recently the opinion coming from a Methodist—any Methodist preacher—that the children of non-professing parents were not entitled to baptism." He condemned such a position as Calvinist.[76] Another correspondent asserted that at least one parent must be in the church and that if McFerrin were right, " . . . why we ought to do like the Roman Catholic priests, kidnap and baptize, forcibly or clandestinely, every baby that we can lay our hands on."[77] The exchange became so extensive that Editor Summers commented: "We should require a very large sheet to be able to publish all that is sent to us on the subject of baptism as mooted by some of our correspondents."[78] Letters on the subject continued to appear, however, throughout the century. In the northern church, Editor Buckley of the New York *Advocate* appeared to be in debate with himself on this very controversial issue. In 1881, he averred that the teachings of the church did not prohibit the baptizing of children of non-members, but he realized that "irreligious people cannot truthfully respond to the questions of the liturgy. . . ." In answer to a question in 1884 about unmarried couples, Buckley replied:

> We certainly should baptize their children, and I cannot imagine why such a question should be asked. We should baptize any child. . . . We would baptize the children in foundling asylums as soon as we would those of the most godly and sanctified people in the Church.

Two years later, he responded that he would refuse to baptize a child if the parents were "living in open sinfulness [because] the parents would lie if they answered the questions in the liturgy, and without that the whole becomes a farce."[79] Buckley's ambivalence was indicative of that which was endemic throughout the church.

The question of eligibility for infant baptism revealed the ultimate ambiguity of the Methodist understanding of the practice. The growing emphasis on the subjective and cognitive aspects was in conflict with the central Wesleyan proclamation of the universality of grace made available by Christ's atonement. The closest approach to a solution was the drawing of a distinction between the theological and the pragmatic. Summers articulated this position in the south by affirming that while all children have the right to receive the sacrament, it must not be administered indiscriminately; provision must be made for responsible care and nurture of baptized children.[80] A very similar position was delineated in the north by Daniel Whedon. He was quite reluctant to limit access to the sacrament due to his belief in general redemption. However, "an indiscriminate baptizing of infants would be a profanation;" the church had the duty to assure proper instruction and training.[81] McClintock and Strong's *Cyclopedia* stated the antilogy succinctly:

> The Methodist Church holds that all infants are redeemed by Christ, and are therefore entitled to baptism, wherever they can receive the instruction and care of a Christian church or family.[82]

ISSUES OF BAPTISM AND CHURCH MEMBERSHIP

Old questions of the relationship between baptism and church membership continued to be mooted throughout the century. Though seemingly clarified by General Conference actions in the 1850s and 60s, the status of baptized children remained problematic. To what exactly did reception of the sacrament admit or entitle children? There was virtually complete agreement that the baptized child had the right to religious nurture and instruction, including "knowledge and love of Methodism."[83] Both branches of the church, however, accepted similar responsibility for unbaptized children as well, when there was opportunity to exercise it. More specifically, baptism was understood to confer upon children some status of church membership. Daniel Whedon and others continued to insist that, "Baptism initiates the infant into the Church of Christ, but not into a particular Church organization, as the Methodist Episcopal Church." Hence, the visible church was protected against the danger of unregenerate members:

> If the infant so grows up in the nurture and admonition of the Lord as never to lose his saved state (no imaginary case) he needs no conversion. He will bring forth the fruits showing him entitled to an unforfeited church-membership. Otherwise, his membership is forfeited, as in any other case of apostasy.[84]

Baptized children were expected to grow up under the "watch care" of the church, but not within its membership, and to affiliate themselves with the denomination of their choice when they became capable of making that decision.[85] For most Methodists, this position was inadequate because it failed to associate baptized children closely enough with the visible church or to provide for their orderly progression into full membership. Some contended that all who had received the sacrament should be recognized as probationers, while others labelled such a view as "an absurdity."[86] Probably the majority opinion was in accord with the Methodist Episcopal Church *Discipline* which provided for the enrolling of children as probationers after they had received instruction in classes.[87] In both north and south, many commentators asserted that children come into the Methodist church by baptism, since "no one can join the general church without coming into some one of the divisions which compose it."[88] Such children should be regarded as part of the visible church at least until they reach accountability.

An even more difficult question was that of the prerequisite for baptized children being accepted into full membership. Was the criteria to be conversion or catechesis? Daniel Whedon, again, represented the more conservative stance. He expressed his approval of the section in the 1856 Methodist Episcopal *Discipline* on children, with the exception of "the want of a sufficient demarcation line requiring in more express terms a regenerate character as condition of unqualified church membership. . . ." Others also expressed apprehension over the threat of unconverted membership, especially in the southern church which no longer required a probationary period.[89] The weight of opinion in both parts of the church was, on the contrary, moving toward admission of children on the basis of their having been exposed and receptive to proper Christian training. A correspondent to the *Nashville Christian Advocate* expressed a typical opinion: "All well-instructed children should be recognized as members between the ages of seven and fourteen years."[90] Persons of this school of thought rarely addressed the question of conversion at all. Their concerns were for children's noetic development in religious matters and for pious, obedient conduct.[91] By these standards, children who were sufficiently mature and "manifest a proper appreciation of the doctrines and privileges of the gospel and a becoming conformity to the requirements of the discipline . . . ought to be admitted by a simple and solemn ceremony to the full privileges and rights of membership. . . ."[92]

American Methodism had never had any rite comparable to Anglican confirmation. Signation, which ritualized reception into the church, had been omitted at least as early as 1786. The periodical literature revealed occasional quarrels with the Episcopalians over this matter. Somewhat surprisingly, the Methodist Episcopal Church, South added the following rubric to its services of infant and adult baptism in 1866: "The Minister may, at his discretion, lay hands on the subject, accompanying the act with a suitable invocation. . . ."[93] This action was not understood as tantamount to the "unscriptural and damaging rite" of confirmation with its "blasphemous or superstitious notion" that the Holy Spirit was being imparted.[94]

The question of a baptized child's right to participate in the sacrament of the Lord's Supper remained in debate. Old Testament Jewish practice was frequently cited as precedent, but not all agreed on what that practice had been. A few argued that all who were circumcised ate the Passover, while most contended that this privilege was enjoyed only when a boy had received instruction and attained the age of twelve.[95] Clearly the most pervasive interpretation was one which viewed baptized children as church members, but in a "state of minority" rather than in full standing. As these children progressed in understanding and in piety through appropriate Christian nurture, they were to be allowed at the Lord's Table.[96] Buckley's reply to an inquirer in the *Advocate* was representative:

> We do not believe in administering the sacrament to children, nor to any children that on their personal character, moral and mental, are not in the opinion of the Church, suitable to be received intelligently on probation. . . . Administering the Lord's Supper to the infant that is not old enough to know what it means is mummery.[97]

Discussions of the moral status of children and of their development into full membership in the church were closely correlated with disputes over the criteria for admission of adults. The context of this debate was different in the two branches of episcopal Methodism, but the theological quandary was the same. What spiritual condition was to be a prerequisite for acceptance into church membership? The northern church in 1864 had added the profession of saving faith as a part of its membership ritual, but this action did not end the controversy. A seminal article by B. H. Nadal of Drew University occasioned extensive exchanges in the periodical literature. Nadal's purpose was to justify the baptism and church membership of infants on the grounds that "regeneration is not a condition of admission into the Church of Christ." In making regeneration essential to adult membership, the church had committed an error which raised the hydra of confusion over the moral status of children. Nadal's position was that one needed to be only a sincere seeker in order to be admitted as a member and that any contrary contention conflicted with the whole previous history of the Christian church.[98] Others expressed apprehension that a requirement of saving faith would result in an attenuated understanding of regeneration in which penitence and diligent striving would be substituted for real spiritual transformation, in order that the explicit criteria be formally met.[99] It is interesting that Pope's *Compendium*, which was the basic theological textbook on the course of study of both the northern and southern churches for a portion of this period, upheld a position at variance with that which was sanctioned by the Methodist Episcopal General Conference:

> All who profess faith in the doctrines of Christ, who are seeking salvation, whose lives do not contradict their profession or impeach their sincerity, may be accepted to baptism; and their children with them. . . . We deny that the visible Church is limited to the regenerate.[100]

Despite these and other expressions of dissension, however, the majority stance of the northern branch was clear and often reiterated:

> That saving faith, as well as evangelical repentance, was a requisite of admission to church membership in the New Testament Church, and that this condition was not ignored or discarded by Mr. Wesley, is our thorough conviction. . . .[101]

The most articulate and tenacious proponent of this position was Daniel Whedon who insisted that the Christian Church does, indeed, "aim to be the Church of the Regenerate." Thus, the Methodist Episcopal Church "is bound to require the full evidences of true justifying faith in its catechumen, in order to admission to its fellowship and its ordinances." Seekers could be admitted only to classes; they were not to be baptized or admitted into membership, lest the church "become secularized."[102]

The process of making converted, regenerate Christians out of repentant seekers was the function of the system of probation prior to full church membership. Throughout protracted debate in the *New York Christian Advocate* in the 1880s, Editor Buckley averred that a person who was sincere should be converted within the probation period; if this did not occur, the period could be extended, but no one should be admitted to full membership who had not come to have saving faith.[103] In an attempt to enhance the significance of the probation period, the Methodist Episcopal Church added to its ritual a form for "Receiving Persons into the Church as Probationers" in 1896.[104]

The Methodist Episcopal Church, South sustained vehement internal debate on the question of requiring an experience of saving faith as a condition for church membership.[105] Ultimately it declined to take such action, even though several of its revered leaders propagandized verbosely on the point. Lovick Pierce contended that the church, to protect its purity, should be hard to get into and easy to leave. J. B. McFerrin insisted that "conversion and saving faith [were] necessary for full membership."[106] Wilbur F. Tillett claimed to be presenting an intermediate view when he denied that the witness of the Spirit was a condition of either salvation or membership. He argued, however, that admitting members merely upon statement of desire was dangerous and un-Wesleyan:

> The Church is designed to be the collective body of regenerate believers. . . . [Its] proper condition of admission . . . is a credible evidence of salvation as manifested in a sincere profession of such repentance of sin and personal faith in Christ as are represented in the Scriptures to be the condition of personal salvation. . . . The true place of all unregenerate persons, even though they be penitents and sincere seekers, is outside and not inside the Church.[107]

Some opined that the dispute was largely a semantic one provoked by the ambiguity of the term "conversion." Thomas Summers attempted to clarify:

> No minister is authorized to baptize anyone who is not converted, in the scriptural sense of turning away from sin, but no one is authorized to refuse baptism to any one who complies with the baptismal stipulation, whether or not he professes to enjoy the witness of justification, which many popularly speak of as "conversion."[108]

Other commentators enunciated a position clearly evincing differences in theology, not simply linguistics. R. Abbey asserted that "all persons should be members of the Church"; the doctrine that conversion must precede membership "is most dangerous and destructive. . . . The Church is the place to be saved. . . ."[109] Southern spokespersons pointed to the "unScriptural and unWesleyan" requirements for membership in the northern church as barriers to movement toward reunion of the two branches of episcopal Methodism. The dominant southern position was well expressed by D. C. Kelley:

> The pastor must come to believe that the purpose to be saved from sin is fixed in the heart, that repentance is sincere, that the faith has the right object and that the purpose of obedience is for life. . . . The New Testament Church as we understand it, was not a church

> of the saved. . . . [The southern church teaches] the doctrine of conscious pardon of the witness of the Spirit . . . but we do not place it at the door of the Church as an obstacle to penitent and sincere approach. . . .

Kelly went on to elucidate his, and his church's, understanding of the relationship between baptism and church membership: "No one will hesitate to acknowledge that baptism gives Church membership, and no condition should be added at variance with the vows there taken." The imposition of any additional requirement would create "the strange spectacle" of a person who was baptized into the Christian church, but who was then "halted at the door of the Methodist Episcopal Church." Such a situation exposed "the absurdity, not to say the fanatical presumption, which places Church membership on any other ground than the scriptural conditions of baptism."[110]

There was considerably less discussion during these years than there had been previously on the issue of eligibility to partake of the Lord's Supper. Some commentators downplayed the relationship between the two sacraments, arguing that baptism was not an essential prerequisite, so much as "sincere penitence and faith in Christ."[111] This emphasis on moral fitness was coupled with ecclesiastical status by those like Daniel Whedon who insisted that only justified Christians were entitled to receive either sacrament: "The 'sign' of regeneration should be given only to the regenerate, and the Lord's Supper only to the Lord's people."[112] The prevalent position was one which recognized that, while there were cases in which exceptions should be made, in general persons should be baptized prior to participating in Communion.[113]

♦ ♦ ♦

The end of the nineteenth century did not bring resolution of the long discussion and debate over baptism and the issues associated with it. Controversy and, indeed, confusion continued in both parts of episcopal Methodism. As one correspondent expressed it in 1900: "The subject of baptism is one that will not down, like Banquo's ghost in Shakespeare's tragedy of Macbeth—at least, not for a time."[114]

CHAPTER VII

Twentieth-Century Consensus and Confusion: 1901–1968

FROM THE BEGINNING OF THE CENTURY TO THE 1939 UNION

Despite the decades of debate in the eighteenth and nineteenth centuries, the theology and practice of baptism remained subjects of controversy within episcopal Methodism as the twentieth century opened. George Hughey, famed for his skill in such disputation, wrote in 1907: "There is no discussion on any theological question, especially in the rural communities, that will draw such crowds and create such interest as a discussion on the subject of baptism."[1] Dissatisfaction with the practice of the church was revealed in an editorial printed in the *Daily Christian Advocate* at General Conference in 1900. Infant baptism, it was charged, had degenerated into a "pretty form," "a christening," which was more of a social function than a religious rite. The writer asserted that the ceremony was to be understood not only as dedication, but also as the testimony of the church that the child belongs to God and not to the devil. A baptized child should be understood as already in the church and should receive proper training to keep him there.[2]

Lack of consensus was revealed later in the conference session when an exchange between delegates was occasioned by a resolution calling upon the publishing house to print church record forms suitable for use as rolls of baptized children. R. Forbes declared that infant baptism was no mere form, but actually brought a child into vital relation to the church, but J. F. Thompson insisted that, "We are not empowered of our God to make Christians of children by baptizing them." The resolution passed.[3] The crux of the problem continued as it had been so long: to avoid both "false rationalism" and "magical sacramentalism."[4] The deeper threat was that infant baptism for American Methodists might be reduced to the position articulated by the Baptist child who when teased by her little Methodist friend saying, "I have been baptized, and you haven't," replied without concern, "I don't care; I have been vaccinated and that is just as good."[5]

Authorized Church Statements on Baptism

In 1905 *The Methodist Hymnal* was published jointly by the Methodist Episcopal and Methodist Episcopal, South Churches. Six hymns are listed in the index for use on baptismal occasions. Charles Wesley's "Come Father, Son and Holy Ghost" was recommended for adult baptism, as it had been in Methodist hymnbooks since 1802. "Stand, Soldier of the Cross" was also appropriate for adults with its call to "Arise, and be baptized . . . ," while "Spirit of the Living God" is much more a general evocation of the Spirit's power than it is a sacramental hymn. For infant baptism, "See Israel's Gentle Shepherd Stand" continued to hold the place it had occupied in hymnals of the northern church since 1836 and the southern since 1847. "This Child We Dedicate to Thee" was carried over from the northern church's 1878 collection. An interesting new hymn was added in response to the Joint Hymnal Commission's recognition of the need for hymns suitable for infant baptism. "O God, great Father, Lord and King" had been written in 1903 by Bishop E. E. Hoss of the Methodist Episcopal Church, South. It grounded the sacrament in the covenant promises of old and beseeched God to "visit us in grace today . . . These little ones in mercy take, and make them thine for Jesus' sake."[6] When, thirty years later, a joint hymnal was produced by the two branches of episcopal Methodism and the Methodist Protestant Church, none of these 1905 hymns was included except the perennial "See Israel's Gentle Shepherd." The only other baptismal hymn was "Friend of the Home" which was also appropriate for infant baptism. This 1935 book, which would be the official hymnal for the unified church until 1964, thus contained no hymn for use at the sacrament of adult baptism.

Significant changes occurred in the baptismal rituals of both branches of episcopal Methodism during these years—changes which clearly reflected the modified theological understandings of the sacrament which had been developing since the nineteenth century. The ritual of the southern church underwent a major revision in 1910 after protracted debate in the General Conference. In the General Address opening the service of infant baptism, the phrase "all men are conceived and born in sin" was replaced by "all men, though fallen in Adam, are born into this world in Christ the Redeemer, heirs of life eternal and subjects of the saving grace of the Holy Spirit." The request that God "will grant to this child . . . that which by nature he cannot have" was eliminated. The reference to John 3:5 which had long been criticized for its alleged implication of baptismal regeneration was replaced with a quotation from Mark 10:13–16. Other changes reduced the sense of immediacy of divine action within the sacramental occasion. The prayer that "he may be baptized with the Holy Ghost, received into Christ's holy Church and be made a lively member of the same" was changed to "so grant unto this child now to be baptized, the continual replenishing of his grace, that he may ever remain in the fellowship of God's holy Church. . . ." The address to the parents was expanded by the addition of a fourth duty: to bring the child, when he has reached the age of discretion and is willing and evinces faith, to publicly "ratify and make his own the act of dedication which you this day perform on his behalf." Unlike in the earlier service, parents were asked to assent aloud to the assumption of these obligations.

Modifications in the rite of adult baptism were less severe. The description of human nature in the opening address was changed from " . . . all men are conceived and born in sin (and that which is born of the flesh is flesh, and they that are in the flesh cannot please God, but live in sin, committing many actual transgressions) . . . " to the more succinct " . . . all men do inherit a nature so fallen that no man, of his own strength, can so live as to please God. . . ." In contrast to the changes in the rite for infants, the prayer that the baptizands receive "that which by nature they cannot have" and that "they be baptized with the Holy Ghost, received into Christ's holy Church and be made lively members of the same" was retained from the earlier ritual. A Scripture reading from Matthew 28:16–20 was added with the former selection from John 3:1–8 being offered as an alternative. Reference to this Scripture in the opening address was, however, retained. In 1914 the General Conference of the southern church added a third service of baptism—"For Children and Youth"—to the traditional rites for "Infants" and for "Such as Are of Riper Years." This action was taken on recommendation of the Sunday School

Board; the service was authored by H. M. Hamill, Superintendent of Teacher Training Work.[7]

Similar significant changes occurred in the baptismal rituals of the northern branch of the church in 1916. In the infant baptism rite the phrase "all men are conceived and born in sin" was replaced by the words "God in his great mercy hath entered into covenant relation with man, wherein he hath included children as partakers of its gracious benefits." Reference to Mark 10:14 replaced John 3:5. In the rite for adults, "all men are conceived and born in sin" became "all men have sinned and come short of the glory of God." The controversial John 3:3 reference was retained; Matthew 28:19 was added as well as a lection from Acts 2:38–42. Further revisions were made in 1932 in both rituals. In the order for infants, the grounding of baptism in the covenant relationship was replaced with the statement "all children are members of the kingdom of God and therefore graciously entitled to Baptism. . . ." A new option—"A Briefer Order for the Baptism of Children"—was added; it included only the address to and vow of the parents, the baptismal formula and prayers. In the adult order, all mention of fallenness and sin was expurgated. The opening address made no reference to human nature or behavior, but asserted that "from apostolic times the Church has regarded Baptism as the sign of God's renewing grace in the heart of the believer, and has recognized that Baptism signifies the acceptance of Jesus Christ as Savior and Lord." Reference to the necessity of being "born anew" was eliminated from this part of the service; John 3:1–8 was retained only as the third of four options for Scripture reading, the others being Acts 2:38–42, Acts 19:1–6, Ephesians 3:14–19. In the baptismal covenant, the long-traditional denunciation of "the devil and all his works, the vain pomp and glory of the world, with all the covetous desires of the same, and the carnal desires of the flesh" disappeared and was replaced by the simple pledge to "by the help of God turn from all sin." Also removed was the assent of the baptizand to the formulation of the faith expressed in the Creed.

With the union of the two branches of episcopal Methodism and the Methodist Protestant Church in 1939, a new ritual for The Methodist Church was authorized. In the order for administration to infants, baptism was grounded in the assertion that "all men are heirs of life eternal and subjects of the saving grace of the Holy Spirit" and in the words of Jesus in Mark 10:14. God was petitioned to grant to the child "the continual replenishing of His grace that he become a worthy member of Christ's holy Church." In the address to the parents, the child was said to be "consecrated to God and to His

Church" by baptism, as in the MEC ritual since 1916. The parents were not asked to promise to lead the child to a public commitment in later years as the southern ritual had required. The shorter option for infant baptism was retained from the practice of the northern branch and the ritual for baptism of children and youth was carried over from the southern resulting in a total of four baptismal orders. The ritual for adults grounded baptism only in the command of Jesus in Matthew 28:19. There was no renunciation of sin or affirmation of the Creed.

Major Issues in Theology and Practice

The writings of Methodists in both the northern and southern branches of the church during the first four decades of the twentieth century revealed significant decline in controversy concerning some of the most mooted issues of the past. While exceptions could still be noted, consensus on the questions of baptismal regeneration, proper mode, and rebaptism had been largely achieved. Similarly, a rationale for infant baptism had been generally accepted. Recapitulation rather than innovation was predominant.

Triumph of long efforts to eradicate any vestiges of baptismal regeneration was evinced by revisions of the rituals to expunge references to John 3:3–5 in the opening addresses and to ground the sacrament in different theological positions. Continuing Methodist sensitivity on this subject, however, was revealed by repeated denials. W. S. Harrison expressed the prevailing position succinctly: "We do not baptize children with any thought that the act of baptism will work any spiritual change to make them acceptable to God; but by baptism we recognize the fact that they are already acceptable to God.[8] Still, there were also indications of reluctance to depreciate the sacrament overmuch. Methodist sources preferred the term "sign" to the alternative "symbol" and explicitly described the stance of the denomination as falling between the extremes of "High-Church sacramentalism" and free church "Socinian-Zwinglianism."[9]

No question of baptismal practice had been so controversial throughout the eighteenth and nineteenth centuries as that of the appropriate mode of bringing together the baptizand and the water. During the first twenty years of the new century writing on the subject continued to be prolific, but the 1920s and 30s saw a marked decline in interest. The dominant position in Methodism was clear: sprinkling, pouring, and immersion were all biblical and valid modes of baptism, but immersion was the least desirable of the three due to practical concerns. Further, the legitimate significance of immersion had been irretrievably obscured by those who insisted upon its practice as the only acceptable mode.[10] This distaste for immersion, in reaction to the Baptists and Disciples who insisted upon it, even determined some interpretation of Scripture—many Methodist authors continued to deny that Romans 6:4 had any reference to water baptism.[11] The course of study requirements for 1918, 1922, 1926, and 1930 in the Methodist Episcopal Church, South included Edmund Fairfield's *Letters on Baptism*. This entire 245-page volume, by a former Baptist who changed his views, was devoted to the contention that the word "baptize" meant "ceremonial purification by water" in any form, not by immersion only.[12] The Methodist consensus was well summarized in the *Sunday School Journal* in 1916:

> What the New Testament leaves open and free it seems to us that none has the right to circumscribe. The Methodist Episcopal Church has taken no part in the controversy as to the mode of baptism except to defend the catholicity of the rite and to refuse to allow its members to be limited to any one mode. . . . It is not against immersion, though it has made a strenuous protest against considering this the only form of baptism, and it was never stronger in its insistence upon freedom for the individual conscience as to this than it is today.[13]

Perhaps as a result of the subsiding of controversy over mode, the issue of rebaptism receded from the realm of public disputation in church literature. Comments on the subject are extremely meager during this period, although it is probable that rebaptism continued to be practiced within Methodism more than it was discussed.[14]

The eligibility of infants to receive baptism continued to be defended by Methodist spokespersons, but with decreased ferocity reflecting the more irenic temper of denominational relationships during this period. The points of emphasis were those which had been trumpeted during the preceding century. The baptism of infants was asserted to be consistent with the practices of both the Old and New Testament communities of faith, as well as the apostolic and historic churches. Theologically the sacrament was grounded in the understanding of infants as members of the divine covenant community in "one unbroken line of succession from God's covenant with Abraham down to this good hour."[15] There was also much less debate on the more specific issue of which infants were to be adjudged eligible to receive baptism. Nolan Harmon in his widely-used *The Rites and Rituals of Episcopal Methodism* articulated a position that would have been sharply assailed in an earlier era but apparently occasioned little dispute in 1926: " . . . no distinction is to be made by the Methodist ministry as to whether the infant for whom baptism is sought be the child of a believer or unbeliever. . . . Whenever a mother has faith to request baptism for a child, a ministry pledged to execute the Ordinances of God has never felt competent to refuse."[16]

The salient understanding of infant baptism was that of a ceremony of dedication, fully as domestic as ecclesial. Olin Curtis of Drew University expressed this view cogently:

> The baptism of an infant is the most forcible recognition and utilization of the home on the part of the Christian church . . . the sacramental acceptance by the church of the consecration unto Christ of a babe by a home. The church officially joins in with the home in dedicating the child unto the Redeemer, and does this by making the child a member of the holy catholic church under the principle of Christian claim. The two rites, infant baptism and adult baptism, are alike only in that both are forms of entrance into the church of Christ.[17]

The periodical literature featured numerous articles reminding both pastors and parents of their duties: "The baptism of children is a vow taken by the parents to dedicate the child to the Lord and train him in the teaching and ways of the Christian religion."[18] In some churches, infants were to be presented for baptism on a particular Sunday designated as Children's Day.[19]

In truth, American Methodists were much more concerned to affirm their traditional practice of baptizing infants than they were to develop coherent and convincing justifications for it. Horace DuBose epitomized this attitude in his comment about the reference to infant baptism in the Articles of Religion: "It states the confident, scriptural, matter-of-fact attitude of Methodism today. It is our heritage and needs no argument."[20]

The Nature and Nurture of Children

The regnant view of the moral nature of infants and young children in the early decades of this century has already been revealed by the changes in the baptismal rituals of both branches of episcopal Methodism. Any sense that infants were born into the world in a state of condemnation or even bearing any burden of moral guilt or sin had been rejected. The only appropriate attribution of sinfulness to an infant was in reference to the child's innate inclination to evil actions—a tendency that threatened to manifest itself as the child grew up. This consensus was so well established that there was little continuation of the old debate about nomenclature. Children might be described as having been born justified, regenerated, converted, or saved, with no interest in distinguishing between the nuances of these terms. Still, Methodist writers repudiated any suggestion of a Pelagian understanding of the birth nature and stressed repeatedly that infants were in a state of grace as a result of the gracious atonement wrought by Christ. Children are born into the Kingdom of God, already recipients of redeeming grace. It is for this reason that they are proper recipients of the sign of baptism which marks them as God's.[21] Packard expressed this view quite clearly:

> We do not baptize an infant to make it a child of God, but because, by virtue of the redemption of Jesus Christ, it is God's child and an heir to the covenanted mercies of God. Baptism is the authoritative declaration of the fact that the child is already redeemed. Being passive in Adam's sin, it is passive in Christ's redemption, and a rightful heir of God through Christ.[22]

What changes are to be anticipated in the lives of these baptized children of God as they grow up? On this point greater divergence of opinion can be observed. In spite of heavy and repeated emphasis on the necessity of training children in the faith and guiding their moral development, there was disagreement among Methodist leaders as to what the expected results might be. Some argued that if children were truly considered to be members of both Christ's heavenly kingdom and his earthly church, if they were consistently taught to understand themselves to belong to Christ, and if they were properly nurtured in the faith, then they could remain Christians throughout their lives. Others contended that, while it might be theoretically possible to so raise a child, in actual fact no child has perfect parents and no child can be isolated from corrupting influences. Therefore all children will fall into sin as they mature and need to be brought back into God's saving grace. Certainly if parents fail in their duty, their children will likely turn away from God and be lost.[23] "It is the lack of faithful parents, not the lack of grace, that accounts for the multitude of children who stray from the Lord's fold."[24] If a child after reaching the age of accountability does indeed turn away from God, it is imperative for the church to strive to bring him or her back to Christ as early in life as possible. An article in the *Sunday School Journal* in 1912 was illustrative of these concepts:

> The normal program is for the child never to be anything but a Christian, and with proper instruction, example, and direction, in most cases it would never be anything else than a Christian. But if the infantile Christian life is neglected by parents, pastors, or teachers,

> and the child becomes a backslider, by all means seek to bring that child back to Christ by as early a decision as possible. From ten to eighteen years of age is the best time. The chances of conversion dwindle after eighteen.[25]

Judging by the references to it in the periodical literature of the church, a book entitled *The Child's Religious Life* was quite influential on the thought of this period. Written by William George Koons, this work utilized the insights of modern psychology to examine religious experiences. Koons contended that a child is born "with a disordered moral nature" but without sin or guilt since these are possible only when there is sufficient free will to make real choices. The child "is born depraved though not a sinner," but with a bent toward committing sin when opportunities arise. God seeks to neutralize and counteract this tendency: "the grace of God, in cooperation with proper religious training, does gradually overcome and supplant in the irresponsible infant the hereditary bias toward evil."

Hence, the child is enabled to "emerge into responsible life unprejudiced toward evil" and even possibly with a tendency to good. This change in tendencies may be called conversion, at least in a limited sense, and usually occurs around the ages of three to five. Conversion in a fuller sense usually occurs in adolescence—from age twelve to sixteen—at the time when free personal choice is becoming a reality. Applying his psychological schema to the church's dealing with children, Koons pointed out that the child is in a state of salvation before reaching the age of responsibility and so is eligible for preparatory membership in the church. He criticized the Methodist Episcopal Church because of its failure to nurture such children appropriately and keep them from wandering from the church and from God until they were old enough to "publicly vow their allegiance to Christ."[26]

During the first decade of the 1900s, there were fairly frequent appeals for conversion which were strongly reminiscent of those typical of a century earlier. Various writers deplored what W. R. Goodwin called "a growing tendency in these latter days to exalt culture above repentance and conversion."[27] As the century progressed, however, such appeals were heard far less frequently. Even when the language of conversion was used, it usually reflected the categories of emotional development being popularized by modern psychology much more than the traditional understanding of spiritual transformation.[28] Firmly denigrated, not only as unnecessary but also as undesirable, was any expectation of crisis conversion following a period of waywardness and sin. The properly nurtured child, it was repeatedly asserted, could be "progressively *claimed* by the Spirit, to the end that he may never need to be reclaimed. . . . Christian nurture ought to obviate the necessity of conversion in the experience" of children and youth.[29] There was frequently expressed and vehement objection to acquiescence to the idea that children would inevitably fall into sin and have to be won back to Christ: "The infant is born a child of God and as such he should remain. I denounce as a diabolical heresy the false doctrine that a child must go to the devil before he can come to Jesus."[30] Carl F. Eltzholtz expressed the emerging consensus in his influential work *The Child: Its Relation to God and the Church* when he argued that there was for every child an essential moment of decision when he or she "steps over from an *unconscious* relation or state of grace and salvation by virtue of the unconditional benefits of the atonement to a *conscious* relation of faith and trust in Christ as his personal Savior."[31]

A characteristic feature of the periodical literature of both the northern and southern branches of the church throughout this period continued to be repeated and emphatic concern for the process of Christian nurture in both church and home. Despite the emphasis on education and nurture which had been pronounced during the latter half of the nineteenth century, all appeared to agree that not enough was being done and that much of what was being done was ineffectual.[32] *The Sunday School Journal* asserted that if the church were to conduct no revivals for a period of twenty years, but instead concentrate upon the nurture and teaching of its children, "a greater growth would be realized than in any previous twenty years of church history.[33] Going beyond the positions articulated by most writers, southern Sunday School editor James Atkins claimed that "the Church of Christ is fundamentally an educational institution."[34] As regards children, this educational responsibility of the church was thought to reside peculiarly in the institution of the Sunday School. While during the earlier century, teachers had been admonished to bring their charges to Christ, so now they were urged to maintain and strengthen the children's inherent relationship to God and to the church: " . . . the culture of spiritual character must be set before us as the supreme purpose for which the Sunday School exists."[35] Little children, belonging to Christ's Kingdom from birth, were to be so nurtured that they would never experience a period during which sin ruled in their lives. If both church and home fulfilled their duties, children might grow progressively and uninterruptedly into a personal relationship to Christ appropriate to their level of maturity without the necessity of falling away and traumatic conversion:

"Better a fence at the top of a precipice than an ambulance at the bottom."[36]

Issues Relating to Church Membership

A great deal of the emphasis upon proper nurture for children was focused upon preparing them to enter upon the responsibilities and privileges of membership in the church. While most agreed that baptized children were to be considered, at least in some degree, members of the universal church of Christ, there were diverse interpretations of their relationship to the denomination and local congregation. Throughout this period, *The Sunday School Journal* consistently and vehemently espoused the place of children in the church. Its writers and editors constantly advocated extensive religious instruction geared toward preparing children for "joining the church." In accord with the oft-cited views of popular psychologists, the early years of adolescence were targeted as the appropriate time for personal commitment to Christ and to the church. As revealed by statistics, the Sunday School was the most potent agency for this work.[37] Many local churches observed an annual Decision (or Commitment) Day when children around twelve years of age were encouraged to declare their loyalty to Christ and desire for membership in the church. There was great concern expressed that such commitments be neither perfunctory or pressured, that they be preceded by careful cultivation and marked by ceremonies of impressive significance.[38]

The northern and southern branches of the Methodist Episcopal Church differed in the forcefulness with which they advocated infant baptism and their understanding of the relationship of baptized children to the church. In the *Discipline* of the northern church throughout this period, it was stated in the section entitled Baptized Children and the Church that:

> We hold that all children, by virtue of the unconditional benefits of the atonement, are members of the kingdom of God, and therefore graciously entitled to Baptism; but, as Infant Baptism contemplates a course of religious instruction and discipline, it is expected of all parents or guardians who present their children for Baptism that they will use all diligence in bringing them up in conformity to the word of God; and they should be solemnly admonished of this obligation, and earnestly exhorted to faithfulness therein.

The following paragraph continued: "We regard all children who have been baptized as placed in visible covenant relation to God, and under the special care and supervision of the Church." In 1912 the General Conference added the phrase "as probationers" to the end of this sentence in order to make the status of baptized children clear. In 1916 the reference was changed to "preparatory members" with the same terminology being used also for adults who were in probationary status. However, the section of the *Discipline* specifying statistical reports to be made by pastors to annual conferences stipulated: "'Baptized Children' shall not be counted as 'Preparatory Members' in making reports of membership." A subsequent paragraph specified the conditions for membership:

> Whenever baptized children shall understand the obligations of religion, and shall give evidence of piety, they may be admitted into Full Membership in the Church, on the recommendation of a leader with whom they have met at least six months in Class, upon publicly assenting before the Church to the Baptismal Covenant, and also to the usual questions on Doctrines and Discipline.

The word "full" was removed from this paragraph in 1908. In 1916 the church added to its ritual a "Form for Receiving Children as Members of the Church." The introductory address of this ritual began:

> Dearly Beloved, these persons here present before you are baptized children of the Church, who, having arrived at the years of discretion, desire now to confirm the vows of their baptism and to enter upon the active duties and the full privileges of membership in the Church of Christ.

This ritual was used until 1928 when the church returned to the use of a single form for receiving persons into full membership. This ritual–used for preparatory members, for persons coming from other churches, or on confession of faith–made clear in its wording that none of these groups was considered to be a member already. It spoke of "seeking admission" into the Methodist Episcopal Church and welcomed persons "to the fellowship of the Church."[39]

In the 1902 *Discipline* of the Methodist Episcopal Church, South, the section concerning the children of the church began: "Let the minister diligently instruct and exhort all parents to dedicate their children to the Lord in baptism as early as convenient." A roll of baptized infants was to be maintained, but they were not to be included in membership statistics. Ministers were directed to care and pray for the children and "cause them to be faithfully instructed in the nature, design, privileges, and obligations of their baptism." The following paragraph continued:

> As soon as they comprehend the responsibilities involved in a public profession of faith in Christ, and give evidence of a sincere and earnest determination to discharge the same, see that they be duly recognized as members of the Church, agreeably to the provisions of the Discipline.

The southern church did not use the terms "probationers" or "preparatory members" for either children or adults. In 1914 the General Conference adopted a ritual for "The Reception and Recognition of Children as Members" which would be used until the 1939 merger. It described the children as, "Having arrived at years of discretion, and now of their own accord appearing before this congregation to take upon themselves the vows and enter upon the privileges and duties of the Church. . . ." The service included the renewal by parents of the vows which they had made at the time of the children's baptism. One of the questions addressed to the children made explicit the sense in this ritual of ongoing relationship with the church rather than initial reception into its membership: "Is it your sincere desire, of your own free will and accord, to continue as members of the Church of Christ, in the communion of the Methodist Episcopal Church, South?"[40]

In the first *Discipline* reflecting the union of the churches in 1939, the section on infant baptism was a combination of the theological rationale used in the north with the south's earnest exhortation to parents to have their infants baptized promptly. Baptized children were described as "in visible covenant relation to God and as Preparatory Members"—a term new to the south. Unbaptized children who are enrolled in the pastors' classes might, with parental consent, be enrolled as preparatory members also. Admission into full membership was contingent upon "evidence of understanding their Christian privileges and obligations and of their Christian faith and purpose. . . ." There were two orders for reception of members into the church. In the one for children and youth, the southern nuance of continuation of membership was replaced by questions to be answered "Before you are admitted into the Church. . . ."[41] None of the various services for reception of persons into church membership was referred to as confirmation during this period, either in the rituals or in other literature. Forms of the verb "confirm" did appear in the rituals, usually with reference to faith or to baptismal vows. In the 1932 order of the Methodist Episcopal Church, the rubric directed the minister to lay his hand upon the head of each kneeling candidate and say: "The Lord defend thee with his heavenly grace and by his Spirit confirm thee in the faith and fellowship of all true disciples of Jesus Christ." This wording was used in the unified church of 1939 in the order for reception of adult members, but did not appear in the service for reception of children and youth.[42]

Other issues relating to church membership during this period dealt specifically with the admission of adults into the Methodist Episcopal Church. The southern branch had, in the nineteenth century, eliminated any required probationary period prior to full membership. In the northern church, the stipulation of "at least six months on Probation" was dropped in 1908, but a footnote in the *Discipline* clarified that, according to a ruling by the bishops in 1912: "The probationary relation is required as a condition precedent to reception into Full Membership. The period of Probation is no longer of definite length, but the probationary (preparatory) membership is imperative." This footnote disappeared in 1928 and with it any requirement of a period of preparatory membership, although the *Discipline* continued to classify church membership in the categories of preparatory and full.[43] Another focus of debate was the so-called doctrinal tests that the General Conference of 1864 had added to the vows of church membership by requiring a profession of "saving faith in the Lord Jesus Christ" and an affirmation of belief "in the doctrines of the Holy Scriptures as set forth in the Articles of Religion of the Methodist Episcopal Church." The "saving faith" reference was modified in 1916 to remove the implication that a person must have experienced regeneration before being admitted to membership. The affirmation of the Articles of Religion was upheld by the General Conference in 1920, but continued to occasion controversy until in 1924 the vow was rephrased to an affirmation of the faith as contained in the New Testament.[44]

The precise relationship between baptism and participation in the Lord's Supper remained ambiguous during this period, but was not a subject of much discussion. In general, while Methodists believed that baptism was appropriately prerequisite, they were unwilling to prescribe rigid limitations on the Lord's Table. *The Sunday School Journal* editors asserted their considerable influence in favor of baptized children being encouraged to partake, but this practice varied widely in different regions of the country and no normative pattern can be identified.[45]

By the time of the 1939 union, the wide-ranging complex of issues associated with the sacrament of baptism had been examined in every minute detail and debated with every conceivable nuance. Controversy had yielded to consensus on many points, but numerous ambiguities were carried over into the new Methodist Church.

THE METHODIST CHURCH: 1940–1968

Although substantive changes in rituals and in polity relating to baptism occurred during the first decades of the twentieth century, debate concerning underlying theological issues was much less prolific than during the preceding century. In an article entitled "The Mystery of Baptism" which appeared in *Religion in Life* in 1951, Paul S. Minear wrote:

> During the past generation there has been in American Christianity a dearth of interest in the doctrine and practice of baptism. There were once heated arguments over the relative merits of immersion and sprinkling, and over the legitimacy of infant baptism. In fact, the debates over such issues were prominent among the ostensible causes for the splintering of American denominations. The heat has been dissipated, and few of us regret the cooler temperatures. We recall the interminable wrangling, the theological hair-splitting, the long chains of biblical proof texts, the specious rationalizations of inherited prejudices, and we are grateful that baptism has ceased to provoke civil war within Protestantism.

But following a brief assessment of the reasons for this less contentious climate of opinion, Minear concluded:

> More important, perhaps, current conceptions of the gospel and of the church have been so chaotic that it has been impossible to maintain a clear-cut doctrine of the sacraments. Church members are so confused or so unimpressed by what happens in baptism that they have been quite unconcerned about how this sacrament is celebrated.
>
> Whatever may be the reasons for their apathy, it is clear that the American churches are now witnessing a resurgence of the ancient issues.[46]

Authorized Church Statements on Baptism

The 1964 *Book of Hymns* which became the official hymnal of the church was, like its 1935 predecessor, seriously deficient in hymns for use on baptismal occasions. Only "See Israel's gentle Shepherd stand" was so listed in the index. Four others were suggested in the "See also" category: "Glorious things of thee are spoken;" "I love thy kingdom, Lord;" "Now thank we all our God;" and "The Church's one foundation." These hymns include only indirect, tangential references to baptism. (In contrast, the index of the 1964 hymnal cited seventeen hymns for use with the Lord's Supper.)[47]

Few changes were made in the baptismal and membership rituals of the reunified church prior to the publication of the 1964 *Book of*

Hymns. An Order for Receiving Persons as Preparatory Members was added in 1940, but was designated as for optional use. That same General Conference modified the Order for Receiving Persons into the Church by approving an alternative form at the end of the service. Restoring the wording previously used in the southern part of the church, this form allowed the congregation to greet new members by saying: " . . . and in token of our brotherly love, we give you the right hand of fellowship, and pray that you may be numbered with His people here, and with His saints in glory everlasting." In 1944, the optional Briefer Order for the Baptism of Infants was eliminated; added was an Order for Receiving Members by Transfer or on Reaffirmation of Faith or in Affiliated Membership.

Although no further substantive changes took place in the ritual until 1964, a commission began working toward major revisions as early as 1956. Trial use of some of new rituals was inaugurated in 1960 accompanied by a commentary written by the General Conference Commission on Worship entitled *Proposed Revisions for the Book of Worship*, or Green Book as it was popularly known. The most significant change that occurred in these trial rituals before their finalization in the 1964 hymnal was the insertion of congregational pledges in the baptismal orders and in the order for confirmation and reception of members.

The rituals adopted by the 1964 General Conference represented major alterations in the baptismal theology of Methodism. The "Introduction to the Order for the Administration of the Sacrament of Baptism" made it clear that the Commission on Worship was quite intentional in making these changes and was attempting to explicate and justify them to the church:

> In revising the Order for the Administration of Baptism, the Commission on Worship has endeavored to keep in mind that baptism is a sacrament, and to restore it to the Evangelical-Methodist concept set forth in our Articles of Religion. . . . Due recognition was taken of the critical re-examination of the theology of the Sacrament of Baptism which is currently taking place in ecumenical circles, and of its theological content and implications.

In order to make the current situation in the church more understandable, the Commission provided a brief historical perspective on baptismal theology in Methodism:

> In preparing the Orders for the Methodists in America, Mr. Wesley carried over into the ritual for the administration of baptism two ideas from the Church of England which are foreign to our

> thinking. A comparison of our present order with the one recommended by John Wesley reveals sharp divergences. These differences in the main center around the teaching of total depravity and baptismal regeneration. Our present ritual bears marks of this conflict, and of the attempts of revisers to retain the form of the ritual for baptism while eliminating the offending elements in the content.
>
> During this process of revision, the idea of baptism as a sacrament was watered down, if not lost altogether. In the main our ministers have acquiesced to the popular notion that baptism is nothing more than a dedication of the child to God by his parents. Indeed, some conceive of baptism as a social event where no Christian conviction is involved. It is looked upon as a mark of respectability in the community. The concept of a dedication differs from that of a sacrament. In a dedication we make a gift of a life to God for him to accept; in a sacrament God offers the gift of his unfailing grace for us to accept. The revision here offered seeks to restore the rite of baptism to its original and historic meaning as a sacrament.[48]

The 1964 order for the administration of baptism contained two rituals—one for use with children, the other for use with youth and adults. This represented a change from the previous order which offered three services—for infants, for children and youth, and for adults. The new ritual included no reference to infants or any explanation for the grouping of youth with adults rather than with children as previously done. The opening rubric of the order, however, was a directive that indicated the expectation: "Our ministers are enjoined diligently to teach the people committed to their pastoral care the meaning and purpose of the Baptism of children and to urge them to present their children for Baptism at an early age." William R. Cannon, chair of the Committee on Ritual and Order of Service, speaking at the General Conference of 1964 referred to this service as being for the "Baptism of infants." He described the service as follows:

> This service emphasizes the divine grace. It is not what we do for ourselves, nor yet what we as parents confer upon our children when we present them in this Holy Rite. Rather, Baptism is what God does. What happens is His divine act, an expression of His mercy, the gift of His love. Consequently, we do not begin this service, the Baptism of infants, with the statement that all men are as of God and subject to life eternal, but we begin with grace and say, "By grace, we are made partakers of the righteousness of Jesus Christ."[49]

The introductory address characterized the baptized infants as "thereby marked as Christian disciples, and initiated into the fellowship of Christ's holy Church." Reference was made , as in all previous infant baptism rituals in Methodism, to Mark 10:14. The parents or sponsors confessed their own faith in Christ and pledged themselves to the Christian nurture of the child at home and in the church. For the first time, a congregational pledge of support was added to the baptismal service. The order for baptism of youth and adults restored the statement of human sinfulness which had been removed from the ritual earlier in the century: "Dearly beloved, forasmuch as all men have sinned and fallen short of the glory of God. . . ." As Cannon described it:

> When you turn to the second Baptismal service, that is Baptism of youth and adults, you finally return to the language of Wesley, to the language of the *Book of Common Prayer*, and here, again, the redemptive element is emphasized, and we know that Baptism saves a man from his sin, and the statement is made that we are all sinners and fallen short of the glory of God and we cannot save ourselves.[50]

Also in 1964, the order for receiving persons into membership was renamed The Order for Confirmation and Reception into the Church. This was the first use of the term "confirmation" in the title of any ritual in the history of Methodism (although the verb form of the word had been used since the 1930s). The service had few substantive changes from the 1939 version. Perhaps most theologically significant was the replacing of the word "ordinances" with "Sacraments" in the opening address.

Major Issues in Theology and Practice

A renewed interest in issues of baptismal theology and practice was apparent among American Methodists in the 1950s and 60s. It was equally clear that significant modifications were emerging, although their outcome was as yet unpredictable. In 1953 Robert W. Goodloe, Professor of Church History at Perkins School of Theology, published his widely-read book *The Sacraments in Methodism*. Goodloe's theology epitomized the optimistic assessment of human moral ability which vitiated any understanding of the sacramental nature of baptism. It was "initiation into the membership of the church [which] is the characteristic use of baptism in all present-day churches," he affirmed approvingly. Goodloe linked orthodox sacramental theology with autocratic, authoritarian political systems such as the Roman Empire and, by implication, the totalitarian regimes of the World War II period:

> And—in every age—a people who are unable to control themselves politically and must depend upon someone to rule over them have

> found that in the matter of salvation the individual assumes that he is unable to exercise saving faith and so must depend upon the priest and the church to do that for him. It was within a society holding that conception of God and man and the state that there developed a Church whose characteristic teachings were original sin and baptismal regeneration. . . . So that today in a great democratic country like America there are those who cling to the Catholic inheritance of original sin and baptismal regeneration; but as democracy increases, in both state and church, the worth of the individual advances, and the "whosoever will" teaching of Jesus is on the march![51]

Goodloe went on to attribute the changes in baptismal understanding evinced in revisions of the Methodist ritual to the growing strength of American democracy:

> But given the solid New Testament teaching of justification by faith, both original sin and baptismal regeneration are on the decline. The first ritual for the baptism of infants in the Methodist Church opened by saying: "Dearly, beloved, for as much as all men are conceived and born in sin"; the corresponding paragraph today reads: "Dearly beloved, forasmuch as all men are heirs of life eternal and subjects of the saving grace of the Holy Spirit." While Methodism was making that transition, the American people joined in the fight for their freedom, the Declaration of Independence was signed, the Constitution of the United States was adopted, and slavery was overthrown; and we stand today the most thoroughly democratic people on the earth. These changes all flow out of our conception of God, man, and society; and in theology the classic phrase for this conception is justification by faith.[52]

Presumably Goodloe would have been chagrined to learn that the official process toward further revision of the ritual, which began just three years after the publication of his book, would issue in the 1964 orders. In that 1964 order of infant baptism, the emphasis was shifted from the moral nature of human beings to the activity of divine grace: "Dearly beloved, Baptism is an outward and visible sign of the grace of the Lord Jesus Christ, through which grace we become partakers of his righteousness and heirs of life eternal." In the 1964 order for baptism of youth and adults, wording quite similar to that which Goodloe had found offensive was restored: "Dearly beloved, forasmuch as all men have sinned and fallen short of the glory of God. . . ."[53]

The direction of impending change in Methodist baptismal theology was clearly articulated in an article by Carl Michalson, Professor of Systematic Theology at Drew University, in 1958. Entitled "Why Methodists Baptize?," the article featured an introductory sentence which read, "Baptism signifies the future–it is not tied to a moment of time." The opening paragraphs expressed Michalson's concern over the current understanding of baptism:

> If there is such a thing as a Methodist theology for the sacrament of Baptism today, it has a wide gulf to span. . . . The conscience of The Methodist Church surely cannot remain easy about the existence of a sacramental practice savoring of a body of belief which is no longer invoked to justify the practice.[54]

Heavy emphasis was placed on the high significance of baptism:

> The Christian witness affirms that there is a Word which pre-exists both baptism and preaching. This Word is the Baptism with which Jesus was baptized [that is,] the Baptism of Jesus' dying and rising. . . . Baptism, however, is more comprehensive than preaching in granting the *seal* of faith, together with the promise.
>
> Preaching refreshes the Church's memory of its baptism. In this sense, Baptism is the unrepeatable Word, while preaching continually repeats. . . .[This is] equally true of infant baptism and adult baptism. . . .
>
> Baptism is, therefore, the basic sacrament. Its priority is logical as well as chronological. For Baptism forms the Church's life. It is the inaugurating, initiating event, engrafting the Church into Jesus' baptism.[55]

Michalson's thought presaged an understanding of baptism with which the church in the 1990s is struggling: baptism as a lifelong process of the workings of grace rather than as a discrete event in time. He found this concept alive in the history of Protestantism:

> The seal remains upon the baptized as the continuous access to a knowledge of God's redeeming grace. As the Westminster catechism states, the efficacy of baptism is not tied to a moment in time. And, as Luther suggests in his smaller catechism, baptismal water signifies not the past but the future, the daily drowning of sins in repentance and rising in righteousness. . . . Repentance of sins in the baptized is not a going on to something beyond baptism but a re-entry into the baptismal grace. . . . Preaching refreshes the Church's memory of its watery foundation and evokes the repentance by which the congregation continually immerses itself in the healing waters.[56]

Further evidence of the shift which was taking place in Methodist thought can be found in the Episcopal Address to the 1960 General Conference. Speaking of the need for revisions in the forms of worship used in the church, the bishops asserted:

> Other Christians are asking us, and we might well ask ourselves: "Do your sacramental practices conform with your historic sacramen-

> tal doctrines? How does your conception of the ministry fit in with either or both?" We recognize that The Methodist Church stands in an anomalous position in the eyes of other major Christian communions with respect to our current practice. An extensive sampling of lay opinion concerning the significance of Baptism and the Lord's Supper, and the obligation of parents to bring their infant children for consecration in Christian baptism "to God and to His Church" has indicated an alarming degree of uncertainty and confusion. All of this points unmistakably to the fact that, in full recognition of the paramount place which preaching has always held in the Methodist tradition, far greater significance than is commonly assigned them must be given to the Sacraments and to the worship service itself.[57]

It is clear that by the early 1960s baptism was again a subject of serious concern and of increasing significance in the life of Methodism. Further, the theological understanding of baptism plainly was undergoing alteration in a direction that placed expanded emphasis upon its nature as a sacrament. In a 1961 series of adult Sunday School lessons entitled "The Sacraments of the Methodist Church," Boston School of Theology Professor L. Harold DeWolf assessed the proposed revisions of the baptismal order, and in effect, the general movement in the church toward renewed interpretation of baptism: "This revised order is much more clearly the ritual of a *Christian sacrament* than was the order used in recent years, and presents so many advantages in sound instruction and worship that it will be followed exclusively in this present study."[58]

Two issues which had long been contentious in the church had ceased by this period to be major foci of debate—appropriate mode of baptism and the repetition of the sacrament later in the life of a believer. John M. Moore included a fairly lengthy discussion of the question of mode in his 1946 book *Methodism in Belief and Action*. After examination of the New Testament evidence, he concluded that each of the three modes had spiritual significance and that all were acceptable. Robert Goodloe devoted an entire chapter to the subject and reached a similar conclusion. In the absence of arguments to the contrary, this may be taken to be the twentieth-century consensus. Although the practice of rebaptism certainly continued, little theological ground existed to support it. Carl Michalson was one of very few writers of the period who dealt with the issue:

> Baptism never loses its effectiveness. It is virtually the indelible Word. That is why the sacrament of Baptism is unrepeatable. . . . Baptism is God's covenant with us to drive out sin. Nothing invalidates that covenant, even sin.[59]

Infant Baptism

Cruel Water
Is there a sound that's quite so dismal
As infants' squalls through rite baptismal? [60]

Surely Methodism's general assessment of infant baptism was not as negative as this ditty, which appeared in *The Christian Home Magazine* in 1950, might imply. However, the understanding of the sacrament as it was received by infants was an area that got much attention in the church press. The crux of the problem was clear: if infants were not born needing baptism to cleanse them from the guilt of original sin and if they were not spiritually regenerated in and through the sacrament, then what justification was there for continuation of the practice? Actually Methodists never even considered terminating the practice of infant baptism, but they did struggle with interpreting its significance. Still fighting the old suspicions of belief in baptismal regeneration with which American Methodism had always struggled, John Moore declared in 1946:

> To believe in baptismal regeneration, that is, in the effecting of a spiritual transformation by a ceremonial use of the physical element of water, is to bring magical power into the ceremony of the sacrament or into the officiating person, and neither has the endorsement of modern intelligence. . . .[The Methodist Church] rejects all sacerdotal and sacramental views of baptism and baptismal regeneration. . . .[61]

For Moore, infants were "baptized not because of what they are but because of what they are to become and to do."[62] Such a proleptic view of infant baptism was also espoused by theologians Harris Franklin Rall and L. Harold DeWolf who defended the practice on the grounds of the unity of the family and asserted that its purpose was to initiate the process of Christian nurture which would issue in an informed decision to commit one's life to Christ.[63] Infants were baptized only "in anticipation of their joining the church [and] no infant baptism is valid which does not issue in adherence to the Kingdom through the church."[64] Robert Goodloe largely ignored the child and emphasized the effects of infant baptism upon others: " . . . the possibility of influencing the tender mind of the growing child in favor of righteousness may be impressed upon congregation and parents more effectively than by any other agency." [65]

Indeed, much of the focus in discussions of infant baptism during the period continued, as in earlier times, to stress the role and responsibilities of parents and the church community and to represent the sacrament as basically a service of dedication and commitment of those who would be in positions to influence the maturing child. This was a constant theme in the church periodical literature of the time.[66] An illustrative example was an article by Anna Laura Gebhard in *The Christian Home*:

> The dedication of parents to the responsibilities to which God has called them by entrusting new life to their keeping and nurture has been formalized in the sacrament of baptism, a symbol of the child's birth into the Christian fellowship. Baptism is a symbol of the dedication of parents to bring up a child in the way he should grow.[67]

It was obvious that in the minds of many Methodist persons no concept of infant baptism as a sacrament existed. Instead, the ceremony was an opportunity for human action, an expression of human choice, "the dedication of a child to God on the part of his parents."[68] Infant and adult baptisms were understood as theologically very different : " . . . the service for adults is symbolic of the washing away of sins, but in the case of the infant it is the outward expression of the parents' intent to relate themselves and their child to God."[69] Such perception of distinction was the logical result of understandings which focused solely on the human participants in the baptismal occasion.

As the dedicatory aspect of infant baptism emerged as the most salient feature of the ceremony in the minds of many, the issue arose of a separate service of infant dedication without the trappings of baptism at all. A legal test of such a service in the Methodist tradition came before the Judicial Council in 1957. The case grew out of an action of the Latin American Central Conference which had adopted the following paragraph for inclusion in the *Discipline* to be used in that area:

> We recognize the right that parents have to dedicate their children to the Lord, postponing baptism until the child accepts Jesus Christ as his Lord and Savior. The dedicated children shall be entered on the permanent records as candidates for membership, in a special section for them. The Minister shall diligently instruct the parents with regard to the vows they assume and he shall exhort them to be ever faithful therein.

In addition the words "in Baptism" were to be omitted from the paragraph in the *Discipline* reading, "It shall be the duty of the Pastor of every charge earnestly to exhort parents and guardians within his constituency to dedicate their children to the Lord *in Baptism* as early as practicable." Citing Article of Religion XVII, the First Restrictive

Rule, and Paragraph 127 of the *Discipline*,[70] the Judicial Council ruled that the actions of the Latin American Central Conference were contrary to the Constitution of The Methodist Church and could not be included in the *Discipline*.[71] This decision was referred to in a footnote in the 1960 and 1964 *Disciplines*.

Questions concerning a service of dedication for infants arose more broadly as the proposed merger of The Methodist Church and the Evangelical United Brethren Church moved toward fruition in 1968. In addition to a service of infant baptism, the EUB Church offered, in a section entitled Additional Rituals, an order for The Dedication of Infants. The order is introduced by this note: "The following ritual is provided for use of Christian parents, or guardians, who desire to reserve the Sacrament of Baptism until a later time when the child makes personal commitment to Christ." The opening address of the service refers to Hannah's bringing Samuel to God and to the parents of Jesus presenting him in the Temple "in an act of dedication." The parents pledge themselves to Christian example and nurture to the end that the child come to accept Christ as Savior. The congregation accepts responsibility to aid the parents in this endeavor.[72] The provenance of this service is unclear, since neither of the constituent denominations had such a ritual until the United Brethren added it in their *Discipline* in 1945—the year just prior to merger with the Evangelical Church.[73]

Evidence from the church publications of the early 1960s revealed that infant baptism was a subject of considerable interest, but of more confusion. An article entitled "The Sacred Event of Baptism" in *The Christian Home* acknowledged this confusion explicitly and manifested it unwittingly by using a picture of an infant baptism to accompany text which spoke of the sacrament in terms only applicable to adults.[74] Lyle Schaller's 1964 article "Who Is Baptizing the Babies?" documented the sharp decline in the number of baptized infants in the last four years.[75] This situation was at least partially the result of the two contradictory interpretations of infant baptism which were coexisting in Methodism during this period. Increasingly at odds with the dedicatory understanding was the burgeoning effort to recover the sacramental view. Carl Michalson's 1958 article expressed seminal ideas:

> Infant baptism is the evangelical sacrament because it does not exact a pledge from man, not even in a delayed way at confirmation. It is the act in which the Church renews God's pledge. . . . The Word of Baptism in either children or adults has the same spiritual efficacy. It does not exact responsibility. It creates the conditions for the

> possibility of responsibility. . . . Baptism in an adult is as difficult to understand as baptism in an infant. For each is the gracious promise and seal of God.[76]

The commentary on baptism in the 1960 *Proposed Revisions for the Book of Worship*, after distinguishing clearly between dedication and sacrament, asserted the necessity of restoring the sacramental meaning which it went on to explicate:

> As a sacrament, baptism is both a *sign* and a *means* of grace. As a sign of God's grace, it recognizes the fact that a child is not made a child of God by baptism. He is born of God, and baptism is the public recognition of that fact. Performed in the face of the congregation, it reminds the people that God takes the initiative in claiming the child for his own. Thus it is the sign and seal of the child's inclusion in Christ's holy Church, and of his inheritance of the kingdom of God. It is the outward acknowledgement that the church consists of all professing believers *together with their children*.

The statement continued by making unequivocal the necessity of human response to the divine grace manifested in baptism:

> But a sacrament is also a means of grace. In our tradition baptism requires a response of faith on the part of the person being baptized if it is to be a means of grace. The physical act of baptism means nothing at all unless it is a personalization of man's relation to God made effective through faith. . . . The sacramental nature of infant baptism can be preserved, if, in baptism, we see the child brought into a new environment of Christ's holy Church. Where the sacramental character of infant baptism is taken seriously by the Church, then the attitude of the congregation and the parents becomes a means of grace in providing an atmosphere of faith and love in which the child grows in the knowledge that he is a child of God's, and the parents, taking the baptismal vows for the child, dedicate themselves to bring the child up in the nurture and admonition of the Lord. Inasmuch as this rite is performed in the presence of the congregation, its administration becomes a means of grace for them also, since it is a repeated reminder to the members of the congregation of our origin and destiny in God, and the renewal of our vows taken at the time of baptism.[77]

The position here being articulated attempted to preserve the dedicatory significance of infant baptism while restoring the sacramental understanding. This trend was expressed in the Sunday School literature of the 1960s as well. In the *Adult Student* Charles S. Hempstead argued that, "a dedication service is a far call from a sacrament of baptism." In dedication, he contended, parents offer the child to God and declare what they will do; in a sacrament, God offers grace in Christ declaring what God has done and will do. Congregation and parents function as means of grace for the baptized child growing up in the faith.[78] In the *Methodist Teacher–Nursery*, Editor of Church School Publications Walter Vernon recognized the responsibility undertaken by parents and congregation, but described infant baptism as "a time of recognition of God's love for this baby and his claim on its life." Vernon insisted that the service was not primarily a dedication; instead, the focus should be on the "God-child relationship that is being dramatized in the occasion."[79]

American Methodists had engaged in rather vehement debate during the nineteenth century over the question of which infants were eligible to receive baptism. The focus of the problem was, of course, the ecclesiastical status of the parents. While the issue had not been resolved, debate had largely ceased in the twentieth century. At the 1964 General Conference, however, the question resurfaced in response to a proposal by a delegate from Chile. He insisted that the ministers in his area were under strong pressure "in a semi-pagan—nominally Roman Catholic milieu . . . to perform . . . what we can describe only as semiblasphemous Baptisms." Supported by a delegate from Malaya, he wanted an amendment to make clear that parents presenting their children for baptism must be members of the Christian church. In the ensuing debate, Albert C. Outler averred:

> One recognizes the issue at stake here, the question to accept the notion that we baptize children only of professed Christian parents is to misunderstand, both the historic and evangelical concept of baptism and the relation of the pastor to those admitted to pastoral care. This would require the pastor to make a judgment even within the Christian church as to whether you will baptize a child of one member or two—this is an ancient and thorny question—it would mean that you restrict the notion of membership in the church to formal membership in the church and deny the whole problem of the latent church in relation to the baptism and this membership of God's people, and it would—in the last instance—require the kind of division in families, it seems to me, to have very seriously inimical to the notion of Baptism, not as baptismal regeneration, but initiation into the people of God.

The motion to amend was lost.[80] However, the baptismal ritual adopted by this General Conference and appearing in the *Book of Hymns* of 1964 did contain the following rubric: "Parents or sponsors presenting a child for Baptism should be members of Christ's holy Church."

It was clear by 1968 that the evolution in theological understanding of infant baptism was in the direction of a more sacramental interpretation. Laurence H. Stookey accented this theme in an article in the *Christian Advocate* written in response to an earlier piece by another author entitled "Put Adults Back in Infant Baptism." Stookey's article was entitled "Put God Back in Infant Baptism." He asserted that the basic problem was that adults are confused about the role of God in baptism. This contemporary confusion, Stookey thought, resulted from the erosion of the doctrines of original sin and baptismal regeneration and from the "historic emphasis on the conversion experience as the rite of initiation into the church." Many Methodists had become, in effect, anabaptists and all sense of baptism as a sacrament had been lost. "God became the recipient of man's gracious decision" rather than the divine initiator and enabler of salvation.[81] Methodism would move into its next period struggling to recover the balance between these elements.

The Nature and Nurture of Children

The bitter and protracted debates over the spiritual status of children which were typical of the nineteenth century had ceased by this point in the twentieth. The prevailing understanding was expressed by Goodloe:

> Children, we believe, are born in innocence, not guilty of inherited sins; they are possessed of a capacity which at the opening of accountability enables them to enter upon the way of salvation or upon the way of sin, depending upon the choice to be made by the child.[82]

Conversion for children was understood as the turning away from the option of evil which free choice made possible—the "turning to God . . . in response to the love, the grace of God."[83] If children receive appropriate nurture, this conversion can occur quite early in life:

> Now our concern as workers in the home and in the church school is how we may bring a child to exercise that act of saving faith back there at the first dawn of moral consciousness, rather than at some distant adult experience after years of rebellion against God have intervened.[84]

Goodloe stressed that children do not naturally grow up as Christians and that, while they must ultimately make their own personal commitments to Christ, faithful instruction and admonition at church and at home were the best determinants of the choices they would make.

This doctrine of Christian nurture was the basis upon which the practice of infant baptism rested:

> . . . we believe that by use of an objective ceremony like that of infant baptism, the possibility of influencing the tender mind of the growing child in favor of righteousness may be impressed upon congregation and parents more effectively than by any other agency.[85]

While writers in the 1960s tended to have a more profound interpretation of the significance of baptism than did Goodloe, the emphasis upon the role of nurture in the Christian life of the child continued to be paramount as it had been in Methodism for so long.[86]

Issues Relating to Church Membership

Mid twentieth-century Methodists were largely agreed that something more than baptism was required for children to be considered full members of the Methodist Church.[87] The 1939 *Discipline* spoke of all baptized children as preparatory members. The pastor was to organize classes—which would meet "at least once a week for a reasonable period"—for the children at age ten " or at an earlier age when it is deemed advisable. . . ." These classes were equally open to unbaptized children who "may, with the consent of their parents or guardians, be recognized and recorded as Preparatory Members" as well. The following year the paragraph stated that, "*When baptized children are organized into classes*" (emphasis mine), they were to be classified as preparatory members. The effect was to loosen further the connection between baptism and church membership. This section of the *Discipline* was reworked in 1944 to state, "All children who are baptized by a Methodist minister and other baptized children under the care of a Methodist church shall be enrolled as preparatory members in the Methodist Church. . . ." The section went on to stipulate that parents of such children "shall be instructed as to the significance of the Sacrament and informed that the children will be enrolled after baptism as preparatory members *unless they determine otherwise*" (emphasis mine). This parental option was eliminated in 1952. The specified age for organization into classes was raised to twelve. In 1948 "a minimum of thirteen sessions" was stipulated for the pastors' classes, but in 1952 the number of classes was left unspecified and the "age of decision" was cited as the time for the organization of children into classes.

The tenuous relationship between baptism and church membership was expressed in the 1952 provision that children on the preparatory roll who reach the age of sixteen without becoming members of any church be transferred to the constituency roll which was defined as "containing the names and addresses of such persons as are not members of the church concerned. . . ." In 1968, obviously as a result of merger with the EUB Church, the preparatory membership roll was redefined to include dedicated as well as baptized children. These changes in legislation regarding the relationship of baptized children to the church revealed that this long-mooted issue remained ambiguous. Dr. Ray W. Ragsdale, longtime secretary of the General Board of Evangelism, articulated the loss to which this situation led:

> We Methodist pastors have been sinfully sloppy in our record keeping. We have failed to give adequate attention to our preparatory rolls with the result that thousands of youth slip through our fingers annually who should have been brought into a lifedetermining commitment to Christ. . . . We have been woefully weak in our membership training programs so that the people of the church inside look and act little different from the people outside.[88]

This 1964 assessment is surprising in view of the immense amount of materials published by The Methodist Church during the 1940s and 50s designed to prepare children for church membership.[89]

At least as early as 1942, the attainment of full church membership was occasionally being referred to as confirmation. *Church School Magazine* was especially inclined toward this usage. An editorial entitled "Have You a Confirmation Class?" indicated that this terminology was novel for the denomination:

> Names are not especially important, but recently we heard a bishop of the Methodist Church suggest *Confirmation Class* as a good term to use in this connection. It is a customary designation in the more ritualistic churches. It has a good historic usage for background though it is not officially recognized in Methodist terminology. Certainly the confirming of persons in faith and practice is the purpose of all such preparation for fellowship in the church of Christ.[90]

A 1947 article called confirmation "the second part of the sacrament of baptism" and stated that a person who was willing to take the vows of "the membership or confirmation covenant . . . is then ready to unite with the church or, as we say in many sections of the country, to be confirmed."[91] Carl Michalson mentioned confirmation in his important 1958 article on baptism as " . . . the congregation's means of continuing to testify to its existence by fulfilling its responsibility to the child."[92] The introduction to the new "Order of Confirmation and Reception into the Church" in the 1960 *Proposed Revisions for the Book of Worship* attempted to explain the adoption of the term:

> In the revision of the ritual, the Commission on Worship has kept in mind that Methodism is no longer a society but a church, while retaining Mr. Wesley's concept of a church as "a fellowship of faithful men." Thus the title "The Order of Confirmation and Reception into the Church" is used. The adoption of this title restores the Sacrament of Baptism to its traditional meaning as a sign and seal of inclusion in Christ's holy Church. Therefore in the Order of Confirmation the person simply confirms the vows taken at the time of his baptism, and, on his own initiative, accepts the privileges and assumes the responsibilities involved in church membership. This is consistent with the New Testament teaching and the essential elements taught in the church universal. It meets the criticism often made of the Methodist Church that its ritual for receiving members into the church is parochial, and not in keeping with the practice of the ecumenical church.[93]

A significant point of note here is that confirmation was understood to function as a rite which tied baptism more closely to church membership. William R. Cannon, presenting this new service to the 1964 General Conference, emphasized the personal, volitional aspect of confirmation:

> For us Protestants, this is not a Sacrament, it is subsidiary to Baptism; it supplements the sacrament of Baptism; it completes it, because the person on his own initiative takes the vows of church membership and joins voluntarily into Christian fellowship.[94]

Closely related to issues of membership was the question of the appropriateness of baptized children participating in the Lord's Supper. There was virtually no discussion of the matter in denominational materials of this period and no prescribed rule of action. The general practice, however, appears to have been to open the Table to children only after they had reached the age of discretion and formally joined the church.

Intentional preparation of persons for full membership in the church had never been limited, in the Methodist tradition, only to children. Instruction had been offered for adults as well—in classes and, for a long period, required as a component of a probation period. The first *Disciplines* of the Methodist Church stipulated that pastors were to see to the instruction of all candidates for membership " . . . in the principles of the Christian life, in the baptismal and membership vows, and in the rules and regulations of The Methodist Church." From 1952 through 1964, instruction was mandated in

". . . the meaning of the Christian faith and the history, organization, and teaching of The Methodist Church; to explain to them the baptismal and membership vows; and to lead them to commit themselves to Jesus Christ as Lord and Saviour." The insertion of the phrase "after the completion of a reasonable period of training" in 1964 restored the concept of a probationary period. In 1968 an amendment made explicit that this instruction was to utilize "materials approved" by the denomination.

Debate in the 1964 General Conference over the new baptismal ritual evinced continuing differences of opinion on the question of relationship between baptism and church membership. Chairman William R. Cannon acknowledged in response to a question from Robert Cushman that he had "grudgingly and of necessity" accepted a change in the infant baptism service by which the reference to a child being *received* into the family of God was replaced by wording which *recognized* the child as a member of that family.[95] A delegate from the New England conference questioned the portion " . . . being received into Christ's holy Church, may continue as a worthy member of the same" in the baptism service for youth and adults. He requested and received assurance that this wording would be revised by the editorial committee "so that the baptism of an adult is not equated with membership in the church."[96] In its final form in the *Book of Hymns* this statement was changed to read, " . . . may be received into Christ's holy Church, and be made a living member of the same." Clearly all dispute on issues of baptism and membership had not been resolved.

♦ ♦ ♦

As The Methodist Church became The United Methodist Church through merger with the Evangelical United Brethren in 1968, the trend in theological understanding of baptism and its complex of related issues was undeniably in the direction of a more sacramental interpretation. Yet, the evangelical heritage still struggled to reassert itself and to resist developments which might deemphasize the necessity of personal commitment to Christ. The old tradition of controversy would continue within the new denomination.

CHAPTER VIII

Debate in The United Methodist Church: 1969–1992

THE UNITED METHODIST CHURCH: 1969–1991

During the first years of its existence The United Methodist Church sought to avoid agitation on theological and liturgical issues which might occasion dissension within the newly established denomination. Certainly this was true in the area of baptismal theology and practice. Longstanding Methodist disagreements were now merged with an Evangelical United Brethren tradition which had always harbored disparate understandings of baptism from the diverse groups constituting its heritage.[1] The official hymnals and rituals of the two predecessor denominations continued to be used despite their differences.

Authorized Church Statements on Baptism

The United Methodist Church did not produce a new official hymnal during the first two decades of its existence, but finally in 1988 the General Conference approved *The United Methodist Hymnal* which was published the following year. Burgeoning interest in the sacrament of baptism was evinced by the inclusion of seven hymns for use at "Baptism, Confirmation, Reaffirmation." The only baptismal hymn in the 1964 Methodist book—"See Israel's gentle Shepherd stand," a fixture in Methodist hymnals since 1836—was finally omitted. With one exception, these seven hymns were of contemporary origin; their words were written between 1969 and 1987. Charles Wesley's "Come, Let Us Use the Grace Divine" had appeared in almost all American Methodist hymnals, but had not been listed for use on baptismal occasions. It was originally used for Covenant Services and so was appropriately recommended in 1989 for services of reaffirmation of the baptismal covenant. "Praise and Thanksgiving Be to God" by H. Francis Yardley was also a hymn of reaffirmation. Ruth Duck's "Wash, O God, Our Sons and Daughters" was pertinent for infant baptism as well as reaffirmation. With their references to Romans 6, "This Is the Spirit's Entry Now" by Thomas E. Herbranson and "We Know That Christ Is Raised" by John Brownlow Geyer were best suited for occasions of adult baptism. The chorus "You Have Put on Christ" was taken from the Rite of Baptism for Children by the International Commission on English in the Liturgy. Explicitly written for infant baptism was "Child of Blessing, Child of Promise" by Ronald S. Cole-Turner. These hymns offered an enriched theological as well as musical appreciation of the significance of baptism.

The General Conference of 1968 defined United Methodist ritual as that contained in the 1959 *Book of Ritual* of The Evangelical United Brethren Church and that in the *Book of Worship for Church and Home* of The Methodist Church. A Commission on Worship was established to begin the process of considering revisions. This Commission solicited suggestions throughout the church and in 1969 sponsored a national convocation on worship where ideas were exchanged by more than two thousand people. In 1972 the Commission on Worship was incorporated into the newly established General Board of Discipleship and authorized to prepare new rituals and orders of worship for the denomination. This work became the responsibility of the General Board of Discipleship's Section on Worship when it was formed the next year. In 1976 *A Service of Baptism, Confirmation and Renewal* was published as one of the series of Supplemental Worship Resources. Laurence H. Stookey, Professor of Preaching and Worship at Wesley Theological Seminary, served as writer and chair of the task force. This material was revised over the next four years and published in 1980 with other services under the title *We Gather Together*. The General Conference of 1980 commended these services for trial use throughout the church during the quadrennium. In 1984 the rituals, which had been further revised, were adopted by the General Conference as additional official rituals for the church—the first such action by The United Methodist Church—and they were published as *The Book of Services* in 1985. After considerable debate and still more revisions, these services were approved by the General Conference of 1988 for incorporation into the hymnal to be published the next year. While thus clearly designated as official ritual for the church, these new services were not stipulated as superseding the older official rituals of the predecessor denominations.

The Services of the Baptismal Covenant elicited greater controversy than any other portion of the ritual. Baptismal Covenant III, for example, was written in great haste during the meeting of the 1988 General Conference. It is a reworking of the traditional services of the Methodist and Evangelical United Brethren churches. Baptismal Covenants I, II, and IV evince the movement in United Methodism toward recovery of its antecedents in the theology and practice of the early Christian church and in the richness of baptismal concepts and images from both the Old and New Testaments. These rituals are characterized by their conjunction of emphasis upon the objective work of divine grace with the subjective action of human response. The efficacy of baptism is clearly described as something that God does, something that God gives. The culmination of the trend in Methodism during the past three decades is evident in this more sacramental understanding. Yet, human beings must pledge themselves to accept God's covenant offer and to participate in it.

The rituals reclaim Wesley's view of salvation as a life-long process rather than as an event. Baptism is portrayed as having its own dynamic quality; from it one looks back to the salvation history in which one is made a participant, and forward to the fulfillment of God's purpose. The reality and power of sin—cosmic, systemic, and personal—are recognized, thus recovering an emphasis lost in early twentieth-century Methodism. Restoration of use of the Apostles' Creed provides content for the faith that baptized persons are professing. Strong emphasis is placed on the corporate nature of the Christian faith and the role of the church as the covenant community. Baptism is understood as initiation into the church. Baptized persons, including infants, are explicitly recognized as members of the church of Christ, of The United Methodist Church and of the local congregation. All of these baptismal services, including Covenant II designed to be used for infants and children, conclude with the recommendation that they be followed immediately by Holy Communion and that the new members receive first. Plainly these rituals depart in many ways from what had become the widespread understandings and practices of baptism in the Methodist and Evangelical United Brethren traditions earlier in the century.

Major Issues in Theology and Practice

Long decades of debate had at last issued in some measure of consensus on at least a few points relating to baptismal theology and practice. Dispute concerning the appropriate mode for administering sacramental water had ceased by this period. The official position of American Methodism had always been to allow free choice of modes; now this had become the common practice. Each mode was understood as most powerfully expressing an aspect of the symbolic significance of the sacrament: sprinkling, the washing away of sin; pouring, the gift of the Holy Spirit; immersion, burial and resurrection to new life. Certainly the prevalent practice continued, however, to be that of sprinkling, largely due to considerations of convenience rather than of theology. In recent years there has been increased emphasis upon the use of sufficient quantities of water to stimulate appreciation of its sacramental import.

In accord with renewed stress on the sacramental nature of baptism, the majority of opinion within United Methodism was opposed to the practice of rebaptism. The 1970 *Companion to the Book of Worship* stated flatly, "Appeals to be rebaptized . . . are to be rejected as gratuitous."[2] To repeat the ritual in response to an individual's experiences was understood to undercut the validity of infant baptism and to deny the action of divine grace. Still, however, minority voices within the church were heard frequently espousing the right of rebaptism for persons who wished to receive it and the denomination had no official legislative directive to settle the question.

Historically much of the controversy on baptismal issues in Methodism had been grounded in different understandings of the moral nature of children and how they were to become or continue to be Christians. By the mid twentieth century these conversion versus nurture debates were much muted if not wholly resolved. While evangelical voices continued to be heard in protest, the Bushnellian approach had clearly won in theory, even when it was poorly carried out in practice.

One theological issue which continues to be debated within United Methodism is the perennially mooted question of baptismal regeneration. The new baptismal rituals in the 1989 hymnal have been received with some reservations by evangelical spokespersons in the church. The focus of this concern is the introduction to the service which contains these words: "Through the Sacrament of Baptism we are initiated into Christ's holy church. We are incorporated into God's mighty acts of salvation, *and given new birth through water and the Spirit"* (emphasis added). The fear is that, irrespective of the intentions of the writers of the ritual, this statement will be interpreted in the church as a clear teaching that regeneration occurs through the medium of and at the time of administration of the baptismal water. Such an interpretation would, of course, undercut the evangelical emphasis upon the necessity of personal repentance and faith. Hence, "this particular phrase may represent a serious obstacle for many United Methodists."[3]

The movement toward a more sacramental theology of baptism in Methodism can be traced from the late 1950s. This understanding emphasizes the objective nature of a sacrament as a channel of divine grace, as a ritual action in which the chief actor is God, rather than the human participants. The 1970 *Companion to the Book of Worship* articulated this view quite clearly:

> . . . infant baptism tells us more about God than it does about infants. . . . The nothingness, the anonymity, the alienation—which are some of the contemporary understandings of original sin—are washed away in baptism. The baptized child is born to new life in Christ. . . . Baptism is more than a "dedication" of the child by the parents inasmuch as a real transaction between God and the child is acknowledged.[4]

During the 1980s, widely read commentators on Methodist theology of worship—notably William H. Willimon, Laurence H. Stookey, and James F. White—have expounded and expanded this position.[5] Baptismal Covenants I, II, and IV in the 1989 hymnal represent the culmination of this evolution in understanding.

While the dedicatory aspects of infant baptism were being downplayed, though not discounted, by the more pervasive recognition of divine action in the sacrament, debate continued over the validity of a separate ceremony of infant dedication. Support for such an option came from some in the Evangelical United Brethren tradition and from the evangelical wing of the denomination.[6] Confusion, even contradiction, existed in the official policy of United Methodism as evidenced by the fact that from 1968 to 1980 dedicated children were required by the *Discipline* to be listed on both the preparatory membership and the constituency rolls. After 1980 dedicated children were no longer designated as preparatory members. In 1972 the General Conference Committee on Rituals voted down a proposal for an infant dedication ritual.[7] However, the service for this purpose from the EUB Church continued to be official ritual for United

Methodism even after the adoption of the new services which appear in the 1989 hymnal.

A question about which Methodism has always been unclear is that of the relationship between baptism and church membership. Since the early decades of the twentieth century, baptized children had been designated as preparatory members with full membership status contingent upon a later ceremony of "joining the church." By at least the 1980s this distinction was drawing sharp criticism on the part of some leaders in the church. The argument was that if baptism truly initiated one into the church of Christ, then one was a full church member without further requisites.[8] In *The Formal Response of the United Methodist Church to Baptism, Eucharist and Ministry* in 1986, the Council of Bishops made these comments:

> *BEM* can help us develop a more consistent conception of what it means to be at the same time a member of Christ's holy Church universal, of The United Methodist Church, and of the local congregation. For many years we have been inclined to distinguish between preparatory and full membership, often describing them without giving due attention to baptism as the one decisive act by which the church brings persons into its membership. We must ask ourselves whether we make The United Methodist Church appear to be more exclusive than the universal Church of Christ itself.[9]

Baptismal Covenants I and II in the 1989 hymnal conclude with a congregational response in which the newly baptized persons, including infants, are addressed as members " . . . in the body of Christ and in this congregation of The United Methodist Church." By contrast, the *Discipline* still retains the sharp distinction between preparatory and full membership.

A closely related issue is that of confirmation which since 1964 has become the common term for what was long referred to as a service of joining the church. The confirmation event has been understood as a person's acceptance into full membership. As William F. Dunkle expressed it in *The Encyclopedia of World Methodism*, in baptism a person "is made a member of the holy, catholic Church;" in confirmation one's "denominational and congregational membership is established."[10] But the distinction in significance has not always been so facile. The Council of Bishops underlined the confused state of Methodist thinking in 1986:

> The very word [confirmation] itself came into our usage fairly recently but without definition. American Methodism originally had no concept of confirmation. The Christian's progress in faith was for long thought to begin with infant baptism, continue in educational

> nurture, be marked decisively by either a "conversion experience" or a "confession of faith in Jesus Christ as personal Savior," and certified by the rite of "joining the church." In this scheme, baptism was given slight weight; and, more deplorable, no mention was made of the giving of the Holy Spirit in baptism, confirmation, or in one's indefinable experience. The splitting of infant baptism from personal confirmation has weakened the concept of the once-done sacrament and hardened the idea of covenant as a voluntary commitment. . . . When something like confirmation returned in name and practice, it bore the marks of individual voluntarism. The person, rather than the Holy Spirit acting through the Church, was the subject of the verb "confirm." This development has robbed both baptism and confirmation of personal appropriation of an objective divine action.[11]

Laurence Stookey acknowledged that the committee which drafted the new baptismal rites would have preferred to eliminate the term "confirmation," but feared that such a change would not be accepted in the denomination. Consequently, ambiguities remained.[12] Indicative of the confused relationship between baptism, confirmation, and church membership is the stipulation in the *Discipline* that baptized persons who have not been confirmed by age nineteen (changed from sixteen in 1980) are to be transferred from the roll of preparatory members to the constituency roll of the church. The new baptismal ritual has removed one point of awkwardness in past practice by eliminating any separate act of confirmation for those baptized as youth or adults.

Another long-disputed question appears to have been answered by the new baptismal rites—that of the participation of baptized children in Holy Communion. At the close of each of the Baptismal Covenants, including the one designated for use with children, there is the recommendation that the service continue with Holy Communion and that the new members receive first. This practice would restore in Methodism the customary observance in the Western church until the twelfth century and in the Eastern church to the present day.

Many aspects of the complex of issues relating to baptism had been dealt with in ways that might appear to be definitive, but unresolved questions and nagging ambiguities remained. The General Conference of 1988 recognized that the adoption of new rituals did not settle baptismal questions for the church. Even at those points which had been clarified in theory, uncertainties about future practice in the churches of United Methodism continued. Therefore, the General Conference accepted a recommendation of the General Board of Discipleship and directed that Board ". . . in consultation with the General Board of Higher Education and Ministry, General Commission on Christian Unity and Inter-religious Concerns, and relevant study commissions, to study the meaning of Baptism as it relates to salvation, membership, confirmation, Holy Communion, and Christian vocation and report their findings and recommendations to the 1992 General Conference." A study committee was appointed to fulfill this mandate and worked from April of 1989 through August of 1991 to develop "a biblical, theological and educational statement" on baptism.

THE GENERAL CONFERENCE OF 1992 AND BEYOND

A document entitled "By Water and the Spirit, A Study of the Proposed United Methodist Understanding of Baptism" was produced by the Baptism Study Committee and approved by the General Board of Discipleship for submission to the 1992 General Conference. The document attempts a comprehensive presentation of the denomination's theological positions relative to baptism and the historical process through which they have been developed. This report was assigned to the Faith and Mission Legislative Committee of the General Conference where it received careful examination and extensive discussion. Several delegates stated that this was the most significant issue being considered by the General Conference. By an almost unanimous vote, the Legislative Committee approved the report with the addition of some specific questions and concerns. In the plenary session, the General Conference received the report by a vote of 840 to 89.

As a result, the document[13] was recommended for denomination-wide study during the 1992–96 quadrennium. The Baptism Study Committee will work with the United Methodist Publishing House in preparing the document and appropriate study materials. Processes will be set up for collecting responses from persons and groups throughout the church. The study committee will then submit a revised form of the document with proposed legislation to the 1996 General Conference.

"By Water and the Spirit" continues the trend in American Methodism of the last three decades of returning to a more sacramental understanding of baptism. It seeks to recover the balance characteristic of the Wesleyan heritage between this sacramental emphasis and the stress on evangelical elements. There are several areas of controversy, but two major ones can be identified from the deliberations at General Conference and are expected to remain prominent throughout the quadrennium of study. One focuses on the service of infant dedication which was included in the Evangelical United Brethren *Book of Worship* and which some persons want retained as official ritual in The United Methodist Church. Unsuccessful attempts were made in the Discipleship Legislative Committee and on the floor of General Conference to have this service placed in *The Book of Worship* which is to be published in the fall of 1992. Bishop George Bashore insisted that the EUB tradition out of which he came did not have a long or extensive heritage of such a service and that its existence had been a source of theological confusion. The second center of debate was concerns about the relationship between baptism and church membership and the concomitant issues of confirmation and conversion. Apprehensions were expressed that any understanding of baptism as making one a member of the church undercut the emphasis upon personal decision and commitment.

It is significant and not surprising that the points of controversy which are emerging as United Methodism seeks clarity and consensus on baptismal issues in the 1990s are continuations of questions which have been debated for more than two hundred years in American Methodism. Several speakers at the General Conference expressed anticipation of the positive effects upon the church of a quadrennium of study of these vital theological concerns. As Mark Trotter, chair of the Baptism Study Committee, put it, " . . . the use of the document as a basis of study could be the means that God uses to revive and recommission the church."

CONCLUSION

The practice and theology of baptism have been subjects of intense concern, prolific interpretation, and vehement debate throughout the history of Methodism in America. Yet, in spite of all that has been said and written, the church today still finds itself painfully lacking in both consensus and clarity. Obviously baptism is not a simple subject. This is true in large part because baptismal questions do not stand alone, but instead are linked to a whole complex of related issues in Christian thought. Underlying baptismal disputes are theological mysteries of the nature of God and how God relates the divine Self to human beings; anthropological dilemmas about the nature of human beings and their relationship to God; soteriological conundrums about what salvation is and how it is to be accomplished for human beings; ecclesiological quandaries about the role of the church in the divine-human encounter and, especially, the function of sacraments as vehicles of divine grace.

One of the presuppositions of this book is that revitalization for contemporary United Methodism will not occur unless or until we are able to achieve substantive clarity and consensus on these crucial issues. A denomination cannot thrive in the absence of some consciousness of identity; a church can claim no sense of purpose without commitment to ultimate values; a people can engage in no mission unless they comprehend their calling. Identity, commitment, and mission—these are quintessential to renewal of the people called United Methodists. Without them we probably cannot survive; without them we surely have no reason to continue to exist. It is my thesis that renewal of the church in the future is contingent upon recovery of the heritage of the past. To go forward requires that we understand where we are and how we arrived here. American Methodism has, in matters of baptismal practice and theology, diverged sharply from its Wesleyan legacy and the classical Christian tradition in which Wesley was rooted. The expectation of objective, sacramental grace has been lost; the call for personal conversion has been muted; the faith is assessed in categories intellectual, rather than spiritual. Perhaps it is impossible ultimately to solve a problem of theology by recourse to history, but such a study may serve to deepen appreciation for the heritage and enkindle enthusiasm for its recovery.

The genius of John Wesley's theology of baptism is to be found in his creative synthesis of objective and subjective elements, of ecclesiastical and evangelical aspects. Wesley understood infant baptism as a sacrament through which divine grace effectuates the cleansing of children from their inherited burden of sin and occasions their spiritual rebirth through the merits of Christ's atonement. This initiating action of God's grace places children within the community of faith and signifies their admission into membership in the church of Christ.

For Wesley, the realities of the human situation are such that, even though carefully nurtured, children fall into actual, personal sin as they grow toward maturity, and, accordingly, their covenant relationship with God is forfeited. The spiritual regeneration begun in infant baptism must, therefore, culminate in an experience of conversion as an adult. To rely upon the residual grace of baptismal regeneration is to "lean [upon a] broken reed."[1] Justification after the age of accountability depends upon a volitional act of response and repentance. For Wesley, spiritual rebirth through which a person comes into saving relationship with God, is a twofold process involving sacramental regeneration as an infant and requiring conversion of heart and mind as an adult. Unfortunately for his Methodist followers, Wesley never articulated his understanding of the relationship between the two aspects of regeneration. Much subsequent confusion has its source in that ambiguity. Early American Methodism was inhospitable to Wesley's emphases upon theocentric action and the objective validity of sacramental grace. These elements tended to be ignored in favor of stress upon the anthropocentric, volitional, and subjective notes more harmonious with the milieu of revivalism. However, by the end of the nineteenth century, changing theological understandings of the spiritual nature of children and of human moral ability had vitiated that part of the heritage as well and American Methodism was becoming increasingly uncomfortable with Wesley's insistence upon the necessity of conversion. In the American ethos, the Wesleyan synthesis was first torn asunder; then both components were repudiated.

During the first half of the twentieth century, an optimistic assessment of human nature prevailed and the interpretation of baptism was based upon it. Children, born innocent, were brought to receive baptism as an act of dedication to God and of parental promise to provide Christian nurture. With an enervated sense of sin, the emphasis was upon catechesis, not conversion; upon cultivation, not transformation, although too frequently these assumptions failed to be carried out in practice. Virtually all sense of baptism as a sacrament—as an act of God's initiating grace—was lost and infant baptism degenerated into a pretty, often sentimental, ceremony of human action. Even the very name became equivocal—the term "christening" was commonly preferred. With no undergirding theology, infant baptism became a vapid, largely meaningless occasion and adult baptism was widely understood as only an act of joining the church.

By the 1960s there was clear evidence of a growing movement in the church to reclaim the meaning of baptism as a sacrament through which God offers grace to human beings and to comprehend baptism as a part of a lifelong process of spiritual growth rather than as an isolated event. These emphases seem, however, both novel and threatening to many United Methodists. Having divorced itself over the decades from its heritage of classical and Wesleyan faith, American Methodism has progressively vitiated both its sacramental ministry and its evangelical mission.

Baptism in contemporary United Methodism continues to be diverse, even nebulous, in theology and confusingly eccentric in practice. At least five major issues can be identified which remain unresolved and controversial. The basic issue is that of the significance of infant baptism and its relationship to a person's subsequent spiritual experiences; other points of controversy have their origins here. Although the baptism of infants has been the historic practice of the overwhelming majority of Christians, it remains poorly understood and often criticized, especially in areas where various strains of baptist and anabaptist influence are strong. Many United Methodists are confused about, and even apologetic for, infant baptism in the absence of clear teaching by their church. Interestingly, throughout the history of Methodism many issues relating to baptism have been the subjects of vehement dispute, but the correctness and desirability of infant baptism has been unquestioned, even when its practice was somewhat neglected. Indeed, a salient characteristic of Methodist doctrine has been the consistent and forceful affirmation of the administering of baptism to infants. Although the rationale for infant baptism has altered enormously, the practice itself has historically remained unquestioned. Methodist defense of infant baptism has been adamant and copious throughout the existence of the church in this country. The current official position of The United Methodist Church—that pastors "shall earnestly exhort all Christian parents or guardians to present their children to the Lord in Baptism at an early age"[2]—has a long and unbroken history.

Clearly, the established position of the denomination is one which goes beyond acceptance to advocacy of baptism of the children of its members. While certainly the church approves the baptism of persons of any age, this position is not correctly understood if it is interpreted as providing United Methodist parents with a free option as to whether or not to have their infants baptized. Neither should the baptism of adults in United Methodism be understood as theologically synonymous with believer's baptism. Advocates of believer's baptism stress the human action of decision and commitment; one undergoes baptism as an act of public profession witnessing to a transaction already consummated between oneself and God; the term "ordinance" is appropriately preferred to "sacrament." Proponents of infant baptism emphasize the action of God, the offer of divine grace in the sacrament. While certainly an adult should come with repentance and faith to receive baptism, he or she comes realizing that the primary actor in the sacrament is God. Persons of all ages are as helpless infants before God—unable to save ourselves through our own volition, dependent upon the prevenient grace of a loving God. Baptist traditions which insist upon the "rebaptism" as adults of persons previously baptized as infants recognize this significant difference in theology much more clearly than do most United Methodists.

Closely related to this issue is the continued debate in the church about infant dedication. In the first half of the present century the dedicatory aspects of baptism virtually crowded out all other meanings. In spite of renewed emphasis upon sacramental understandings, many—perhaps most—United Methodists today still think and speak of infant baptism largely in this attenuated manner. The persistent use of the term "christening" for infant baptism evinces the deep-rooted sense that infant baptism is different, is not the real thing. This confusion is exacerbated by the existence of the option of services of infant dedication based upon theological presuppositions which not only differ from, but actually contradict United Methodist understandings.[3]

One of the issues occasioning widespread discomfort and dispute in the church today is that of confirmation. It is clear from statistics showing the loss of members that present practices are simply not working. Confirmation services too often function as ceremonies of graduation from the church rather than as rituals of deeper commitment.[4] Confirmation classes are often poorly conducted, but unfortunately, even when done competently, they too frequently fail to articulate any theological relationship between the grace received in infant baptism and this adolescent occasion of personal pledge. Underlying this problem in contemporary United Methodism is a historical legacy of disparate interpretations of confirmation in the Christian tradition. Confirmation has been understood as a sacramental means of grace through which the Holy Spirit strengthened a person for holy living, as a public profession of personal faith when one was sufficiently mature to make such a decision, as a ceremonializing of the conclusion of the catechetical process, and as a service in which one became a member of the church. Because confirmation has no clear function in the United Methodist tradition and since the use of the term itself is so recent in the denomination, it is not surprising that confusion and vacuity abound.

Perhaps because it is an issue of both theology and polity, the question of relationship between baptism and church membership continues to be troublesome. Currently there is a real discrepancy between the sacramental theology expressed in the services of the baptismal covenant and the membership polity prescribed by the *Discipline*. If baptized persons are through the sacrament initiated into membership in the church of Jesus Christ, The United Methodist Church, and the local congregation, then what does it mean to designate some of them as preparatory members? This dilemma of contradiction is intensified by the *Disciplinary* requirement that persons who reach age nineteen without having been confirmed will have their names removed from the preparatory membership roll and placed on the constituency roll. The baptism which such persons received as infants is thus totally discounted as without significance when they are listed with persons who have never been baptized nor even associated with the church in any meaningful way. If we believe that in baptism God does something in the life of a child, we cannot nullify or disregard this relationship with Christ and Christ's church.

Practical questions of church governance and statistics can easily be handled by distinguishing between baptized members and professing members without denigrating the act of God in baptism by treating it as provisional or ephemeral.

If all recipients of the sacrament of baptism, regardless of age, are accepted as members of the church, the old question of children's participation in the sacrament of Holy Communion should disappear. This is certainly envisioned in the rituals of the 1989 hymnal which recommend following each occasion of baptism with serving of the eucharistic meal. The answer to the related question of the participation of unbaptized adults is much less clear. Methodism's long tradition of the open table should continue to be cherished, but persons who choose to commune regularly should be nurtured toward baptism in which they are claimed by God and profess their faith in Christ in whose meal they partake.

Perhaps no more vexing problem of baptismal theology and practice persists today than that of the propriety of "rebaptism." In the absence of any plainly articulated and widely disseminated position, practice in the denomination is various. There has been no official directive on this issue in twentieth- century Methodism, even though the consensus of theological thinkers is clear. If baptism is truly viewed as a sacramental act in which God is acting to claim our lives and initiate us into the church of Christ, it is by definition nonrepeatable. God is faithful and always does what God has promised to do. Subsequent human unfaithfulness may violate the covenant of baptism, but no human behavior can invalidate the action of God. We do need often to return to the covenant made in baptism and to reaffirm it from our perspective. Encouragement and opportunities for both private and public, personal and corporate reaffirmations should be given by the church. Requests for "rebaptism" will dwindle when the theological significance of the sacrament is clearly taught and when meaningful occasions for ritualizing subsequent spiritual experiences are effectively offered.

What we seek to discover—or to rediscover—are the answers to the question of how the church produces faithful Christians and the role of baptism in that process. Examination of the heritage of United Methodism from the tradition of classical and Wesleyan Christianity yields fundamental principles in which such answers must be grounded. We must recover a bipolar conception of baptism in which both its divine and human aspects will be appreciated. Baptism is theocentric: God is the protagonist. Baptism is objective: a real transaction occurs which is not contingent upon the recipient. Baptism is a sacrament: divine grace is channeled into human lives. Baptism is the quintessential celebration of the prevenient grace of God which was so foundational to Wesley's entire theology. God's love is prior to all else; God's grace is initiating, outreaching. God's love precedes each child into life and in baptism claims that child as God's own precious one for whom Christ lived and died. But, because God has given us the freedom of will to accept or to reject saving grace, baptism also has human dimensions. In order for baptism to be fulfilled, we must receive and respond; realize and repent our brokenness; commit our lives to following Christ as Savior and Lord; allow the Holy Spirit to make us holy; and devote ourselves to ministries of justice, peace, and reconciliation.

Baptism, then, is not so much event as it is process. Like the Christian life for which it is both empowerment and metaphor, baptism is dynamic, not static; a journey, not a destination; a quest, not an acquisition. Baptism is promise, the fulfilling of which requires a lifetime and beyond. It is prolepsis–representing in the now that which will be accomplished in the future, but representing that anticipated fruition so powerfully as to make it real even now.

It is only when baptism is viewed from these perspectives that the significance of the baptism of infants can be comprehended. Methodists have always defended infant baptism, but have done so on grounds which have been uncertain and shifting. The practice of infant baptism is often objected to from two contrasting points of view. Some critics argue that the decision to receive the sacrament should be postponed until the person is sufficiently mature to make an informed and responsible decision. Infant baptism is denigrated as meaningless because the child cannot comprehend it and arbitrary because the child has no choice. Other objectors contend that infant baptism as commonly practiced is without significance because it is administered indiscriminately without regard for the faith and commitment of the parents or the nurture which the child will receive. The question of eligibility to be baptized has been long debated in Methodism and opinions remain diverse. While the rubrics of the ritual stipulate that "Parents or sponsors should be members of Christ's holy church," the practice of local congregations and pastors varies greatly.

Fundamental to the question of eligibility is that of the grounds upon which any infants receive baptism. In classical Christianity and in Wesley, infants were to be baptized in order to free them from the guilt and punishment concomitant with their inheritance of original sin. The concept of original sin–in the sense of total depravity and culpability—did not long survive in the American environment. The optimistic assessment of human moral nature which emerged in this country necessitated a quite different rationale for infant baptism. By at least the very early twentieth century, infants were being baptized on grounds completely opposite those put forth in the past. Instead of receiving the sacrament because they were born with the stain of evil which needed to be removed, they were baptized because they were heirs of the atoning grace of Christ and born members of the Kingdom of God. Simply put, infants who had for so long in Christian practice been baptized because they were so wicked, were now baptized because they were so innocent. While perhaps few contemporary United Methodists would decry this revolution in appraisal of the moral nature of infants, the loss of a substantive concept of original sin has proven problematic. It is difficult, probably impossible, to enable persons to apprehend their need for salvation without first restoring their consciousness of sin. With utter rejection of any view that they are born damned, even infants can be understood, at least proleptically, as sinners in need of the redeeming grace of God proffered in the sacrament of baptism. Infants and small children, then, are proper recipients of baptism both because they are born in salvific relationship to God and because they are born burdened with the sinful nature that will be manifest as they grow up.

These assertions must, however, not be interpreted to mean that all children are equally appropriate recipients of the sacrament. Baptism is predicated upon the expectation that a child will be nurtured, both at home and in church, in Christian faith and discipleship. If this is not the case, the process of salvation will likely be truncated and the workings of baptismal grace abortive. A child who is born and raised in the community of faith is different from one who is not. The influences of the environment in which that child lives will condition her or him quite differently from the experiences of children in nonChristian ambiences. This process commences even before birth; modern science teaches us that the process of socialization for infants begins in the womb. Baptism is an act of the church to which God has given the privilege and responsibility of administering it. It is neither given nor received by individuals alone. Every baptized person, especially infants and children, should be incorporated into a covenant community for education, edification, and example. An intentional, continual process of nurture is the coupling needed to link infant baptism to more mature experiences of personal conversion and commitment. When baptized persons are ready, in adolescence or later, to commit their lives to the Lordship of Christ and to assume for themselves the responsibilities of church membership and Christian discipleship, they publicly profess their baptismal faith. Such occasions celebrate human response to the gift of divine grace, the burgeoning of baptismal grace. For persons baptized as adults a similar development occurs. It is perhaps more important than ever to emphasize this as the church struggles with its missionary role in an increasingly secular society. No one, of any age, comes to Christ as anything more than a helpless child, but neither is anyone to remain childish in faith but to grow, nourished by the covenant community, toward Christian maturity. Throughout this lifelong process of the outworking of grace, the church provides opportunity for appropriate ritualization of subsequent spiritual experiences—continued conversion, deepened commitment, tested faithfulness, repentance and return, crisis and change, renewed challenge, reoriented ministry, new responsibility. The grace which God offers fully in our baptism is appropriated by us only gradually, sometimes lost, but always freely available when we will receive it.

For contemporary United Methodists the recovery of our heritage of baptismal theology and practice means revitalized apprehension of the divine grace given in the sacrament and renewed appreciation of the human response of faith. To live lives of commitment and discipleship grounded in the unfathomable love of God is truly to remember our baptism. Because we have been baptized by water and by the Spirit, we share a loving relationship with the God made known to us in Jesus Christ, the God who claimed us for God's own in our baptism.

SELECTED BIBLIOGRAPHY

PRIMARY SOURCES CONSULTED

Books and Pamphlets

Abbey, R. "Baptismal Demonstrations," Nashville: Southern Methodist Publishing House, 1859.

———. *Christian Cradlehood or, Religion in the Nursery*. Nashville: Southern Methodist Publishing House, 1881.

Allen, John. *Christian Baptism*. Columbia, S.C.: Christian Neighbor Office, 1870.

Anderson, Josephus. *Our Church: A Manual for Members and Probationers of the Methodist Episcopal Church, South*. Nashville: Southern Methodist Publishing House, 1860.

Anderson, William K. *A Church Membership Manual for Methodist Pastors*. Nashville: Methodist Publishing House, 1943.

Annan, William. *Difficulties of Arminian Methodism*. Pittsburgh: Luke Loomis, 1838.

Archibald, Francis A. *Methodism and Literature*. Cincinnati: Walden and Stowe, 1883.

Asbury, Francis. *The Journal and Letters*. 3 vols. Edited by Elmer T. Clark, J. Manning Potts, and Jacob S. Payton. London: Epworth Press and Nashville: Abingdon Press, 1958.

Atkins, James. *The Kingdom in the Cradle*. Nashville and Dallas: Publishing House of the Methodist Episcopal Church, South, 1905.

Atkinson, John. *The Class Leader: His Work and How to Do It.* New York: Phillips and Hunt, and Cincinnati: Walden and Stowe, 1882.

Atkinson, John. *Memorials of Methodism in New Jersey.* Philadelphia: Perkinpine and Higgins, 1860.

Atmore, Charles. *An Appendix to The Methodist Memorial.* Manchester: W. Shelmerdine and Co., 1802.

Baker, Osmon C. *A Guide-Book in the Administration of the Discipline of the Methodist Episcopal Church.* New York: Carlton and Lanahan, 1870.

Ballard, C. L. "Lexical Facts versus Immersionists' Follies." Dallas: Smith and Lamar, n.d.

Bangs, Heman. *The Autobiography and Journal.* New York: N. Tibbals and Son, 1872.

Bangs, Nathan. *A History of the Methodist Episcopal Church,* 4 vols. New York: Carlton and Porter, 1853–57.

———. *The Life of the Rev. Freeborn Garrettson.* New York: J. Emory and E. Waugh, 1832.

———. *An Original Church of Christ.* New York: T. Mason and G. Lane, 1837.

Banks, John S. *A Manual of Christian Doctrine.* Edited by John J. Tigert. Nashville, Dallas and Richmond: Publishing House of the Methodist Episcopal Church, South, Lamar and Barton, Agents, 1924. (First published in 1897).

"Baptism According to the Holy Scriptures." No title page.

Baptism, Eucharist and Ministry. Faith and Order Paper Number 111. Geneva: World Council of Churches, 1982.

Baptism, Eucharist and Ministry 1982–1990. Faith and Order Paper Number 149. Geneva: World Council of Churches, 1990.

"Baptize—What Does It Mean?" Doctrinal Series - Number 1. New York: Nelson and Phillips, 1872.

Bartlett, L. *"Uncle Joe Little": Life and Memoirs of Joseph Russell Little.* Toronto: William Briggs, 1903.

Bascom, Henry B. *The Little Iron Wheel: A Declaration of Christian Rights and Articles Showing the Despotism of Episcopal Methodism.* Nashville: South Western Publishing House, Graves, Marks and Rutland, 1856.

Beggs, Stephen R. *Pages from the Early History of the West and Northwest.* Cincinnati: Methodist Book Concern, 1868.

Bennett, William W. *Memorials of Methodism in Virginia 1772–1829.* Richmond: By the Author, 1871.

Bibbins, Ruthella Mary. *How Methodism Came: The Beginnings of Methodism in England & America.* Baltimore: The American Methodist Historical Society of the Baltimore Annual Conference, 1945.

Binney, Amos and Steele, Daniel. *Binney's Theological Compend Improved.* Cincinnati: Curts and Jennings, and New York: Eaton and Mains, 1875. (First published in 1839).

Boland, J. M. *A Bible View of Baptism.* Nashville: Southern Methodist Publishing House, 1883.

Bond, J. W. "A Lecture on Infant Baptism and the Mode of Baptism." Jefferson City: Tribune Printing Co., 1882.

Boyd, G. F. "Seed Thoughts." Sanger, Texas: Courier Print, n.d.

Bradley, Charles F.; Patten, Amos W., and Stuart, Charles M. *Life and Selected Writings of Francis Dana Hemenway.* Cincinnati and Chicago: Cranston and Stowe, 1890.

Breyfogel, S.C. *Landmarks of the Evangelical Association.* Reading, Pa: Eagle Book Print, 1888.

Brooks, Charles L. *All About Infant Baptism.* Nashville: Publishing House of the Methodist Episcopal Church, South, 1923.

Brooks, John. *The Life and Times.* Nashville: Nashville Christian Advocate Office, 1848.

Brown, Henry. *Arminian Inconsistencies and Errors.* Philadelphia: William S. and Alfred Martien, 1856.

Browning, C. "Why I Am a Methodist: Fundamental Doctrines of Methodism." (Essays from "Asbury Memorial No. of Christian Advocate - Nashville), Ford, Va.: H. H. Smith, n.d.

Brownlow, William G. *Baptism Examined, or the True State of the Case to which Is Prefixed a Review of the Assaults of the "Banner & Pioneer."* Jonesborough, Tenn.: Whig Office, 1842.

———. *The Great Iron Wheel Examined or, Its False Spokes Extracted, and an Exhibition of Elder Graves, Its Builder.* Nashville: Published for the author, 1856.

Brunson, Alfred. *A Western Pioneer: or, Incidents of the Life and Times,* 2 vols. Cincinnati: Walden and Stowe, and New York: Phillips and Hunt, 1880.

Bryant, S. S. *A Sermon on the Nature and Mode of Baptism.* Greensborough, N.C.: Swaim and Sherwood, 1843.

———. *A Sermon on the Obligation and Benefits of Infant Baptism.* Greensborough, N.C.: Swaim and Sherwood, 1843.

Bumpass, S. D. *Sermon on Baptism.* Greensborough, N.C.: Swaim and Sherwood, 1847.

Burgess, John. *Pleasant Recollections of Characters and Works of Noble Men.* Cincinnati: Cranston and Stowe, 1887.

Burke, J. W. *Autobiography: Chapters from the Life of a Preacher.* Macon, Ga.: J. W. Burke and Co., 1884.

Burns, William Henry. *Crisis in Methodism*. Chicago and Boston: The Christian Witness Co., 1909.

Bushnell, Horace. *Christian Nurture*. New York: Charles Scribner's Sons, 1876. (First published in 1847).

Cameron, Hugh H. and Koehler, George E. "Our Congregation Surrounds the Baptized Child," in *Children in the Faith Community* series. Nashville: Discipleship Resources, n.d.

Carhart, J. Wesley. *Four Years on Wheels; or Life as a Presiding Elder*. Oshkosh, Wisconsin: Allen and Hicks, 1880.

Carroll, Andrew. *Moral and Religious Sketches and Collections with Incidents of Ten Years' Itinerancy in the West*, Vol. I. Cincinnati: Methodist Book Concern, 1857.

Carter, J. C. *Plain Words for Plain People on the Mode of Baptism*. Nashville: Publishing House of the Methodist Episcopal Church, South, 1907.

Cartwright, Peter. *Autobiography of Peter Cartwright*, Edited by Charles L. Wallis. New York and Nashville: Abingdon Press, 1956.

———. *Fifty Years as a Presiding Elder*. Cincinnati and New York: 1871.

The Catechisms of the Wesleyan Methodists. New York: N. Bangs and J. Emory, 1825.

Caughey, James. *Earnest Christianity Illustrated; or Selections from the Journal*. Boston: For Sale by J. P. Magee, 1856.

[Chandler, A.] "The Scripture Directory to Baptism." New York: J. Leavitt, 1831.

Chapman, James L. *Baptism*. Nashville: Methodist Episcopal Church, South, 1856.

———. *Tracts for the Times on Infant Baptism*. Nashville: Methodist Episcopal Church, South, 1855.

Chase, Abner. *Recollections of the Past*. New York: Conference Office, 1848.

Cherry, Clinton M. *The Beliefs of a Methodist Christian*. Nashville: Tidings, 1952.

Chreitzberg, A. M. *Early Methodism in the Carolinas*. Nashville: Publishing House of the Methodist Episcopal Church, South, Barbee and Smith, Agents, 1897.

Clark, Davis W. *The Methodist Episcopal Pulpit: A Collection of Original Sermons from Living Ministers of the Methodist Episcopal Church*. Collected and edited by George Peck. New York: Lane and Scott, 1850.

Clarke, Adam. *Christian Theology*. New York: T. Mason and G. Lane, 1840. (First published in 1835).

———. *Preacher's Manual*. New York: T. Mason and G. Lane, 1837.

Clement, James A. *An Exposition of the Pretensions of Baptists to Antiquity*. Nashville: For the Author, 1881.

Coke, Thomas. *Extracts of the Journals of the Late Rev. Thomas Coke's Several*

Visits to America, The West Indies, Etc. Dublin: Methodist Book Room, 1816.

John Nelson Cole Papers. Scrapbook, 1892–98. Raleigh, NC.

Coles, George. *My First Seven Years in America.* Edited by D. P. Kidder. New York: Carlton and Phillips, 1852.

Comfort, Silas. *An Exposition of the Articles of Religion of the Methodist Episcopal Church.* New York: Conference Office, 1847.

The Consultation on Common Texts. *A Celebration of Baptism.* Nashville: Abingdon, 1988.

Cooke, Richard J. *Christianity and Childhood; or, the Relation of Children to the Church.* Cincinnati: Cranston and Stowe, and New York: Hunt and Eaton, 1891.

———. *History of the Ritual of the Methodist Episcopal Church.* New York: Eaton and Mains, 1900.

Cox, Ethalmore V., compiler. "A Statement of Facts on Baptism." Granbury, Texas, n.d.

Creighton, Joseph H. *Life & Times.* Lithopolis, Ohio: J. H. Creighton, 1899.

Crooks, George R. *Life and Letters of the Rev. John M'Clintock, DD, LLD.* New York: Nelson and Phillips, and Cincinnati: Hitchcock and Walden, 1876.

Crowther, Jonathan. *A True and Complete Portraiture of Methodism or the History of the Wesleyan Methodists.* New York: Daniel Hitt and Thomas Ware, 1813.

Curtis, Olin Alfred. *The Christian Faith Personally Given in a System of Doctrine.* New York and Cincinnati: The Methodist Book Concern, 1905.

Daniels, W. H., ed. *Memorials of Gilbert Haven, Bishop of the Methodist Episcopal Church.* Boston: B. B. Russell and Co., 1880.

Davis, L. D. *Life in the Itinerancy, in Its Relations to the Circuit and Station, and to the Minister's Home and Family.* New York: Carlton and Porter, 1856.

[Davis, Lucius Daniel] *The Itinerant Side or, Pictures of Life in the Itinerancy.* New York: Carlton and Porter, 1857.

Deems, Charles F., ed. *Annals of Southern Methodism for 1855.* New York: J. A. Gray's Fire-Proof Printing Office, 1856.

DeWolf, L. Harold. *A Theology of the Living Church.* New York: Harper and Brothers, 1953.

Ditzler, J. *Baptism.* Nashville: Publishing House of Methodist Episcopal Church, South, 1898.

Dixon, James. *Methodism in Its Origin, Economy, and Present Position.* New York: G. Lane and P. P. Sandford, 1843.

Doane, N. *Infant Baptism Briefly Considered.* New York: Nelson and Phillips, and Cincinnati: Hitchcock and Walden, 1875.

Doub, Peter. "Discourses on Christian Communion and Baptism." Raleigh: William C. Doub - Star Office, 1854.

Dow, Lorenzo. *Perambulations of Cosmopolite; or Travels and Labors*. New York: Richard Valentine, 1855.

Drury, A. W. *Outlines of Doctrinal Theology*. Dayton, Ohio: The Otterbein Press, 1914.

The Journal of William Duke, 1774–1776. Abstract by Edwin Schell from original in Diocesan Library, Peabody Institute, Baltimore.

Dunkle, William F., Jr. and Quillan, Joseph D., Jr. *Companion to the Book of Worship*. Nashville and New York: Abingdon, 1970.

Durrett, John. *Baptism According to the Scriptures*. Nashville: Publishing House of the Methodist Episcopal Church, South, 1923.

Dyer, John L. *The Snow-Shoe Itinerant: An Autobiography*. Cincinnati: Cranston and Stowe, 1890.

Edge, Caroline B. "Preparing Parents and the Congregation for the Baptism of Infants and Children," in *Worship Alive* series. Nashville: Discipleship Resources, n.d.

Edwards, John Ellis. *Life of Rev. John Wesley Childs*. Richmond and Louisville: John Early, 1852.

Edwards, Peter. *Candid Reasons for Renouncing the Principles of Anti-Paedobaptism. Also a Short Method with the Baptists*. Philadelphia: Presbyterian Board of Publication, 1795.

Ellison, J. W. "Baptism: The Question Settled." Nashville: Publishing House of the Methodist Episcopal Church, South, 1889.

Eltzholtz, Carl F. *The Child: Its Relation to God and the Church*. New York and Cincinnati: The Methodist Book Concern, 1921.

Emory, John. *A Defence of Our Fathers*. New York: Phillips and Hunt, 1880. (First published in 1829).

Emory, Robert. *History of the Discipline of the Methodist Episcopal Church*. Revised by W. P. Strickland. New York: Carlton and Porter, 1843.

Erwin, James. *Reminiscences of Early Circuit Life*. Toledo, Ohio: Spear, Johnson and Co., 1884.

Etter, John W. *The Doctrine of Christian Baptism*. Dayton, Ohio: Press of United Brethren Publishing House, 1888.

Extracts of Letters, Containing Some Account of the Work of God since the Year 1800. Written by the Preachers and Members of the Methodist Episcopal Church, to their Bishops. New York: Ezekiel Cooper and John Wilson, 1805.

Fairfield, Edmund B. *Letters on Baptism*. Boston and Chicago: The Pilgrim Press, 1893.

Ffirth, John, compiler. *Experience and Gospel Labours of the Rev. Benjamin Abbott*. New York: B. Waugh and T. Mason, 1833.

Finley, James B. *Sketches of Western Methodism: Biographical, Historical, and Miscellaneous.* Cincinnati: Methodist Book Concern, 1857.

Finney, Thomas M. *The Life and Labors of Enoch Mather Marvin.* St. Louis: James H. Chambers, 1881.

Fisher, Orceneth. *The Christian Sacraments.* St. Louis: Southwestern Book and Publishing Co., 1858, 1871.

———. *History of Immersion, as a Religious Rite.* St. Louis: Southwestern Book and Publishing Co., 1871. (First published in 1858).

———. *The Wilderness of Judea.* St. Louis: Southwestern Book and Publishing Co., 1871.

Fisk, Wilbur. *Calvinistic Controversy Embracing a Sermon on Predestination and Election and Several Numbers on the Same Subject.* New York: T. Mason and G. Lane, 1837.

Flaharty, J. J. *Glimpses of the Life of the Rev. A. E. Phelps and His Co-Laborers.* Cincinnati: Hitchcock and Walden, 1878.

Fletcher, John. *Works,* 9 vols. London: John Mason, 1860.

Ford, H. M. "The Baptism of John." Nashville: Publishing House of the Methodist Episcopal Church, South, 1889.

Foster, John O., arr. *The Catechism of the Methodist Episcopal Church . . . in Concert Exercise Form.* New York: Hunt and Eaton, and Cincinnati: Cranston and Stowe, 1891.

Fry, Benjamin St. James. *The Life of Rev. Enoch George.* Edited by Daniel P. Kidder. New York: Carlton and Phillips, 1852.

———. *The Life of Rev. William M'Kendree.* Edited by Daniel P. Kidder. New York: Carlton and Phillips, 1852.

———. *The Life of Rev. Richard Whatcoat.* Edited by Daniel P. Kidder. New York: Lane and Scott, 1852.

Gaddis, Maxwell P. *Brief Recollections of the late Rev. George W. Walker.* Cincinnati: Swormstedt and Poe, 1857.

———. *Foot-Prints of An Itinerant.* Cincinnati: Methodist Book Concern, 1856.

Gamertsfelder, S. J. *Systematic Theology.* Cleveland: C. Hauser, 1913.

Garrison, S. Olin. *Probationer's Handbook.* New York: Eaton and Mains, and Cincinnati: Jennings and Pye, 1887.

Gavitt, Elnathan Corrington. *Crumbs from My Saddle Bags or, Reminiscences of Pioneer Life and Biographical Sketches.* Toledo: Blade Printing and Paper Co., 1884.

Giles, Charles. *Pioneer: A Narrative of the Nativity, Experience, Travels, & Ministerial Labours.* New York: G. Lane and P. P. Sandford, 1844.

Godbey, W. B. *Baptism: Mode and Design.* Louisville: Kentucky Methodist Publishing Co., 1896.

God's Children in Worship, Teacher's Guide. Grades K-2 by Susan M. Isbell;

Grades 2–4 by Larry Beaman and Barbara Bruce. Nashville: Discipleship Resources, 1988.

Goodloe, Robert W. *The Sacraments in Methodism*. Nashville and New York: The Methodist Publishing House, 1953.

Gorrie, P. Douglas. *Episcopal Methodism, as It Was and Is*. Auburn: Derby and Miller, 1852.

———. *The Lives of Eminent Methodist Ministers*. Auburn: Derby and Miller, 1852.

Graves, J. R. *The Great Iron Wheel Or Republicanism Backwards, and Christianity Reversed*. Nashville: Graves, Marks and Rutland and New York: Sheldon, Lamport and Co., 1855.

Gregg, Samuel. *Infant Church Membership; or, the Spiritual and Permanent Character of the Abrahamic Covenant*. Edited by D. W. Clark. Cincinnati: Swormstedt and Poe, 1854.

Hall, B. M. *The Life of Rev. John Clark*. New York: Carlton and Porter, 1857.

Hamline, Leonidas L. *Works: Sermons*. New York: Carlton and Lanahan, and Cincinnati: Hitchcock and Walden, 1869.

Harford, R. L. *An Itinerant's Portfolio: Sermons, Lectures, and Miscellany*. San Francisco: H. G. Parsons and Co., 1885.

Harkness, Georgia. *What Christians Believe*. Nashville and New York: Abingdon, 1965.

Hawley, Bostwick. *Manual of Methodism; or, The Doctrines, General Rules, and Usages of the Methodist Episcopal Church, with Scripture Proofs and Explanations*. New York: Carlton and Lanahan, and Cincinnati: Hitchcock and Walden, 1869.

Hayes, G. H. *Children in Christ; or, the Relation of Children to the Atonement, the Ground of their Right to Christian Baptism*. Cincinnati: Elm St. Printing Co., 1884.

Henkle, Moses M. *The Life of Henry Bidleman Bascom*. Louisville: Morton and Griswold, 1854.

———. *Primary Platform of Methodism; or, Exposition of the General Rules*. Louisville: Southern Methodist Book Concern, 1853.

Hersey, John. *An Inquiry into the Character & Conditions of Our Children*. Richmond: Samuel Shepherd and Co., 1832.

Hewson, William. "Baptism and Immersion." Nashville: Publishing House of the Methodist Episcopal Church, South, 1888.

Hibbard, B. *Memoirs of the Life and Travels*. New York: Piercy and Reed, 1843. (First published in 1825).

Hibbard, Freeborn G. *Christian Baptism*. New York: Carlton and Phillips, 1853. (First published in 1841).

———. *The Religion of Childhood; or, Children in Their Relation to Native*

Depravity, to the Atonement, to the Family, and to the Church. Cincinnati: Poe and Hitchcock, 1864.

Hickman, Frank S. *Can Religion Be Taught? Evangelical Religion Faces the Question*, ed. by E. B. Chappell. Nashville: Cokesbury Press. 1929.

Hickman, Hoyt. *A Primer for Christian Worship.* Nashville: Abingdon, 1984.

———. "When United Methodists Baptize." Nashville: Discipleship Resources, n.d.

———. "Your Church Welcomes Your Baby." Nashville: Discipleship Resources, n.d.

Hill, James W., ed. *The North Texas Conference Pulpit.* Nashville: Southern Methodist Publishing House, 1880.

Hillman, Joseph. *The History of Methodism in Troy, New York.* Troy: Joseph Hillman, 1888.

Hiner, R., compiler. *Kentucky Conference Pulpit.* Nashville: Publishing House of the Methodist Episcopal Church, South, 1874.

Hobart, Chauncey. *Recollections of My Life: Fifty Years of Itinerancy in the Northwest.* Red Wing, Minn.: Red Wing Printing Co., 1885.

Holliday, Fernandez. *Life and Times of Rev. Allen Wiley, A.M.* Cincinnati: Swormstedt and Poe, 1853.

Houston, J. C. *Sprinkling: Christian Baptism.* New York: Eaton and Mains, 1895.

Howell, Peter. *The Life and Travels.* Newbern, N.C.: W. H. Mayhew, 1849.

Hudson, Hilary T. *The Methodist Armor; or, A Popular Exposition of the Doctrines, Peculiar Usages, and Ecclesiastical Machinery of the Methodist Episcopal Church, South.* Nashville, Dallas, Richmond: Publishing House of the Methodist Episcopal Church, South, Smith and Lamar, Agents, 1882.

Hughes, T. *The Condition of Membership in the Christian Church Viewed in Connexion with the Class-Meeting System in the Methodist Body.* London: Hodder and Stoughton, 1868.

Hughey, G. W. *Baptismal Remission; or, the Design of Christian Baptism.* Cincinnati: Cranston and Stowe, and New York: Hunt and Eaton, 1891.

———. *The Scriptural Mode of Christian Baptism.* Kansas City: Hudson Press, 1907.

Hunter, William, ed. *Original Sermons, by Ministers of the Pittsburgh, Erie, and Western Virginia Conferences of the Methodist Episcopal Church.* Pittsburgh: Methodist Book Depository, 1850.

Incognito. *Proselyters Defeated.* Nashville: Southern Methodist Publishing House, 1859.

Jackson, Green P. *Sunshine and Shade in a Happy Itinerant's Life.* Nashville and Dallas: Publishing House of the Methodist Episcopal Church, South, Smith and Lamar, Agents, 1904.

Jackson, Samuel. *Methodism and Children: Being Selections from the Manuscripts*. London: 1867.

———. *Samuel Jackson and the Children of Methodism*. London: Hamilton, Adams and Co., 1875.

Jarratt, Devereaux. *An Argument Between Anabaptist and Paedo-Baptist on the Subject and Mode of Baptism*. 1803.

Jimeson, A. A. *Notes on the Twenty-five Articles of Religion as Received and Taught by Methodists in the United States.* Cincinnati: Applegate, Pounsford and Co., 1868. (First published in 1853).

Kean, Laurence. *A Plain and Positive Refutation of the Rev. Samuel Pelton's Unjust and Unfounded Charges Entitled "The Absurdities of Methodism."* New York: J. and J. Harper, 1823.

Knudson, Albert C. *The Doctrine of Redemption*. Nashville and New York: Abingdon, 1933.

Koons, William George. *The Child's Religious Life*. New York: Eaton and Mains and Cincinnati: Jennings and Pye, 1903.

Lednum, John. *History of the Rise of Methodism in America, containing Sketches of Methodist Itinerant Preachers from 1736–1785*. Philadelphia, 1859.

Lee, Jesse. *A Short History of the Methodists in the United States of America; Beginning in 1766 and Continued until 1809*. Baltimore: Magill and Clime, 1810.

Lee, Leroy M. *The Life and Times of the Rev. Jesse Lee*. Richmond: John Early, 1848.

Lee, Luther and Smith, E. *The Debates of the General Conference of the Methodist Episcopal Church, May, 1844*. New York: O. Scott, 1845.

Lee, N. H. *Immersionists against the Bible; or the Babel Builders Confounded.* Edited by Thomas O. Summers. Nashville: Southern Methodist Publishing House, 1881.

Levington, John. *Scripture Baptism Defended, and Anabaptist Notions Proved to be Anti-Scriptural Novelties*. Chicago: Poe and Hitchcock, 1866.

Lewis, Davis. *Recollections of a Superannuate: or, Sketches of Life, Labor, and Experience in the Methodist Itinerancy*. Edited by S. M. Merrill. Cincinnati: Methodist Book Concern, 1857.

Lockwood, John P. *The Western Pioneers; or, Memorials of the Lives and Labours of the Rev. Richard Boardman & the Rev. Joseph Pilmoor.* London: Wesleyan Conference Office, 1881.

"A Lutheran-United Methodist Statement on Baptism." Division of Theological Studies of the Lutheran Council in the U.S.A. and the General Commission on Christian Unity and Interreligious Concerns of The United Methodist Church, 1979.

M'Anally, D. R. *History of Methodism in Missouri*. Vol. I. St. Louis: Advocate Publishing House, 1881.

McClintock, John. *Analysis of Watson's Theological Institutes designed for the Use of Students and Examining Committees*. New York: Hunt and Eaton, and Cincinnati: Cranston and Stowe, 1842.

McClintock, John and Strong, James, eds. *Cyclopedia of Biblical, Theological, and Ecclesiastical Literature*. Vol I. New York: Harper and Brothers, 1869.

McClintock, John. *Sketches of Eminent Methodist Ministers*. New York: Carlton and Phillips, 1854.

McConnell, Francis J. *By the Way: An Autobiography*. New York and Nashville: Abingdon-Cokesbury, 1952.

McLean, John. *Sketch of Rev. Philip Gatch*. Cincinnati: Swormstedt and Poe, 1854.

McTyeire, Holland N. *A History of Methodism*. Nashville: Southern Methodist Publishing House, 1885.

———. *A Manual of Discipline of the Methodist Episcopal Church, South*. Nashville: Southern Methodist Publishing House, 1870.

———. *Passing Through the Gates, and Other Sermons*. Edited by John T. Tigert. Nashville: Publishing House of the Methodist Episcopal Church, South. J. D. Barbee, Agent, 1890.

Mahaffey, James E. *The Bible Mode of Baptism*. Columbia, S.C.: The State Co., 1910. (First published in 1894).

Mahon, R. H. *The Token of the Covenant, or the Right Use of Baptism*. Nashville: Southern Methodist Publishing House, 1886.

Marine, F. E. *Sketch of Rev. John Hersey, Minister of the Gospel of the Methodist Episcopal Church*. Baltimore: Hoffman and Co., 1879.

Marvin, Enoch M. *The Doctrinal Integrity of Methodism*. St. Louis: Advocate Publishing House, 1878.

Massey, John E. and Coulling, J. D. *Baptism: Its Mode, Subjects and Design*. New York: Sheldon and Co., 1861.

Mellen, T. L., ed. *In Memoriam: Life and Labors of the Rev. William Hamilton Watkins, D.D.* Nashville: Southern Methodist Publishing House, 1886.

A Member of the Tennessee Conference. *Methodism in a Nutshell: A Plain and Comprehensive View of the Usages and Doctrines of the Methodist Church*. Nashville: Publishing House of the Methodist Episcopal Church, South, Barbee and Smith, Agents, 1893. (First published in 1879).

Mercein, T. F. Randolph. *Childhood and the Church*. New York: Anson D. F. Randolph, 1858.

———. *Natural Goodness: or, Honour to Whom Honour is Due.* New York: Carlton and Phillips, 1855.

Merrill, Stephen M. *Christian Baptism: Its Subjects and Mode.* Cincinnati: Cranston and Stowe, and New York: Phillips and Hunt, 1876.

———. *A Digest of Methodist Law; or, Helps in the Administration of the Discipline of the Methodist Episcopal Church.* Cincinnati: Cranston and Stowe, and New York: Phillips and Hunt, 1885.

Merritt, Timothy. "Anabaptism Disproved and the Validity and Sufficiency of Infant Baptism Asserted in Two Letters from a Minister to His Friend." New York: T. Mason and G. Lane, 1837.

Methodism Pamphlets. Vol. I, nos. 1–15. "A Rod for Doctor Kemp; or an Examination of His Tract upon Conversion," by a Layman. Baltimore: George Dobbin and Murphy, 1807.

Methodist Episcopal Church. Classbooks 1829–48. Shepherdstown, W.Va.

Methodist Episcopal Church, South. Classbooks 1851–79. Pleasant Hill, Ala.

Milburn, William Henry. *Ten Years of Preacher-Life: Chapters from an Autobiography.* New York: Derby and Jackson, 1859.

Miley, John. *Systematic Theology,* 2 vols. New York: Hunt and Eaton, 1893.

Miller, C. W. *Infant Baptism.* St. Louis: Southwestern Book and Publishing Co., 1872.

Miller, W. G. *Thirty Years in the Itinerancy.* Milwaukee: I. L. Hauser and Co., 1875.

Mitchell, Charles F. *The Story of My Life.* Weatherford, Oklahoma: 1940.

Moede, Gerald F., ed. *The COCU Consensus: In Quest of a Church of Christ Uniting.* Consultation on Church Union, 1985.

Moody, Granville. *A Life's Retrospect.* Edited by Sylvester Weeks. Cincinnati: Cranston and Stowe and New York: Hunt and Eaton, 1890.

Moore, John M. *Methodism in Belief and Action.* New York and Nashville: Abingdon-Cokesbury, 1946.

Morris, B. Wistar. *Presbyterian, Baptist and Methodist Testimony to Confirmation.* New York: E. P. Dutton and Co., 1875.

Morris, Thomas A. *Sermons on Various Subjects.* Cincinnati: L. Swormstedt and A. Poe, 1852.

Neely, Thomas Benjamin. *Doctrinal Standards of Methodism including the Methodist Episcopal Churches.* New York and Chicago: Fleming H. Revell Co., 1918.

Newell, E. F. *Life and Observations.* Worcester: S. W. Ainsworth, 1847.

Nichols, J. H. *Theological Grub-Ax: A Treatise on Infant Baptism.* Nashville: Publishing House of the Methodist Episcopal Church, South, 1908. (First published in 1882).

Olin, Stephen. *The Life and Letters.* 2 vols. New York: Harper and Brothers, 1853.

The Works of Stephen Olin. 2 vols. New York: Harper and Brothers, 1852.

Ownbey, Richard L. *Evangelism in Christian Education*, edited by Lucius H. Bugbee and C. A. Bowen. Nashville: Abingdon- Cokesbury, 1941.

Packard, Wilbur F. "Infant Baptism: Reasonable, Scriptural, Ancient and Apostolic." Houston: 1913.

Paddock, Z. *Memoir of Rev. Benjamin G. Paddock*. New York: Nelson and Phillips, 1875.

Paine, Robert. *Life and Times of McKendree*. Nashville: Publishing House of the Methodist Episcopal Church, South, 1869.

Paris, J. *Baptism, Its Mode, Its Design and Its Subjects*. Baltimore: Methodist Protestant Book Rooms, 1852.

Parker, Z. A. *The People's Hand-Book*. Nashville: Publishing House of the Methodist Episcopal Church, South, 1893. (First published 1885).

Pearne, Thomas Hall. *Sixty-one Years of Itinerant Christian Life in Church and State*. Cincinnati: Curts and Jennings, and New York: Eaton and Mains, 1898.

Peck, George. *Early Methodism within the Bounds of the Old Genesee Conference from 1788 to 1828*. New York: Carlton and Porter, 1860.

Peck, J. M. *"Father Clark," or the Pioneer Preacher*. New York: Sheldon, Lamport and Blakeman, 1855.

Peebles, Isaac L. *Falling From Grace and Baptism*. Nashville and Dallas: Publishing House of the Methodist Episcopal Church, South, 1905.

Perkins, E. L., compiler. *Scrapbook of Methodism in North Carolina*. 2 vols.

Peterson, P. A. *Handbook of Southern Methodism: Being a Digest of the History and Statistics of the Methodist Church, South from 1845 to 1882*. Richmond: J. W. Fergusson and Son, 1883.

———. *History of the Revisions of the Discipline of the Methodist Episcopal Church, South*. Nashville: Publishing House of the Methodist Episcopal Church, South, J. D. Barbee, Agent, 1889.

Phillips, William. *Campbellism Exposed; or, Strictures on the Peculiar Tenets of Alexander Campbell*. Cincinnati: Cranston and Curtis, and New York: Hunt and Eaton, 1837.

Phinney, William R.; Rowe, Kenneth E.; and Steelman, Robert B.; eds. *Thomas Ware, a Spectator at the Christmas Conference: A Miscellany on Thomas Ware and the Methodist Christmas Conference*. Rutland, Vt.: Academy Books, 1984.

Phoebus, George A., compiler. *Beams of Light on Early Methodism in America Chiefly Drawn from the Diary, Letters, Manuscripts, Documents, and Original Tracts of the Rev. Ezekiel Cooper*. New York: Phillips and Hunt, and Cincinnati: Cranston and Stowe, 1887.

Phoebus, William. *An Essay on the Doctrine and Order of the Evangelical Church in America as Constituted at Baltimore in 1784.* New York: Abraham Paul, 1817.

Pilmore, Joseph. *The Journal of Joseph Pilmore, Methodist Itinerant, for the Years August 1, 1769 to January 2, 1774.* Edited by Frederick E. Maser and Howard T. Maag. Philadelphia: Message Publishing Co., for the Historical Society of the Philadelphia Annual Conference of the United Methodist Church, 1969.

Pitts, F. E. *A Book on Baptism: Chiefly Designed as a Refutation of the Errors and Infidelity of Campbellism.* Nashville: Western Methodist Office, 1835. (Presbyterian Historical Society, Philadelphia, 1986).

Pope, William Burt. *A Compendium of Christian Theology.* 3 vols. New York: Phillips and Hunt, and Cincinnati: Walden and Stowe, 1880.

Porter, James. *A Compendium of Methodism: Embracing the History and Present Condition of Its Various Branches in All Countries.* Boston: George C. Rand, 1852.

———. *A Comprehensive History of Methodism.* Cincinnati: Hitchcock and Walden, and New York: Nelson and Phillips, 1876.

Potts, J. H. *Pastor and People; or, Methodism in the Field.* New York: Phillips and Hunt, and Cincinnati: Hitchcock and Walden, 1879.

Rall, Harris Franklin. *The Christian Faith and Way.* New York and Nashville: Abingdon-Cokesbury, 1947.

Ralston, Thomas N. *Elements of Divinity.* Nashville: A. H. Redford, Agent for Methodist Episcopal Church, South, 1876. (First published in 1847).

Raven, A. R. "Baptism in Another Nutshell . . . " Shelby, NC, 1883.

Raymond, Miner. *Systematic Theology.* 3 vols. Cincinnati: Hitchcock and Walden, 1877–80.

Reddy, William. *Inside Views of Methodism or, A Handbook for Inquirers and Beginners.* New York: Carlton and Porter, 1859.

Redford, A. H. *The History of Methodism in Kentucky.* Vol. I. Nashville: Southern Methodist Publishing House, 1868.

———. *Western Cavaliers Embracing the History of the Methodist Episcopal Church in Kentucky from 1832 to 1844.* Nashville: Southern Methodist Publishing House, 1876.

Regester, Samuel. *Children and the Church.* Nashville: Southern Methodist Publishing House, 1874.

Reid, James W. and Frank L. *Life, Sermons and Speeches of Rev. Numa F. Reid, DD, Late of the North Carolina Conference.* New York: E. J. Hale and Son, 1874.

Richardson, Simon Peter. *The Lights and Shadows of Itinerant Life: An Autobiography.* Nashville and Dallas: Publishing House of the Methodist Episcopal Church, South, 1901.

Rishell, Charles W. *The Child as God's Child.* New York: Eaton and Mains and Cincinnati: Jennings and Graham, 1904.

Robison, James. *Recollections of Rev. Samuel Clawson.* Pittsburgh: Charles A. Scott, 1883.

Rosser, L. *Baptism: Its Nature, Obligation, Mode, Subjects and Benefits.* Richmond: By the author, 1854.

———. *Reply to "Evils of Infant Baptism," by Robert C. Howell, D.D., Pastor of the Second Baptist Church, Richmond, Va.* Richmond: By the author, 1855.

Rowe, Gilbert T. *The Meaning of Methodism.* Nashville: Cokesbury Press, 1926.

Sandford, Peter P. "Christian Baptism." New York: Conference Office, 1832. (First published in 1829).

———. *Memoirs of Mr. Wesley's Missionaries to America.* New York: G. Lane and P. P. Sandford, 1843.

Scudder, M. L. *American Methodism.* Hartford, Conn.: S. S. Scranton and Co., 1868.

Seaman, Samuel A. *Annals of New York Methodism 1766–1890.* New York: Hunt and Eaton, and Cincinnati: Cranston and Stowe, 1892.

Shaffer, Hiram M. *A Treatise on Baptism in Two Parts.* Cincinnati: For the author, 1847.

Sheets, Herchel H. *Our Sacraments: A United Methodist View of Baptism and Communion.* Nashville: Discipleship Resources, 1986.

Sheldon, Henry C. *System of Christian Doctrine.* New York: Eaton and Mains and Cincinnati: Jennings and Graham, 1903.

Sherman, David. *History of the Revisions of the Discipline of the Methodist Episcopal Church.* New York: Hunt and Eaton, and Cincinnati: Cranston and Stowe, 1890.

Shinn, Asa. *An Essay on the Plan of Salvation.* Baltimore: Neal, Wills and Cole, 1813.

Shipman, William H. *The Doctrinal Test.* New York and Cincinnati: The Methodist Book Concern, 1922.

Shipp, Albert M. *The History of Methodism in South Carolina.* Nashville: Southern Methodist Publishing House, 1884.

Shuler, Robert P. "A Sermon on Infant Baptism: The Bible on It." Fort Worth: Paxton and Evans, Printers, 1908.

Simons, Volney M. *Infant Salvation: A Discourse.* St. Albans, Vt.: E. B. Whiting, 1860.

Simpson, Matthew. *Cyclopedia of Methodism.* Philadelphia: Everts and Stewart, 1878.

Simpson, Robert Drew, ed. *American Methodist Pioneer: The Life and Journals of The Rev. Freeborn Garrettson, 1752–1827.* Rutland, Vt.: Academy Books, 1984.

Slicer, Henry. *An Appeal to the Candid of All Denominations: in which the Obligation, Subjects, and Mode of Baptism are Discussed.* New York: G. Lane and P. P. Sandford, 1842. (First published in 1835).

Smith, George G. *Childhood and Conversion.* Nashville: Publishing House of the Methodist Episcopal Church, South, Barbee and Smith, Agents, 1891.

———. *The Life and Times of George Foster Pierce, DD., LLD.* Sparta, Ga.: Hancock Publishing Co., 1888.

———. *The Life and Letters of James Osgood Andrew.* Nashville: Southern Methodist Publishing House, 1882.

Smith, I. *Reasons for Becoming a Methodist.* New York: Carlton and Porter, 1850.

Smith, J. C. *Reminiscences of Early Methodism in Indiana.* Indianapolis: J. M. Olcott, 1879.

Smith, John L. *Indiana Methodism: A Series of Sketches and Incidents Grave and Humorous Concerning Preachers and People of the West.* Valparaiso, Indiana: 1892.

Spayth, Henry G. *History of the Church of the United Brethren in Christ.* Circleville, Ohio: Conference Office, 1851.

Spreng, Samuel P. *The Life and Labors of John Seybert, First Bishop of the Evangelical Association.* Cleveland: Lauer and Mattill, 1888.

The Standard Catechism. New York and Nashville: Abingdon, 1905, 1929.

Stanford, Thomas. *Sermons and Other Writings on Various Subjects.* Nashville: Publishing House of the Methodist Episcopal Church, South, 1892.

Stapleton, A. *Annals of the Evangelical Association of North America and History of the United Evangelical Church.* Harrisburg: Publishing House of the United Evangelical Church, 1900.

Stevens, Abel. *The Centenary of American Methodism.* New York: Carlton and Porter, 1865.

———. *History of the Methodist Episcopal Church in the United States of America.* 4 vols. New York: Carlton and Porter, 1865–67.

———. *Life and Times of Nathan Bangs, D.D.* New York: Carlton and Porter, 1863.

Stevenson, D. *Elements of Methodism in a Series of Short Lectures Addressed to One Beginning a Life of Godliness.* Claremont, N.H.: 1879.

Stewart, John. *Highways and Hedges; or Fifty Years of Western Methodism.* Cincinnati: Hitchcock and Walden, and New York: Carlton and Lanahan, 1872.

Stookey, Laurence Hull. *Baptism: Christ's Act in the Church.* Nashville: Abingdon, 1982.

Strickland, W. P. *Autobiography of Rev. James B. Finley or Pioneer Life in the*

West. Cincinnati: Jennings and Pye, and New York: Eaton and Mains, 1853.

———., ed. *Autobiography of Dan Young, A New England Preacher of the Olden Time*. New York: Carlton and Porter, 1860.

———. *The Genius and Mission of Methodism Embracing What Is Peculiar in Doctrine, Government, Modes of Worship, etc.* Boston: Charles H. Peirce and Co., 1851.

Stuart, George R. *What Every Methodist Should Know*. Nashville, Dallas, Richmond: Publishing House of the Methodist Episcopal Church, South, Lamar and Barton, Agents, 1922.

Summers, Thomas O. *Baptism: A Treatise on the Nature, Perpetuity, Subjects, Administrator, Mode, and Use of the Initiating Ordinance of the Christian Church*. Richmond and Louisville: John Early for the Methodist Episcopal Church, South, 1853.

———. *Commentary on the Ritual of the Methodist Episcopal Church, South*. Nashville: A. H. Redford, Agent, 1874.

———., ed. *Methodist Pamphlets for the People*. Vol. II. Nashville: E. Stevenson and F. A. Owen, Agents for the Methodist Episcopal Church, South, 1857.

———., ed. *Sermons & Essays by Ministers of the Methodist Episcopal Church, South*. Nashville: E. Stevenson and F. H. Owen, Agents for the Methodist Episcopal Church, South, 1857.

Sutherland, Helen L.; Brant, Rachel M.; Landis, Oral F. *Being a Christian: A Catechism for Junior Boys and Girls*. Dayton, Ohio: Board of Publication for Board of Christian Education of the Evangelical United Brethren Church, 1950.

Swallow, Silas Comfort. *III Score & X or Selections, Collections, Recollections of Seventy Busy Years*. Harrisburg, Pa.: United Evangelical Publishing House, n.d.

Sweet, William Warren. *Religion on the American Frontier: 1783–1840*. Vol. IV: *The Methodists: A Collection of Source Materials*. New York: Cooper Square Publishers, Inc., 1964.

———, ed. *The Rise of Methodism in the West being the Journal of the Western Conference 1800–1811*. New York and Cincinnati: The Methodist Book Concern, 1920.

Swift, W. A. "Why Baptize by Pouring and Baptize Babies?" Methodist Publishing House, 1932.

Taylor, C. *Apostolic Baptism: Facts and Evidences on the Subjects and Mode of Christian Baptism*. New York: B. H. Bevier, 1843.

Taylor, Landon. *The Battle Field Reviewed*. Chicago, 1881.

Thomson, Edward. *Life of Edward Thomson, DD, LLD*. Cincinnati: Cranston and Stowe, and New York: Phillips and Hunt, 1885.

Thrall, Homer S. *A Brief History of Methodism in Texas*. Nashville: Publishing

House of the Methodist Episcopal, Church, South, Barbee and Smith, Agents, 1894.

Thrift, C. T. "A Modern Scholar, Modern Scholarship and the Form of Baptism." Clayton, N.C.: 1922.

———. "Why John the Baptist Sprinkled the Multitudes at the River Jordan." Clayton, N.C.: 1921.

Tigert, Jno. J. *A Constitutional History of American Episcopal Methodism*. Nashville and Dallas: Publishing House of the Methodist Episcopal Church, South, Smith and Lamar, Agents, 1904. (First published in 1894).

Tillett, Wilbur F. *Personal Salvation*. Nashville and Dallas: Publishing House of the Methodist Episcopal Church, South, 1902.

Todd, Robert W. *Methodism of the Peninsula*. Philadelphia: Methodist Episcopal Book Rooms, 1886.

Triggs, John J. *A Treatise on Christian Baptism*. Augusta: James McCafferty, 1842.

Vincent, H. *History of the Camp-Meeting and Grounds at Wesleyan Grove, Martha's Vineyard*. Boston: Lee and Shepard, 1870.

Wakeley, J. B. *The Bold Frontier Preacher: A Portraiture of Rev. William Cravens of Virginia*. Cincinnati: Hitchcock and Walden, and New York: Carlton and Lanahan, 1869.

———. *The Heroes of Methodism*. Toronto: William Briggs, 1855.

———. *Lost Chapters Recovered from the Early History of American Methodism*. New York: Carlton and Porter, 1858.

Ware, Thomas. *Sketches of the Life and Travels*. New York: T. Mason and G. Lane, 1839.

Warren, William. *Introduction*. Cincinnati: Poe and Hitchcock, 1865.

Watson, J. V. *Tales and Takings, Sketches and Incidents, from the Itinerant and Editorial Budget*. New York: Carlton and Porter, 1856.

Watson, Richard. *Theological Institutes; or a View of the Evidences, Doctrines, Morals and Institutions of Christianity*. 2 vols. New York: George Lane, 1840.

Watters, William. *Short Account of the Christian Experience and Ministerial Labors*. Alexandria: E. Snowden, 1806.

Wesley, John. *The Appeals to Men of Reason and Religion*. Gerald R. Cragg, ed. Volume 11 of *The Works of John Wesley*. Oxford: Clarendon Press, 1975.

———. *Explanatory Notes upon the New Testament*. London: Epworth Press, 1954.

———. *John Wesley*. Albert C. Outler, ed. New York: Oxford University Press, 1964.

———. *John and Charles Wesley: Selected Writings and Hymns*. Frank Whaling, ed. New York: Paulist Press, 1981.

———. *The Journal of the Rev. John Wesley, A.M.* Nehemiah Curnock, ed. 8 vols. London: Epworth Press, 1909–16.

———. *The Letters of John Wesley*. John Telford, ed. 8 vols. London: Epworth Press, 1931.

———. *The Poetical Works of John and Charles Wesley*. George Osborn, ed. 13 vols. London: Wesleyan-Methodist Conference Office, 1870.

———. *Wesley's Standard Sermons*. E. H. Sugden, ed. 2 vols. London: Epworth Press, 1961.

———. *The Works of the Rev. John Wesley*. Joseph Benson, ed. Volume XIII. London: Thomas Cordeux, 1812.

———. *The Works of the Rev. John Wesley, A.M.* Thomas Jackson, ed. 14 vols. London: Wesleyan Conference Office, 1872.

———. *The Works of the Rev. John Wesley, A.M.* John Emory, ed. Volume VI. New York: J. Emory and B. Waugh, 1831.

Whedon, Daniel D. *Essays, Reviews, and Discourses*. New York: Phillips and Hunt, and Cincinnati: Cranston and Stowe, 1887.

———. *Statements: Theological and Critical*. Collected and edited by J. S. and D. A. Whedon. New York: Phillips and Hunt, and Cincinnati: Cranston and Stowe, 1887.

Wheeler, Henry. *One Thousand Questions and Answers concerning the Methodist Episcopal Church*. New York: Eaton and Mains, 1898.

Wheeler, W. D. "Baptism: Its Design and Mode." DeLeon, Texas, n.d.

White, James F. *Introduction to Christian Worship*. Nashville: Abingdon, 1980.

———. *Sacraments as God's Self Giving*. Nashville: Abingdon, 1983.

Williams, William G. *Baptism: A Discussion of the Words "Buried with Christ in Baptism."* Cincinnati: Jennings and Pye, and New York: Eaton and Mains, 1901.

Willimon, William H. *Remember Who You Are: Baptism, a Model for Christian Life*. Nashville: The Upper Room, 1980.

———. *The Service of God: Christian Work and Worship*. Nashville: Abingdon, 1983.

———. "Your Child Is Baptized." Nashville: Discipleship Resources, n.d.

Williston, Seth. *Sermons on Doctrinal and Experimental Subjects*. Hudson: A. Stoddard, 1812.

Wise, Daniel. *Popular Objections to Methodism Considered and Answered: or The Convert's Counsellor*. Boston: J. P. Magee, 1856.

Wright, John F. *Sketches of the Life and Labors of James Quinn*. Cincinnati: Methodist Book Concern, 1851.

Periodicals

Adult Student. Published in Nashville by the Methodist Episcopal Church, South and The Methodist Church: 1908–67.

Arminian Magazine. "Consisting of Extracts and Original Treatises on General Redemption." Published by John Dickins in Philadelphia: Volume I, 1789; Volume II, 1790.

Baltimore Christian Advocate. Published by Baltimore Conference of the Methodist Episcopal Church, South: 1870–1901.

Baltimore Methodist. Published by the Methodist Episcopal Church: 1879–1911.

Catalyst. Published in Atlanta by The United Methodist Church: 1972, irregularly.

Child Guidance in Christian Living. Published in Nashville by The Methodist Church: 1941–64.

Christian Home. Published in Nashville by the Methodist Episcopal Church, South: The Methodist Church; and The United Methodist Church: 1935+.

Christian Neighbor. Published in Columbia, South Carolina: 1868–1901.

Church School. Published in Nashville by The Methodist Church and The United Methodist Church: 1947+.

Circuit Rider. Published in Nashville by the United Methodist Publishing House: 1976+.

Epworth Era. Published in Nashville by Methodist Episcopal Church, South: 1894–1931.

Epworth Herald. Published in Chicago by the Epworth League: 1890–1940.

Good News. Published in Wilmore, Kentucky by the Forum for Scriptural Christianity: 1967+.

London Quarterly and Holborn Review. Published in London: 1853- 1968.

The Methodist. Published in New York: 1860–82.

Methodist History. Published at Lake Junaluska, North Carolina and Drew University, New Jersey: 1962+.

Methodist Magazine. Published in Philadelphia: 1797–98.

Methodist Magazine. Published in Baltimore: 1855–57.

Methodist Quarterly Review (MQR). Published in New York by the Methodist Episcopal Church, 1818–1932. Published as a monthly entitled *Methodist Magazine*, 1818–28; as *Methodist Magazine and Quarterly Review*, 1830–41; as *Methodist Quarterly Review*, 1841–85; and as *Methodist Review*, 1886–1932.

Methodist Quarterly Review, South (*MQRS*). Published in Louisville and Nashville: 1847–1930. Published as *Quarterly Review of the Methodist Episcopal Church, South*, 1847-61, 1879-86, 1889–94; as *Southern*

Methodist Review, 1887-88; as *The Methodist Review*, 1895-1903, 1906-8. Suspended in 1862-78.

Methodist Teacher–IV-VI. Published in Nashville by The Methodist Church: 1964-68.

Methodist Teacher–Nursery. Published in Nashville by The Methodist Church: 1964-68.

Nashville Christian Advocate. Published by the Methodist Episcopal Church and Methodist Episcopal Church, South: 1832-1940. (Originally titled *South-Western Christian Advocate*).

New Christian Advocate. Published in Chicago by The Methodist Church: 1956-59.

New Orleans Christian Advocate. Published by the Methodist Episcopal Church, South: 1851-1946.

New York Christian Advocate. Published by the Methodist Episcopal Church: 1826-1956.

North Carolina Christian Advocate. Published by the Methodist Episcopal Church, South 1855-1919. *Raleigh* and *Western (Asheville) Christian Advocates* merged in 1894 to form this periodical.

Quarterly Review. Published in Nashville by the General Board of Higher Education and Ministry of The United Methodist Church: 1980+.

Religion in Life. Published in Nashville and New York by the Methodist Episcopal Church, The Methodist Church and The United Methodist Church: 1932-80.

Sacramental Life. Published in Cleveland by the Order of Saint Luke: 1988+.

Southern Methodist Pulpit. Published in Richmond by the Methodist Episcopal Church, South: 1848-52.

Southern Methodist Recorder. Published in Farmville, Blackstone and Richmond, Virginia by the Methodist Episcopal Church: 1893-1903.

Sunday School Advocate. Published in New York and Cincinnati by the Methodist Episcopal Church: 1842-1921.

Sunday School Journal for Teachers. Published by the Methodist Episcopal Church: 1860-1932. (Also titled *Church School Journal*).

Sunday School Magazine. Published in Nashville by the Methodist Episcopal Church, South: 1871-1941. (Also titled *Church School Magazine*).

Sunday School Teacher. Published in Chicago by Adams, Blackmer and Lyon: 1866-68.

Together–The Midmonth Magazine for Methodist Families. Published in Nashville by The Methodist Church and The United Methodist Church: 1956-73.

Youth Leader. Published in Nashville by The United Methodist Church: 1968+.

Western Christian Advocate. Published in Cincinnati by the Methodist Episcopal Church: 1834–1929.

World Parish. Published in Lake Junaluska, N.C. by The Methodist Church: 1948–62.

Zion's Herald. Published in Boston by the Methodist Episcopal Church; official paper of the New England Conference: 1823+.

Official Church Documents

The Book of Services Containing the General Services of the Church, Adopted by the 1984 General Conference. Nashville: The United Methodist Church, 1985.

Collection of Interesting Tracts, Explaining Several Important Points of Scripture Doctrine.
New York: D. Hitt and T. Ware, 1814.
New York: J. Soule and T. Mason, 1817.
New York: N. Bangs and Jn. Emory, 1825.
New York: Nelson and Phillips, 1861.

Companion to the Book of Services. Supplemental Worship Resources 17. Nashville: Abingdon Press, 1988.

Daily Christian Advocates.
Methodist Episcopal Church 1876–1939
Methodist Episcopal Church, South 1882–1938
The Methodist Church 1940–66
The United Methodist Church 1968–88.

Discipline of the Evangelical United Brethren Church. Dayton: 1947–67.

Discipline of the Church of the United Brethren in Christ including Origin, Doctrine, and Constitution. Dayton: 1885–1949.

Doctrines and Discipline of the Evangelical Church. Cleveland and Harrisburg: Evangelical Publishing House, 1923.

Doctrines and Discipline of the Methodist Episcopal Church.

Minutes of Several Conversations Between the Rev. Thomas Coke, LL.D., The Rev. Francis Asbury and Others, at a Conference Begun in Baltimore, in the State of Maryland, on Monday, the 27th of December, in the Year 1784. Composing a Form of Discipline for the Ministers, Preachers and Other Members of the Methodist Episcopal Church in America. Philadelphia, 1785.

The General Minutes of the Conferences of the Methodist Episcopal Church in America, forming the Constitution of the said Church, 1786.

A Form of Discipline, for the Ministers, Preachers, and Members of the Methodist Episcopal Church in America. Considered and approved at a Conference Held at Baltimore, in the State of

Maryland, on Monday the 27th of December, 1784.... New York, 1787.

Same title, Elizabethtown, 1788.

Same title, New York, 1789.

A Form of Discipline, for the Ministers, Preachers, and Members (now comprehending the Principles and Doctrines) of the Methodist Episcopal Church in America, Considered and approved at a Conference held at Baltimore, in the State of Maryland, on Monday the 27th of December, 1784. Philadelphia: Printed by R. Aitken, sold by John Dickins, 1790.

Same title as 1790. Philadelphia: Printed by Joseph Crukshank, sold by John Dickins, 1791.

The Doctrines and Discipline of the Methodist Episcopal Church in America, Revised and Approved at the General Conference Held at Baltimore, in the State of Maryland, in November, 1792.... Philadelphia: Printed by Parry Hall, sold by John Dickins, 1792.

The Doctrines and Discipline of the Methodist Episcopal Church in America, Revised and Approved at the General Conference Held at Baltimore, in the State of Maryland, November, 1792; ... To Which Are Added, the Minutes of the General Conference Held at Baltimore, October 20th, 1796. Philadelphia: Printed by Henry Tuckniss, sold by John Dickins, 1797.

The Doctrines and Discipline of the Methodist Episcopal Church in America. With Explanatory Notes, by Thomas Coke and Francis Asbury. Philadelphia: Printed by Henry Tuckniss, sold by John Dickins, 1798.

The Doctrines and Discipline of the Methodist Episcopal Church in America. Philadelphia: Printed by Solomon W. Conrad, for Ezekiel Cooper, 1801.

The Doctrines and Discipline of the Methodist Episcopal Church. New York: T. Kirk, 1804.

Beginning in 1808, the *Doctrines and Discipline* were published quadrennially, following General Conference.

Doctrines and Discipline of the Methodist Episcopal Church, South. Published quadrennially following General Conference, 1846–1938, except for 1862.

Journals of the General Conference of The Methodist Church. Published after each General Conference, 1940–64.

Journals of the General Conference of the Methodist Episcopal Church: Volume I: 1796–1836. New York: Carlton and Phillips, 1855. Published as separate volumes following each General Conference, 1836–1936.

Journals of the General Conference of the Methodist Episcopal Church, South. Published after each General Conference, 1846–1938.

Journals of the General Conference of The United Methodist Church. Published after each General Conference, 1968–88.

Minutes of the Methodist Conferences Annually Held in America, from 1773 to 1794, inclusive. Philadelphia: Printed by Henry Tuckniss, sold by John Dickins, 1795.

Minutes of the Annual Conferences of the Methodist Episcopal Church, Vol. I, 1773–1828. Vol. II, 1829–39. New York: Mason and Lane, 1840. Vol. III, 1839–45. New York: Carlton and Porter, 1846.

Proposed Revisions of the Book of Worship for Church and Home. Nashville: Methodist Publishing House, 1960.

Report of The United Methodist Book of Worship Committee to the 1992 General Conference, Daily Christian Advocate, Advance Edition, Volume III. Nashville: The United Methodist Publishing House, 1992.

Response of The United Methodist Church to "One Baptism, One Eucharist and a Mutually Recognized Ministry." Drafted by a Task Force assigned by the Ecumenical and Interreligious Concerns Division, the Board of Global Ministries, and Designated by the Council of Bishops, 1977.

Hymnals

The Book of Hymns: Official Hymnal of the United Methodist Church. Nashville: The United Methodist Publishing House, 1964, 1966.

A Collection of Hymns for Public, Social, and Domestic Worship. Richmond: John Early, 1847.

A Collection of Hymns and Tunes for Public, Social, and Domestic Worship. Nashville: Southern Methodist Publishing House, 1885.

A Collection of Hymns for the Use of the Methodist Episcopal Church, Principally from the Collection of the Rev. John Wesley. New York: N. Bangs and T. Mason, 1821.

A Collection of Hymns, for the Use of the Methodist Episcopal Church: Principally From the Collection of the Rev. John Wesley. Revised and Corrected, With a Supplement. New York: G. Lane and P. P. Sandford, 1842.

The Epworth Hymnal. New York: Phillips and Hunt and Cincinnati: Cranston and Stowe, 1885. No. 2, 1891.

Hymnal of the Methodist Episcopal Church, with Tunes. New York: Phillips and Hunt, 1882.

Hymn Book of the Methodist Episcopal Church, South. Nashville: Publishing House of the Methodist Episcopal Church, South, 1889.

Hymns for the Use of the Methodist Episcopal Church, revised edition. New York:

Carlton and Lanahan, and Cincinnati: Hitchcock and Walden, 1849.

The Lesser Hymnal. A Collection of Hymns, Selected Chiefly From the Standard Hymn-Book of the Methodist Episcopal Church. New York: Nelson and Phillips, 1875.

The Methodist Harmonist Containing a Collection of Tunes from the Best Authors, Embracing Every Variety of Metre, and Adapted to the Worship of the Methodist Episcopal Church. New York: B. Waugh and T. Mason, 1833.

The Methodist Hymnal. New York: Eaton and Mains, and Cincinnati: Jennings and Graham, 1905.

The Methodist Hymnal. New York, Cincinnati, Chicago: The Methodist Book Concern, 1935.

The Methodist Pocket Hymn Book, revised and improved. New York: Ezekiel Cooper and John Wilson, 1807.

The Methodist Pocket Hymn Book, revised and improved. New York: J. Soule and T. Mason, 1817.

The New Hymn and Tune Book. A Collection of Hymns and Tunes for Public, Social, and Domestic Worship. Nashville: Southern Methodist Publishing House, 1881.

A Pocket Hymn-Book Designed as a Constant Companion for the Pious, 11th edition. Philadelphia: Pritchard and Hall, 1790.

A Selection of Hymns from Various Authors. New York: John Wilson and Daniel Hitt, 1808.

Songs of Zion: A Supplement to the Hymn-Book of the Methodist Episcopal Church, South, revised edition. Nashville: A. H. Redford, 1874.

The United Methodist Hymnal: Book of United Methodist Worship. Nashville: The United Methodist Publishing House, 1989.

SECONDARY SOURCES CONSULTED

Alexander, Gross. *A History of the Methodist Church, South.* New York: Charles Scribner's Sons, 1911.

Ayres, Samuel G. *Methodist Heroes of Other Days.* New York and Cincinnati: Methodist Book Concern: 1916.

Baillie, John. *Baptism and Conversion.* New York: Charles Scribner's Sons, 1963.

Baker, Frank. *A Charge to Keep: An Introduction to the People Called Methodists.* London: Epworth Press, 1947.

———. *From Wesley to Asbury.* Durham: Duke University Press, 1976.

———. *John Wesley and the Church of England.* Nashville and New York: Abingdon Press, Inc., 1975.

Baker, Gordon Pratt, ed. *Those Incredible Methodists: A History of the Baltimore Conference of The United Methodist Church.* Baltimore: Commission on Archives and History, 1972.

Baketel, Oliver S. *Concordance to the Methodist Hymnal.* New York: Eaton and Mains, and Cincinnati: Jennings and Graham, 1907.

Barclay, Wade Crawford. *History of Methodist Missions.* 4 vols. New York: The Board of Missions and Church Extension of The Methodist Church, 1949–50.

Behney, J. Bruce and Eller, Paul H. *The History of the Evangelical United Brethren Church.* Nashville: Abingdon Press, 1979.

Bishop, John. *Methodist Worship in Relation to Free Church Worship.* Scholars Studies Press Inc., 1975.

Borgen, Ole E. *John Wesley on the Sacraments.* Nashville and New York: Abingdon Press, 1972.

Bowen, C. A. *Child and Church: A History of Methodist Church-School Curriculum.* New York and Nashville: Abingdon Press, 1960.

Bowmer, John C. *The Sacrament of the Lord's Supper in Early Methodism.* London: Dacre Press, 1951.

Bruce, Dickson Davies, Jr. "And They All Sang Hallelujah: Plain-Folk Camp-Meeting Religion, 1800–45." Ph.D. dissertation, University of Pennsylvania, 1971. (University Microfilms.)

Bucke, Emory S., gen. ed. *Companion to the Hymnal.* Nashville: Abingdon, 1970.

———. *The History of American Methodism,* 3 vols. Nashville and New York: Abingdon Press, 1964.

Buckley, James M. *Constitutional and Parliamentary History of the Methodist Episcopal Church.* New York: Eaton and Mains, 1912.

———. *A History of Methodists in the United States.* New York: The Christian Literature Co., 1896.

Button, Carl Lloyd. "The Rhetoric of Immediacy: Baptist and Methodist Preaching on the Trans-Appalachian Frontier." Ph.D. dissertation, University of California, Los Angeles, 1972. (Ann Arbor: University Microfilms.)

Byrne, Donald E., Jr. *No Foot of Land: Folklore of American Itinerants.* Metuchem, N.J.: The Scarecrow Press, 1975.

Cameron, Richard M. *Methodism and Society in Historical Perspective.* New York and Nashville: Abingdon Press, 1961.

Cannon, William R. *The Theology of John Wesley with Special Reference to the Doctrine of Justification.* Nashville and New York: Abingdon Press, 1949.

Chappell, E. B. *The Church and Its Sacraments*. Nashville, Dallas, Richmond, San Francisco: Publishing House of the Methodist Episcopal Church, South, Lamar and Whitmore, Agents, 1921.

———. *Evangelism in the Sunday School.* Nashville, Dallas, Richmond, San Francisco: Publishing House of the Methodist Episcopal Church, South, Lamar and Whitmore, Agents, 1921.

Chiles, Robert E. *Theological Transition in American Methodism: 1790–1935*. New York and Nashville: Abingdon Press, 1965.

Cho, John Chongnahm. "John Wesley's View on Baptism." *Wesleyan Theological Journal* 7 (Spring 1972): 60–73.

Cleveland, Catharine C. *The Great Revival in the West 1797–1805*. Chicago: University of Chicago Press, 1916.

Copas, Jack M. "Infant Baptism: A Practice in Search of a Theology," *The Drew Gateway* 52 (Fall 1981): 21–32.

Crawford, Benjamin Franklin. *Changing Conceptions of Religion as Revealed in One Hundred Years of Methodist Hymnology–1836–1935*. Carneige, Pa.: Carneige Church Press, 1939.

———. *Religious Trends in a Century of Hymns*. Carneige, Pa.: Carneige Church Press, 1938.

Cushman, Robert E. "Baptism and the Family of God." Pages 79–102 in *The Doctrine of the Church*. Dow Kirkpatrick, ed. Nashville and New York: Abingdon Press, 1964.

Davies, Horton. *Worship and Theology in England: From Watts and Wesley to Maurice, 1690–1850*. Princeton: Princeton University Press, 1961.

Davies, Rupert and Rupp, Gordon. *A History of the Methodist Church in Great Britain*. Volume I. London: Epworth Press, 1965.

Dearing, Trevor. *Wesleyan and Tractarian Worship*. London: Epworth Press, 1966.

Dixon, Neil. *Troubled Waters*. London: Epworth Press, 1979.

Drury, Augustus W. *Baptism: Its Place in the Church Visible*. Dayton, Ohio: United Brethren Publishing House, 1902.

———. *History of the Church of the United Brethren in Christ*. Dayton, Ohio: The Otterbein Press, 1924.

———. *The Life of Rev. Philip William Otterbein*. Dayton, Ohio: United Brethren Publishing House, 1884.

Dubose, Horace M. *The Symbol of Methodism*. Nashville and Dallas: Publishing House of the Methodist Episcopal Church, South, 1907.

Dunlap, E. Dale. "Baptism and the Christian Life: A United Methodist View." *The Perkins School of Theology Journal* 34 (Winter 1981): 4–12.

Eller, Paul H. *Those Evangelical United Brethren*. Dayton, Ohio: Otterbein Press, 1950.

English, John C. "The Heart Renewed: John Wesley's Doctrine of Christian

Initiation." *The Wesleyan Quarterly Review* 4 (May-August 1967): 112–92.

———. "The Sacrament of Baptism According to the Sunday Service of 1784," *Methodist History* 5 (January 1967): 10–16.

Everett, Daryl Stephen. "Some Current Practices Relating to Infant Baptism in Five Protestant Denominations: Implications for Pastoral Care." Ann Arbor, Michigan: University Microfilms International, 1980.

Fisher, J. D. C. *Confirmation Then and Now.* London: Alcuin Club/S.P.C.K., 1978.

Galliers, Brian J. N. "Baptism in the Writings of John Wesley." *Proceedings of the Wesley Historical Society* 32 (June 1960): 121–24 and (September 1960): 153–57.

Gewehr, Wesley M. *The Great Awakening in Virginia, 1740-1790.* Durham: Duke University Press, 1930.

Goodpasture, B. C. and Moore, W. T., arr. and ed. *Biographies and Sermons of Pioneer Preachers.* Nashville: B. C. Goodpasture, 1954.

Guettsche, Walter Louis. "Background for United Methodist Baptismal Doctrine and Practice: The Wesleyan Tradition." D.Min. dissertation, Perkins School of Theology, Southern Methodist University, Dallas, April 20, 1974. (Typewritten.)

Hall, Thor. "The Meaning of Church Membership." University of Tennessee at Chattanooga, 1975. (Typewritten).

Hamill, H. M., ed. *Manual of Southern Methodism Including Church History, Doctrine, Polity, and Missions.* Nashville, Dallas, Richmond: Publishing House of the Methodist Episcopal Church, South, Smith and Lamar, Agents, 1909.

Harmon, Nolan B., Jr., ed. *The Encyclopedia of World Methodism,* 2 vols. Nashville: United Methodist Publishing House, 1974.

———. *The Rites and Rituals of Episcopal Methodism.* New York: Lamar and Barton, 1926.

———. *Understanding the Methodist Church.* Nashville: The Methodist Publishing House, 1955.

Harrison, W. S. *The Articles of Religion as Amended, Supplemented and Explained.* Nashville, Dallas, Richmond: Publishing House of the Methodist Episcopal Church, South, Smith and Lamar, Agents, 1914.

Head, Jean and David. *Martin Is Baptized.* London: The Epworth Press, 1962.

Hildebrandt, Franz. *From Luther to Wesley.* London: Lutterworth Press, 1951.

Holifield, E. Brooks. *The Covenant Sealed: The Development of Puritan Sacramental Theology in Old and New England, 1570–1720.* New Haven and London: Yale University Press, 1974.

———. *The Gentleman Theologians: American Theology in Southern Culture, 1795–1860.* Durham: Duke University Press, 1978.

Holland, Bernard G. *Baptism in Early Methodism.* London: Epworth Press, 1970.

Johnson, Charles A. *The Frontier Camp Meeting.* Dallas: Southern Methodist University Press, 1955.

Jones, John G. *A Complete History of Methodism as Connected with the Mississippi Conference of the Methodist Episcopal Church, South,* 2 vols. Nashville and Dallas: Publishing House of the Methodist Episcopal Church, South, 1908.

Kirkpatrick, Dow, ed. *The Doctrine of the Church.* New York and Nashville: Abingdon Press, 1964.

Lang, Edward M., Jr. "The Theology of Francis Asbury," 1972. Thesis, Northwestern University (Typewritten.)

Langford, Thomas A. *Practical Divinity: Theology in the Wesleyan Tradition.* Nashville: Abingdon Press, 1983.

———. *Wesleyan Theology: A Sourcebook.* Durham, N.C.: The Labyrinth Press, 1984.

Lankard, Frank Glenn. *A History of the American Sunday School Curriculum.* New York and Cincinnati: Abingdon Press, 1927.

Lindstrom, Harald. *Wesley and Sanctification: A Study in the Doctrine of Salvation.* London: Epworth Press, 1946.

Logan, James C. "Baptism - The Ecumenical Sacrament and the Wesleyan Tradition" pp. 323–29 in *Wesleyan Theology Today: A Bicentennial Theological Consultation.* Edited by Theodore Runyon. Nashville: Kingswood Books, The United Methodist Publishing House, 1985.

McEllhenney, John G. with Frederick E. Maser, Charles Yrigoyen, Jr. and Kenneth E. Rowe. *Proclaiming Grace and Freedom.* Nashville: Abingdon Press, 1982.

McKinley, William. *A Story of Minnesota Methodism.* Cincinnati: Jennings and Graham, and New York: Eaton and Mains, 1911.

Maser, Frederick E. *Robert Strawbridge: First American Methodist Circuit Rider.* Rutland, Vt.: Academy Books, 1983.

Muelder, Walter G. *Methodism and Society in the Twentieth Century.* New York and Nashville: Abingdon Press, 1961.

Nagler, Arthur Wilford. *Pietism and Methodism: The Significance of German Pietism in the Origin and Early Development of Methodism.* Nashville, Dallas, Richmond: Publishing House of the Methodist Episcopal Church, South, Smith and Lamar, Agents, 1918.

North Carolina Annual Conference of the United Methodist Church. *The Conference Programs, Recommendations and Reports, 1985.* Raleigh: Derreth Printing Co., 1985.

Norwood, Frederick A. *Church Membership in the Methodist Tradition.* Nashville and New York: Methodist Publishing House, 1958.

———. *Sourcebook of American Methodism.* Nashville: Abingdon Press, 1982.

Nottingham, Elizabeth K. *Methodism and the Frontier: Indiana Proving Ground.* New York: Columbia University Press, 1941.

Nutter, Charles S. and Tillett, Wilbur F. *The Hymns and Hymn Writers of the Church.* New York and Cincinnati: Methodist Book Concern, 1911.

Palmer, Louis DeForest. *Heroism and Romance: Early Methodism in Northeastern Pennsylvania.* Saylorsburg, Penn.: Engel-Truitt Press, 1950.

Parris, John R. *John Wesley's Doctrine of the Sacraments.* London: Epworth Press, 1963.

Patterson, Louis Dale. "The Ministerial Mind of American Methodism: The Courses of Study for the Ministry of the Methodist Episcopal Church, Methodist Episcopal Church, South, and Methodist Protestant Church: 1880–1920." Ph.D. dissertation. Drew University, 1984. (University Microfilms International, Ann Arbor, 1984.)

Payton, Jacob Simpson. *Our Fathers Have Told Us: The Story of the Founding of Methodism in Western Pennsylvania.* Cincinnati: The Ruter Press, 1938.

The Perkins School of Theology Journal 34 (Winter 1981). Southern Methodist University, Dallas.

Pettit, Norman. *The Heart Prepared: Grace and Conversion in Puritan Spiritual Life.* New Haven and London: Yale University Press, 1966.

Phares, Ross. *Bible in Pocket, Gun in Hand: The Story of Frontier Religion.* Garden City: Doubleday, 1964.

Phelan, Macum. *A History of Early Methodism in Texas 1817–1866.* Nashville: Cokesbury, 1924.

Plyler, A. W. *The Iron Duke of the Methodist Itinerancy: An Account of the Life and Labors of Reverend John Tillet of North Carolina.* Nashville: Cokesbury Press, 1925.

Prince, John W. *Wesley on Religious Education: A Study of John Wesley's Theories and Methods of the Education of Children in Religion.* New York and Cincinnati: The Methodist Book Concern, 1926.

Rattenbury, J. Ernest. *The Eucharistic Hymns of John and Charles Wesley.* London: Epworth Press, 1948.

Reist, Irwin, "John Wesley's View of the Sacraments: A Study in the Historical Development of a Doctrine." *Wesleyan Theological Journal* 6 (Spring 1971): 41–54.

Rigg, James H. *The Churchmanship of John Wesley.* London: Wesleyan-Methodist Book-Room, 1878, 1886.

Sanders, Paul S. "An Appraisal of John Wesley's Sacramentalism in the

Evolution of Early American Methodism." Doctorate of Theology dissertation, Union Theological Seminary, 1954.

———. "John Wesley and Baptismal Regeneration." *Religion in Life* 23 (1953-54): 591-603.

———. "The Sacraments in Early American Methodism." *Church History* 26, No.4 (1957):355-69.

Schilling, S. Paul. *Methodism and Society in Theological Perspective*. New York and Nashville: Abingdon, 1960.

Schmidt, Martin. *John Wesley: A Theological Biography*. Volume I. Nashville and New York: Abingdon Press, 1972.

Scott, Leland H. "Methodist Theology in America in the Nineteenth Century." Ph.D. dissertation, Yale, 1954. (*Microcard Theological Studies*, Vol. 20.)

Smeltzer, Wallace Guy. *Methodism on the Headwaters of the Ohio: The History of the Pittsburgh Conference*. Nashville: Parthenon Press, 1951.

Smith, George G. *The History of Georgia Methodism from 1786 to 1866*. Atlanta: A. B. Caldwell, 1913.

Smith, H. Shelton. *Changing Conceptions of Original Sin*. New York: Charles Scribner's Sons, 1955.

Snow, M. Lawrence. "Confirmation and the Methodist Church." *The Versicle* 13, No. 4 (1965): 3-17.

Sparrow Simpson, W. J. *John Wesley and the Church of England*. London: Society for Promoting Christian Knowledge, 1934.

Stoeffler, F. Ernest. "Infant Baptism: Entry into Covenant." *Christian Advocate* 6 (May 24, 1962): 10-11.

Stookey, Laurence H. "Three New Initiation Rites." *Worship* 51 (January 1977): 33-49.

Sweet, William Warren. *The American Churches: An Interpretation*. New York and Nashville: Abingdon - Cokesbury Press, 1947.

———. "The Churches as Moral Courts of the Frontier." *Church History* 2 (March 1933): 3-21.

———. *Methodism in American History*. New York and Cincinnati: Methodist Book Concern, 1933.

———. *Religion in the Development of American Culture 1765–1840*. New York: Scribner, 1952.

———. *Revivalism in America: Its Origin, Growth, and Decline*. New York: Charles Scribner's Sons, 1945.

Swift, Wesley F. "The Sunday Service of the Methodists." *Proceedings of the Wesley Historical Society* 29 (March 1953):12-20, 31 (March 1958):112-18, 32 (March 1960):97-101.

Tees, Francis. *Methodist Origins*. Nashville: The Parthenon Press, 1948.

Thurian, Max, ed. *Churches Respond to BEM*, Faith and Order Paper 132. Geneva: World Council of Churches, 1986.

Tippy, Worth Marion. *Frontier Bishop: The Life and Times of Robert Richford Roberts*. New York and Nashville: Abingdon Press, 1958.

Vernon, Walter. *Methodism in Arkansas: 1816–1976*. Little Rock: Joint Committee for the History of Arkansas Methodism, 1976.

Wade, William Nash. "A History of Public Worship in the Methodist Episcopal Church and Methodist Episcopal Church, South, from 1784 to 1905." Ph.D. Dissertation, University of Notre Dame, 1981. (Ann Arbor: University Microfilms, International)

Wainwright, Geoffrey. *Christian Initiation*. London: Lutterworth Press, 1969.

Weisberger. Bernard A. *They Gathered at the River: The Story of the Great Revivalists and Their Impact Upon Religion in America*. Boston and Toronto: Little, Brown and Co., 1958.

Wheeler, Henry. *History of the Exposition of the Twenty-five Articles of Religion of the Methodist Episcopal Church*. New York: Eaton and Mains, and Cincinnati: Jennings and Graham, 1908.

Williams, Colin. *John Wesley's Theology Today*. Nashville and New York: Abingdon Press, 1960.

Williams, Samuel. *Pictures of Early Methodism in Ohio*. Cincinnati: Jennings and Graham, and New York: Eaton and Mains, 1909.

NOTES

Introduction

1. *North Carolina Christian Advocate,* January-March, 1983.

2. North Carolina Annual Conference of The United Methodist Church, *The Conference Programs, Recommendations and Reports, 1985,* Section IV, p. 36.

3. B. Keith Rowe, principal of the Methodist Theological College in Auckland, New Zealand quoted in *United Methodist Newscope,* July 25, 1986, p. 1.

4. "Adult baptism" and "believer's baptism" should not be viewed as synonymous terms. Believer's baptism is not defined primarily by the age of the baptizand, but by the understanding that the act of baptism connotes a prior spiritual experience of salvation which is being ritually ratified. The believer is performing a public act of profession and commitment.

5. In traditional theological interpretation, there can be no such thing as "rebaptism." Though the rite itself may be repeated, no new baptism takes place because God has already bestowed sacramental grace on the first occasion, initiating the recipient into the visible and invisible church. God's action in baptism cannot be repeated, nor does it need to be.

6. The only extensive treatment of a similar subject which I have located is the doctoral dissertation by Paul S. Sanders at Union Theological Seminary in 1954, entitled "An Appraisal of John Wesley's Sacramentalism in the Evolution of Early American Methodism." My focus, sources, and conclusions are quite different from those of Sanders, though his work has been seminal in my thought.

Chapter I

1. J. Ernest Rattenbury, *The Eucharistic Hymns of John and Charles Wesley* (London: Epworth Press, 1948), p. 89.

2. *The Works of the Rev. John Wesley*, Vol. VI (New York: J. Emory and B. Waugh, 1831), p. 15.

3. Albert C. Outler, ed., *John Wesley* (New York: Oxford University Press, 1964), pp. 317–18; John E. English, "The Heart Renewed: John Wesley's Doctrine of Christian Initiation," *The Wesleyan Quarterly Review* 4 (May–August 1967): 171–72; Ole E. Borgen, *John Wesley on the Sacraments* (Nashville and New York: Abingdon Press, 1972), pp. 20–26.

4. Nehemiah Curnock, ed., *The Journal of John Wesley, A.M.* 8 vols. (London: Epworth Press, 1909–16), 1:111; John R. Parris, *John Wesley's Doctrine of the Sacraments* (London: Epworth Press, 1963), p. 25.

5. Martin Schmidt, *John Wesley: A Theological Biography*, Vol. I (Nashville and New York: Abingdon Press, 1972), p. 138.

6. *Journal* 1:361 and Parris, *Doctrine of the Sacraments*, p. 26.

7. Bernard G. Holland, *Baptism in Early Methodism* (London: Epworth Press, 1970), p. 31.

8. *Journal* 1:390.

9. Ibid., p. 394.

10. Ibid.

11. Holland, *Baptism*, p. 33. Wesley was ultimately forced to flee surreptitiously from Georgia, when he realized that the hostility of local political authorities made a fair trial on the charges against him an impossibility. The indictments, while based on his ecclesiastical practices, were motivated largely by personal resentments against him. The details can be traced in Wesley's journal entries for 1736 and 1737. A cogent account is in Stuart C. Henry's "Early Contacts in America," in *History of American Methodism*, Vol. I, ed. Emory S. Bucke (New York and Nashville: Abingdon Press, 1964), pp. 46–68.

12. Quoted from Charles Wesley's diary in *Journal* 2:93.

13. *Journal* 3:434.

14. This is the version in Outler, *John Wesley*, pp. 317–32.

15. Frank Baker, *John Wesley and the Church of England* (Nashville and New York: Abingdon Press, 1970), p. 156.

16. "Popery Calmly Considered," 10:150 in Thomas Jackson, ed., *The Works of The Rev. John Wesley, A.M.*, 14 vols. (London: Wesleyan Conference Office, 1872). Cf. "A Roman Catechism with a Reply," p. 114 in Jackson, *Works* X.

17. John Telford, ed., *The Letters of John Wesley*, 8 vols. (London: Epworth Press, 1931), 5:330.

18. *Letters* 7:203–4.

19. Frank Baker makes the curious comment that, "Wesley was quite clear that only in the most exceptional circumstances should baptism be performed by a layman;" Baker, *Wesley and Church of England*, p. 157. He

provides no documentation here and the remark is unclear since I have found no mention elsewhere that Wesley ever countenanced lay baptism.

20. *Journal* 1:167.

21. Ibid., pp. 210–11.

22. Ibid., p. 386. Although immersion was authorized, its use was rare; Anglican baptisms were commonly by the mode of pouring.

23. Holland, *Baptism*, p. 29 and Schmidt, *Theological Biography*, 1:152.

24. Jackson, *Works* 12:56.

25. Joseph Benson, ed., *The Works of the Rev. John Wesley*, Vol. XIII (London: Thomas Cordeux, 1812), pp. 428–29.

26. *Explanatory Notes upon the New Testament* (London: Epworth Press, 1854).

27. Outler, *Wesley*, p. 319.

28. Baker, *Wesley and Church of England*, p. 156. While an advocate, Wesley was not an innovator in the use of this mode. In 1645 the British Parliament ratified *The Directory for the Public Worship of God* which had been adopted by the Westminster Assembly of Divines. Both this document and the Westminster Confession of Faith follow the precedent of John Calvin in sanctioning sprinkling as a baptismal mode. Wesley was certainly familiar with this tradition, although it cannot be proven that he was influenced by it.

29. *Journal* 2:469.

30. Wesley F. Swift, "The Sunday Service of the Methodists," *Proceedings of the Wesley Historical Society* 29 (March 1953):19.

31. *Letters* 3:36–37.

32. *Journal* 1:270–71.

33. These observations are based on accounts in John Wesley's *Diary* and in Charles Wesley's *Journal*, cited in Holland, *Baptism*, pp. 90–95.

34. Quoted in Holland, *Baptism*, p. 94.

35. *Journal* 1:393.

36. Holland, *Baptism*, p. 95.

37. *Journal* 1:391.

38. Ibid.

39. Jackson, *Works* 1:57.

40. Holland, *Baptism*, p. 95 n.2.

41. Benson, *Works* 13:432.

42. Baker, *Wesley and Church of England*, p. 246.

43. Benson, *Works* 13:433–34.

44. Baker, *Wesley and Church of England*, p. 432 and Paul S. Sanders, "An Appraisal of John Wesley's Sacramentalism in the Evolution of Early American Methodism." (Ph.D. thesis, Union Theological Seminary, 1954), p. 262.

45. Benson, *Works* 13:433.

46. John C. Bowmer, *The Sacrament of the Lord's Supper in Early Methodism* (London: Dacre Press, 1951), p. 11.

47. R. Green, *The Conversion of John Wesley* cited in Holland, *Baptism*, p. 21.

48. Holland, *Baptism*, p. 28.
49. Jackson, *Works* 10:116.
50. *Journal* 1:390–91.
51. Ibid., p. 386.
52. Paul S. Sanders, "John Wesley and Baptismal Regeneration," *Religion in Life* 23 (1953–54):592.
53. Horton Davies, *Worship and Theology in England: From Watts and Wesley to Maurice, 1690–1850* (Princeton: Princeton University Press, 1961), p. 205.
54. Holland, *Baptism*, pp. 101–2.
55. English, "Heart Renewed," pp. 112–92.
56. Ibid., p. 150.
57. Outler, *Wesley*, p. 178.

Chapter II

1. Ibid., pp. 317–32.
2. Ibid., p. 321.
3. Jackson, *Works* 9:316.
4. Ibid., p. 321.
5. *Letters* 6:239–40.
6. Outler, *Wesley*, p. 321.
7. George Osborn, ed., *The Poetical Works of John and Charles Wesley*, 13 vols. (London: Wesleyan-Methodist Conference Office, 1870), 10:445–46. Although the thinking of the Wesley brothers was not identical on every detail, the basic theological doctrines expressed in Charles's hymns are assumed to be congruent with the views of John.
8. F. Ernest Stoeffler, "Infant Baptism: Entry into the Covenant," *Christian Advocate* 6 (May 24, 1962):10.
9. Quoted in Borgen, *Sacraments*, pp. 166–67.
10. Robert E. Cushman, "Baptism and the Family of God," pp. 79–102 in Dow Kirkpatrick, ed., *The Doctrine of the Church* (Nashville and New York: Abingdon Press, 1964), p. 81.
11. Outler, *Wesley*, pp. 319, 322.
12. Ibid., p. 322.
13. E. Dale Dunlap, "Baptism and the Christian Life: A United Methodist View," *The Perkins School of Theology Journal* 34 (Winter 1981):8.
14. John Chongnahm Cho, "John Wesley's View on Baptism," *Wesleyan Theological Journal* 7 (Spring 1972):68.
15. *Sermons on Several Occasions* (London: Epworth Press, 1944), pp. 136–37.
16. Outler, *Wesley*, p. 322.
17. Ibid., p. 323.
18. Ibid.
19. Osborn, *Poetical Works* 9:31.
20. Quoted in Borgen, *Sacraments*, p. 234.

21. *N. T. Notes*, Romans 6:3-6.
22. Ibid., Colossians 2:11-12.
23. Frank Whaling, ed., *John and Charles Wesley: Selected Writings and Hymns* (New York: Paulist Press, 1981), p. 268.
24. *N. T. Notes*, Romans 6:3.
25. Jackson, *Works*, 6:414.
26. Osborn, *Poetical Works* 13:114-15.
27. Brian J. N. Galliers, "Baptism in the Writings of John Wesley," *Proceedings of the Wesley Historical Society* 32 (June 1960):123.
28. *Journal* 1:166-67.
29. Holland, *Baptism*, p. 57.
30. *Journal* 4:286.
31. "Treatise on Baptism," Outler, *Wesley*, p. 324.
32. Outler, *Wesley*, p. 97.
33. *Letters* 3:36.
34. *N. T. Notes*, Mark 16:16.
35. Osborn, *Poetical Works* 11:98.
36. *Letters* 4:38.
37. Outler, *Wesley*, p. 323.
38. *N. T. Notes*, John 3:5.
39. Osborn, *Poetical Works* 10:445-46.
40. *Journal* 4:365.
41. Outler, *Wesley*, pp. 322-23.
42. Wall 1:639 quoted in Holland, *Baptism*, p. 22.
43. *Sermons*, p. 523.
44. Outler, *Wesley*, p. 323.
45. William R. Cannon, *The Theology of John Wesley with Special Reference to the Doctrine of Justification* (Nashville and New York: Abingdon Press, 1946), p. 129.
46. James H. Rigg, *The Churchmanship of John Wesley* (London: Wesleyan-Methodist Book-Room, 1878, 1886).
47. Henry Wheeler, *History and Exposition of the Twenty-five Articles of Religion of the Methodist Episcopal Church* (New York: Eaton and Mains, 1908), p. 301.
48. See Sanders, "Appraisal of Wesley's Sacramentalism" and "Wesley and Baptismal Regeneration"; Swift, "Sunday Service"; Holland, *Baptism*; Wheeler, *History and Exposition*; English, "Heart Renewed"; Baker, *Wesley and Church of England*.
49. Sanders, "Wesley and Baptismal Regeneration," p. 598.
50. Rupert Davies and Gordon Rupp, *A History of the Methodist Church in Great Britain*, Volume I (London: Epworth Press, 1965), p. 268.
51. English, "Heart Renewed," p. 179.
52. Davies and Rupp, *Methodist Church in Great Britain*, p. 269.
53. Holland, *Baptism*, p. 135.
54. Baker, *Wesley and Church of England*, p. 247.
55. Swift, *Sunday Service*, p. 18.

56. Baker, *Wesley and Church of England*, p. 390 n. 52.

57. Colin Williams, *John Wesley's Theology Today* (Nashville and New York: Abingdon, 1960), p. 119.

58. *Sermons*, p. 162.

59. Ibid., p. 175.

60. Gerald, R. Cragg, ed., *The Appeals to Men of Reason and Religion.* Volume 11 of *The Works of John Wesley* (Oxford: Clarendon Press, 1975), p. 107.

61. Cho, "View on Baptism," p. 64.

62. *Sermons*, p. 172.

63. Ibid., pp. 172–73.

64. Cushman, "Family of God," pp. 83–84.

65. *Sermons*, p. 525.

66. See "The Great Privilege of Those That Are Born of God," *Sermons*, pp. 178–84.

67. Osborn, *Poetical Works* 10:446–47.

68. *Journal* 1:465.

69. Borgen, *Sacraments*, p. 173.

70. In "The Doctrine of Original Sin," Jackson, *Works* 9:295.

71. Outler, *Wesley*, p. 323.

72. *Journal* 2:275–76.

73. John Baillie, *Baptism and Conversion* (New York: Charles Scribner's Sons, 1963), p. 83. Baillie, however, claims erroneously that, "Wesley altogether dissociated regeneration from baptism," p. 84.

74. Holland, *Baptism*, p. 39.

75. Ibid., p. 70.

76. Ibid., p. 66.

77. Outler, *Wesley*, p. 324.

78. *Works* 13:413.

79. Outler, *Wesley*, p. 330.

80. *Works* 13:427.

81. Outler, *Wesley*, p. 329.

82. Ibid., p. 330.

83. *Works* 13:419.

84. Osborn, *Poetical Works* 10:322.

85. Ibid., 7:71–72.

86. *N. T. Notes*, Acts 10:47.

87. Ibid., Acts 22:16.

88. Cragg, *Appeals*, p. 111.

89. Jackson, *Works* 12:122.

90. Osborn, *Poetical Works* 5:389.

91. *Journal* 2:135.

92. Holland, *Baptism*, pp. 45–51, 82.

93. *Journal* 4:189, 5:195, 7:133.

94. Ibid., 2:211.

95. *N. T. Notes*, I Peter 3:21.

96. *Journal* 6:49.
97. Osborn, *Poetical Works* 5:388-89.
98. Cushman, "Family of God," p. 82.

Chapter III

1. Henry Maynard was born on August 12, 1757; the exact date of his baptism is unrecorded, but it almost surely occurred in 1762 at the home of his brother John Maynard. See Ruthella Mary Bibbins, *How Methodism Came: The Beginnings of Methodism in England and America* (Baltimore: The American Methodist Historical Society of the Baltimore Annual Conference, 1945), pp. 29-31 and Frederick E. Maser, *Robert Strawbridge: First American Methodist Circuit Rider* (Rutland, Vermont: Academy Books, 1983), p. 25.

2. An exception for Strawbridge was apparently made at the 1773 preachers' conference, to allow him to continue to administer the sacraments "under the particular direction" of the supervisor appointed by Wesley. While this stipulation is not contained in the official minutes, it is acknowledged by Asbury. See Francis Asbury, *The Journal and Letters*, 3 vols. Edited by Elmer T. Clark, J. Manning Potts, and Jacob S. Payton (London and Nashville: Epworth Press and Abingdon Press, 1958), 1:85. After 1775 Strawbridge was left without an appointment because of his adamancy on this issue. The tradition that Strawbridge was ordained by a German Reformed minister, Benedict Swope, is probably spurious. See Maser, *Strawbridge* for a full account of the historical facts.

3. "Every preacher in connexion with Mr. Wesley and the brethren who labour in America is strictly to avoid administering the ordinances of Baptism and the Lord's Supper." *Minutes of the Methodist Conferences Annually Held in America from 1773 to 1794, inclusive* (Philadelphia: Henry Tuckniss, 1795). Numerous references in Asbury's *Journal* make it clear that he fully agreed with Wesley on this point. An interesting example is his comment in 1775 on the possibility of going to minister in Antigua: "But there is one obstacle in my way—the administration of the ordinances. It is possible to get the ordination of a presbytery; but this would be incompatible with Methodism: which would be an effectual bar in my way." (1:149).

4. Asbury commented in his *Journal* in 1780: "I have laboured to get our friends well affected to the Episcopal Church; what could I do better, when we had not the ordinances among us?" (1:353). Certain Anglican clergymen gained Asbury's approbation for their character and their support of the Methodists, notably Devereaux Jarratt in Dinwiddie County, Virginia and Samuel Magaw in Baltimore, Maryland.

5. For detailed accounts of "the sacramental controversy," see Asbury, *Journal*, 1:381 n.; Nathan Bangs, *A History of the Methodist Episcopal Church*, 4 vols. (New York: Carlton and Porter, 1853-57); Robert Drew Simpson, ed. *American Methodist Pioneer: The Life and Journals of the Rev. Freeborn Garrettson, 1752-1827* (Rutland, Vermont: Academy Books, 1984); Abel Stevens, *History of the Methodist Episcopal Church in the United States*, 4 vols. (New York: Carlton

and Porter, 1865-67); Jonathan J. Tigert, *A Constitutional History of American Episcopal Methodism* (Nashville and Dallas: Publishing House of the Methodist Episcopal Church, South, Smith and Lamar, Agents, 1904).

6. Jacob Simpson Payton, *Our Fathers Have Told Us: The Story of the Founding of Methodism in Western Pennsylvania* (Cincinnati: The Ruter Press, 1938), p. 40; Stevens, *History*, 2:295; Thomas Coke, *Extracts of the Journals of the late Rev. Thomas Coke's Several Visits to America, the West Indies, Etc* (Dublin: Methodist Book Room, 1816), p. 49. Thomas Ware in *Sketches of the Life and Travels* (New York: T. Mason and G. Lane, 1839) related incidences where the demand for baptisms of infants was so overwhelming that he could maintain no record of the numbers. Asbury's *Journal* contains dozens of references to his administration of the sacrament.

7. Asbury, *Journal*, 1:54, 109, 3:31.

8. The first such official document was published in 1785. Patterned on its English counterpart, it was entitled *Minutes of several conversations between the Rev. Thomas Coke, L.L.D., the Rev. Francis Asbury and Others . . . 1784*. In 1786, "The General Minutes of the Conferences of the Methodist Episcopal Church in America, forming the constitution of the said Church" was appended to Wesley's *Sunday Service*. For the next five years (1787-91) a new title was used—*A Form of Discipline for the Ministers, Preachers, and Members of the Methodist Episcopal Church in America*. In the eighth edition, 1792, the title was changed to *The Doctrines and Discipline of the Methodist Episcopal Church in America*. This nomenclature became standard for the church. (Hereinafter, the term *Discipline*, with the appropriate date, will be used to refer to the documents described above.) Doctrinal statements were a part of the *Disciplines* from the beginning; separate doctrinal tracts were published with the *Disciplines* from 1788 to 1798 and from 1801 to 1808. The 1798 edition included extensive "Explanatory Notes" by Coke and Asbury. Beginning in 1814, the doctrinal tracts were published in a separate volume entitled *A Collection of Interesting Tracts, explaining several important points of Scripture Doctrine. Published by order of the General Conference*. This publication was discontinued in 1892. For a comprehensive treatment of these documents see Frank Baker, "The Doctrines in the *Discipline*: a study of the forgotten theological presuppositions of American Methodism," *Duke Divinity School Review* 31 (1966): 39-55 or Frank Baker, *From Wesley to Asbury* (Durham: Duke University Press, 1976), pp. 162-82.

9. Dickins was appointed as book steward for the Methodist Episcopal Church in 1789—the first step toward the development of the Methodist Publishing House.

10. Norman Pettit, *The Heart Prepared: Grace and Conversion in Puritan Spiritual Life* (New Haven and London: Yale University Press, 1966), pp. 212-14.

11. *A Form of Discipline. . . .* (Philadelphia: R. Aitken and Son, 1790), pp. 180-251.

12. Freeborn Garrettson (1752-1827) was one of the most significant of the native-born American preachers during the early period of Methodism. His influence in the founding years was second only to that of Asbury.

13. Early Methodist societies were divided into classes of approximately twelve members in order to facilitate the overseeing of each person's spiritual progress. The leaders of these classes were lay persons who often functioned also as the stewards or financial officers of the societies.

14. Simpson, *Garrettson*, pp. 203-4.

15. Note that the "ordinances" that the Baptists were here opposing were those of the Church of England, since there were no ordained Methodist preachers administering the sacraments before 1784.

16. Asbury, *Journal*, 1:176.

17. A. H. Redford, *The History of Methodism in Kentucky*, Vol. I (Nashville: Southern Methodist Publishing House, 1868), pp. 289-90.

18. Asbury, *Journal*, 1:305, 344, 379.

19. Tigert, *Constitutional History*, pp. 106-7. The option of sprinkling allowed by the 1779 Fluvanna conference is of interest because some scholars cite Wesley's *Sunday Service* of 1784 as containing the first ritual to recommend sprinkling as a valid mode. See Baker, *Wesley and Church of England*, p. 246 and Swift, *Sunday Service*, p. 19. Baker points out, however, that Wesley had expressed his approval of sprinkling for infants as early as 1755 (p.156).

20. Robert Emory, *History of the Discipline of the Methodist Episcopal Church*. Revised by W. P. Strickland (New York: Carlton and Porter, 1843), pp. 45, 203.

21. *Doctrines and Discipline of the Methodist Episcopal Church, 1792* (Philadelphia: Parry Hall, 1792), p. 234.

22. Asbury, *Journal*, 1:458.

23. *Doctrines and Discipline of the Methodist Episcopal Church, 1798* (Philadelphia: Henry Tuckniss, 1798), pp. 118-19.

24. Ibid., p. 119.

25. Nathan Bangs, *The Life of the Rev. Freeborn Garrettson* (New York: J. Emory and E. Waugh, 1832), pp. 144-45.

26. Simpson, *Garrettson*, p. 279.

27. *Minutes of Several Conversations between the Rev. Thomas Coke, L.L.D. and the Rev. Francis Asbury and Others . . . 1784* (Philadelphia: Charles Cist, 1785), pp. 175-77.

28. *Discipline*, 1798, p.22.

29. E. F. Newell, *Life and Observations* (Worchester: S. W. Ainsworth, 1847), pp. 43-44.

30. *Arminian Magazine*, I (1789):498-99. This American Methodist magazine, which was published for only two years, was patterned on John Wesley's journal of the same name.

31. Stevens, *History*, 2:309-10.

32. Asbury, *Journal*, 2:26

33. Emory, *History of Discipline*, pp. 45, 203.

34. Asbury, *Journal*, 2:142-43.

35. John Atkinson, *Memorials of Methodism in New Jersey* (Philadelphia: Perkinpine and Higgins, 1860), pp. 58–59, 239.

36. Asbury, *Journal*, 1:42.

37. *A Form of Discipline . . .* (New York: W. Ross, 1787), p. 35.

38. *Journals of the General Conference of the Methodist Episcopal Church: Volume I: 1796–1836* (New York: Carlton and Phillips, 1855), p. 37.

Chapter IV

1. Robert W. Todd, *Methodism of the Peninsula* (Philadelphia: Methodist Episcopal Book Rooms, 1886), p. 169.

2. Since 1788, doctrinal tracts on various subjects had been bound with the *Disciplines*. Apparently motivated by the increasing unwieldiness of the volume, the General Conference of 1812 authorized the publication of a separate book of doctrinal commentaries. The first edition was published in 1814 under the title *A Collection of Interesting Tracts, explaining several important points of Scripture Doctrine*.

3. Edwards's work was well received in this country; at least nine editions were published by 1844.

4. The contents of these documents have been discussed in Chapter II.

5. This selection had been published in the *Methodist Magazine*—forerunner of the *Methodist Quarterly Review*—in 1823, under the title "The Antiquity of Infant Baptism Supported, and that of Popery Disproved, From the Works of Chrysostom."

6. Carlton R. Young, *Companion to the Hymnal* (Nashville: Abingdon Press, 1970), p. 55.

7. *A Pocket Hymn-Book, Designed as a Constant Companion for the Pious* (Philadelphia: Pritchard and Hall, 1790).

8. *The Methodist Pocket Hymn Book, revised and improved: designed as a constant Companion for the pious of all denominations* (New York: Ezekiel Cooper and John Wilson, 1807). See page 70 for Charles Wesley's "Come, Father, Son, and Holy Ghost."

9. *A Collection of Hymns for the use of the Methodist Episcopal Church, Principally from the Collection of the Reverend John Wesley, M.A., late Fellow of Lincoln College, Oxford* (New York: N. Bangs and T. Mason, 1821).

10. *A Collection of Hymns . . . with a Supplement* (New York: N. Bangs and T. Mason, 1836). Hymn 674 was Charles Wesley's "God of eternal truth and love"—see page 44 for text—but with stanza two omitted, apparently due to objection to its reference to the burden of Adamic guilt.

11. *Western Christian Advocate*, 12/29/1843.

12. Circuit rider Peter Cartwright commented in his *Autobiography* after an unplanned swim in a swelling river: " . . . my books and clothes had all turned Campbellite." Peter Cartwright, *Autobiography*, edited by Charles L. Wallis (New York and Nashville: Abingdon Press, 1956), p. 221.

13. Pitts's book, published by the Western Methodist Office in Nashville, is now quite rare. A copy on microfilm was graciously made available to me by the Presbyterian Historical Society of Philadelphia.

14. Ibid., p. 67.

15. Ibid., pp. 86-87.

16. The *Christian Advocate* began publication in New York in September, 1826 and was adopted as the organ of the Methodist Episcopal Church at the General Conference of 1828. To meet demand in the growing West, the General Conference of 1832 authorized the *Western Christian Advocate* which began publication in Cincinnati in 1834. In 1836, the General Conference approved *Christian Advocates* to be produced in Charleston, Richmond and Nashville. *Zion's Herald* started publication in Boston in 1823 and became the organ of New England Methodism. The *Methodist Magazine*, begun as a monthly in 1818, changed to a quarterly in 1830 as the *Methodist Magazine and Quarterly Review*, with a further title change in 1840 to the *Methodist Quarterly Review*.

17. *MQR*, 7-1839.

18. For specifics, see various issues of *Zion's Herald* for 1836.

19. An example was a humorous account of the planned immersion of two former slaves in Indiana in 1840. After the Baptist preacher had struggled with great difficulty and limited success to immerse the corpulent woman in a few inches of muddy creek water, her husband decided to postpone his own baptism until conditions were more favorable. John L. Smith, *Indiana Methodism: A Series of Sketches and Incidents Grave and Humorous Concerning Preachers and People of the West* (Valparaiso, Indiana: 1892), pp. 44-46. Methodist editors also chortled over advertisements in Baptist newspapers for "India Rubber Baptismal Vests and Pants." "Were these the appendages of apostolic baptism?" they inquired, lampooning the Baptist claim to be faithful to New Testament precedents. See *Western Christian Advocate*, 11/26/1841.

20. *Autobiography*, p. 336.

21. John W. Riggins in the *Western Christian Advocate*, 12/30/1842.

22. *Western Christian Advocate*, 12/30/1836.

23. *Extracts of Letters, Containing Some Account of the Work of God since the Year 1800. Written by the Preachers and Members of the Methodist Episcopal Church to their Bishops* (New York: Ezekiel Cooper and John Wilson, 1805), p. 114.

24. J. B. Wakeley, *The Heroes of Methodism* (Toronto: William Briggs, 1855), p. 447.

25. Allen Wiley, *Western Christian Advocate*, 1/9/1846.

26. William Phoebus, *An Essay on the Doctrine and Order of the Evangelical Church in America as Constituted at Baltimore in 1784* (New York: Abraham Paul, 1817), p. 69.

27. For examples, see *New York Christian Advocate*, 6/13/1828.

28. S. S. Bryant, *A Sermon on the Nature and Mode of Baptism* (Greensborough, N.C.: Swaim and Sherwood, 1843), p. 22.

29. Voluminous discussion of the subject appeared in the periodical literature of the period. Comprehensive treatments are found in sermons and books; three examples are: Peter P. Sandford, "Christian Baptism." (New York: Conference Office, 1829); Henry Slicer, *An Appeal To The Candid of All Denominations: in which the Obligation, Subjects, and Mode of Baptism are Discussed* (New York: G. Lane and P. P. Sandford, 1835); John J. Triggs, *A Treatise on Christian Baptism* (Augusta: James McCafferty, 1842).

30. An intriguing variant of the historical argument is that of Charles Taylor, an English scholar and engraver who was editor of *Calmet's Dictionary of the Bible.* Taylor's arguments for infant baptism and for sprinkling or pouring were based on archaeological evidence. His work was much admired by American Methodists who often cited and reprinted it. Taylor contended that in the early church a ritual washing by immersion, done either by the candidate or by others, preceded baptism by pouring. This immersion signified death to the old life of sin, but it was preliminary to baptism and not part of the sacrament itself. *Apostolic Baptism: Facts and Evidences on the Subjects and Mode of Christian Baptism* (New York: B. H. Bevier, 1843), pp. 135ff.

31. Newell, *Life and Observations,* p. 45.

32. Sandford, *Christian Baptism,* p. 7.

33. Timothy Merritt, "Anabaptism Disproved and the Validity and Sufficiency of Infant Baptism Asserted in Two Letters from a Minister to His Friend." (New York: T. Mason and G. Lane, 1837), p. 5.

34. *Journals of the General Conference 1796–1836,* pp. 496–97.

35. *Autobiography,* p. 231. See also *Western Christian Advocate,* 4/1/1836 and *Zion's Herald,* 4/22/1831.

36. *Journal,* pp. 56–57. McFerrin would have a distinguished career as an editor and publishing house agent in the Methodist Episcopal Church, South.

37. Benjamin St. James Fry, *The Life of Rev. William M'Kendree.* Edited by Daniel P. Kidder (New York: Carlton and Phillips, 1852), pp. 60–62.

38. Heman Bangs, *The Autobiography and Journal* (New York: N. Tibbals and Son, 1872), p. 43.

39. *Zion's Herald,* 3/6/1831; *New York Christian Advocate,* 4/3/1840.

40. Nathan Bangs, *History* 4:419–20.

41. An interesting glimpse of the influence of other groups besides the Baptists was found in a letter from Delaware blaming the small number of infant baptisms on the Quaker tradition of the area. *New York Christian Advocate,* 4/25/1834.

42. *Zion's Herald,* 12/30/1840.

43. *New York Christian Advocate,* 10/13/1841; *Zion's Herald,* 6/4/1843.

44. Watson's *Theological Institutes* was widely read by American Methodists from its first publication in six parts, 1823–29, and appeared on the required course of study for ministers throughout the century.

45. Richard Watson, *Theological Institutes; or a View of the Evidences, Doctrines, Morals and Institutions of Christianity*, 2 volumes (New York: George Lane, 1840), 2:344-45. Brackets in the original.

46. Wilbur Fisk, *Calvinistic Controversy Embracing a Sermon on Predestination and Election and Several Numbers on the Same Subject* (New York: T. Mason and G. Lane, 1837), p. 183.

47. "Anabaptism Disproved," pp. 16-20.

48. William Annan, *Difficulties of Arminian Methodism* (Pittsburgh: Luke Loomis, 1838), p. 218. Annan was a Presbyterian minister in Pennsylvania who attacked Methodism, pointing out theological contradictions on this subject and others.

49. Watson, 4:630.

50. Jonathan Crowther, *A True and Complete Portraiture of Methodism or the History of the Wesleyan Methodists* (New York: Daniel Hitt and Thomas Ware, 1813), p. 192.

51. Sandford, "Christian Baptism," pp. 15-17 and p. 1.

52. *Western Christian Advocate*, 3/15/1839.

53. *New York Christian Advocate*, 4/11/1828, 9/5/1828; *Zion's Herald*, 9/5/1828. There is much more discussion of this question in these periodicals than in those published in parts of the country where the Calvinist presence was less significant.

54. "Anabaptism Disproved," p. 20.

55. Scott was best known for his activism against slavery. In the same year that this article appeared, he withdrew from the Methodist Episcopal Church and led what became the Wesleyan Methodist Connection.

56. *Zion's Herald*, 2/9, 3/2, 4/6, 5/4, 6/1/1842.

57. Luther Lee and E. Smith, *The Debates of the General Conference of the M. E. Church*, May, 1844 (New York: O. Scott, 1845). Six restrictive rules were passed by the 1808 General Conference to provide a basis of constitutional authority for the church. These rules were not to be altered except by joint action of all the annual conferences and a two-thirds majority of the General Conference.

58. Quoted in Elizabeth K. Nottingham, *Methodism and the Frontier: Indiana Proving Ground* (New York: Columbia University Press, 1941), p. 164.

59. Devereaux Jarratt, *An Argument Between Anabaptist and Poedo-Baptist on the Subjects and Mode of Baptism*, 1803.

60. *Journal and Letters*, 2:459, 3:414-15.

61. See Amos Binney and Daniel Steele, *Binney's Theological Compend Improved* (Cincinnati: Curts and Jennings, New York: Eaton and Mains, 1875); S. S. Bryant, *A Sermon on the Obligation and Benefits of Infant Baptism* (Greensborough, North Carolina: Swaim and Sherwood, 1843); Asa Shinn, *An Essay on the Plan of Salvation* (Baltimore: Neal, Wills and Cole, 1813); Slicer, *Appeal to the Candid*.

62. Jarratt, *An Argument*.

63. *Methodist Magazine* 1:212.

64. See page 14 in Chapter I for this note. *New York Christian Advocate*, 4/17/1844. While Curry's statement is technically correct, it is somewhat curious in view of the fact that Wesley's *Treatise* was published in the *Collection of Interesting Tracts* as one of the denomination's official statements on baptism from 1825 to 1861.

65. John Hersey, *An Inquiry into the Character and Conditions of Our Children* (Richmond: Samuel Shepherd and Co., 1832), p. 12.

66. Lawrence Kean, *A Plain and Positive Refutation of the Rev. Samuel Pelton's Unjust and Unfounded Charges Entitled "The Absurdities of Methodism"* (New York: J. and J. Harper, 1823), p. 321.

67. Ware, *Sketches*, pp. 103, 115, et al.

68. *Zion's Herald*, 2/25/1824 and 1/27/1841 for examples. Cartwright, *Autobiography*, p. 129 and *Fifty Years as a Presiding Elder*, (Cincinnati and New York: 1871), pp. 62–64. See also [A. Chandler], "The Scripture Directory to Baptism." (New York: J. Leavitt, 1831).

69. Newell, *Life and Observations*, p. 163 and John Stewart, *Highways and Hedges; or Fifty Years of Western Methodism* (Cincinnati: Hitchcock and Walden and New York: Carlton and Lanahan, 1872), p. 126.

70. 8/28/1840.

71. Pp. 16–17, 21–22.

72. Simpson, p. 399.

73. *Zion's Herald*, 4/22/1840.

74. Bryant, *Infant Baptism*, p. 22.

75. Quoted in William Warren Sweet, *Religion on the American Frontier: 1783–1840.* Vol. IV: *The Methodists: A Collection of Source Materials* (New York: Cooper Square Publishers, Inc., 1964), p. 728.

76. Slicer, pp. 51–54.

77. References in the *Discipline* to "society" were not changed to "church" until 1816; even then, the self-understanding of Methodism was more sectarian than ecclesiastical.

78. See *Western Christian Advocate*, 3/11/1836 and Z. Paddock, *Memoir of Rev. Benjamin G. Paddock* (New York: Nelson and Phillips, 1875), pp. 64–65.

79. 7/31/1835.

80. *Western Christian Advocate*, 11/25/1836.

81. Lee and Smith, *Debates, 1844*, pp. 17–18. These rules included John Wesley's General Rules for the United Societies which did not require baptism as a prerequisite for membership.

82. See *Zion's Herald*, 9/10/1834 and William G. Brownlow, *Baptism Examined, or the True State of the Case to which Is Prefixed a Review of the Assaults of the "Banner and Pioneer."* (Jonesborough, Tennessee: Whig Office, 1842), p. 178.

83. This legal probationary period remained in the Methodist Episcopal Church, South until 1866 and in the Methodist Episcopal Church until 1908.

84. See "The Rules of the United Societies" reprinted in Outler, *Wesley*, p. 178.

85. For examples see Sandford, "Christian Baptism," pp. 7-8; Brownlow, *Baptism Examined*, p. 171; Triggs, *Treatise*, p. 4.

86. *Zion's Herald*, 4/26/1833.

87. *Western Christian Advocate*, 5/4/1838.

88. *Autobiography*, pp. 303-4.

89. *Western Christian Advocate*, 5/1/1840.

90. Ibid., 8/19/1842.

91. It should be made clear that even an adult who was both baptized and converted could not be admitted into full church membership before the end of the probationary period. These months of trial relationship allowed the church to evaluate the applicant's experience and conduct, as well as providing opportunity for the applicant to become familiar with the rules, doctrines, and practices of the denomination.

92. The doctrine of close communion ("close" rather than "closed" communion is the term consistently used in the sources) had many complex variations in nineteenth-century Baptist views. Some congregations admitted only those who had been baptized into that particular local church. Others required a specific style or formula of baptism to have been employed. Some groups put emphasis upon the necessity of having been immersed by a minister who had himself been validly immersed and tracing this line back into history—a Baptist version of apostolic succession.

93. See Newell, *Life and Observation*, pp. 69-70; *Western Christian Advocate*, 1/23/1835, 3/13/1835; *Zion's Herald*, 6/22/1842.

94. Quoted in *Zion's Herald*, 1/11/1843.

95. The Methodist Episcopal Church split in 1844 into a northern component which retained the original name and a southern component called the Methodist Episcopal Church, South. The divisive issues were largely those of slavery and episcopal authority. Reunion was not achieved until 1939.

Chapter V

1. *A Collection of Hymns for Public, Social and Domestic Worship* (Richmond: John Early, 1847).

2. Ibid.

3. *Hymns for the Use of the Methodist Episcopal Church*, revised edition (New York: Carlton and Lanahan; Cincinnati: Hitchcock and Walden, 1849).

4. Ibid.

5. *Nashville Christian Advocate*, 12/6/1850. For detailed treatments of this issue, see Thomas N. Ralston, *Elements of Divinity*, (Nashville: A. H. Redford, Agent for the Methodist Episcopal Church, South, 1876), pp. 948-52 and the series of articles by John Luccock appearing in the *Western Christian Advocate* from 4/29 to 6/24 of 1857.

6. James R. Graves, *The Great Iron Wheel or Republicanism Backwards and Christianity Reversed* (Nashville: Graves, Marks and Rutland and New York: Sheldon, Lamport and Co., 1855).

7. For examples, see *New York Christian Advocate,* 7/11 and 8/29, 1850; *Western Christian Advocate,* 8/22/1860.

8. See Z. Paddock's review of G. S. Farber's *Sermons on the Doctrine of Regeneration, Methodist Quarterly Review,* 10/1854.

9. These views were articulated at length in many sources. Examples include A. A. Jimeson, *Notes on the Twenty-five Articles of Religion as Received and Taught by Methodists in the United States* (Cincinnati: Applegate, Pounsford and Co., 1868), pp. 284–88; an article by G. W. Langhorne in the *Methodist Quarterly Review,* 7/1855; Freeborn G. Hibbard, *Christian Baptism* (New York: Carlton and Phillips, 1853; and Thomas O. Summers, *Baptism: A Treatise on the Nature, Perpetuity, Subjects, Administrator, Mode, and Use of the Initiating Ordinance of the Christian Church* (Richmond and Louisville: John Early, 1853).

10. *Methodist Quarterly Review, South,* 4/1859.

11. Ibid., 1/1861 and Thomas O. Summers, editor, *Methodist Pamphlets for the People, Volume II* (Nashville: E. Stevenson and T. A. Owen, Agents for the Methodist Episcopal Church, South, 1857).

12. For examples see *New York Christian Advocate,* 8/29/1850, 7/3/1851 and 3/1/1860; *Western Christian Advocate,* 4/25/1860. Minor adjustments made in the ritual have previously been noted, however no substantive change in the use of John 3:5 occurred until the twentieth century.

13. See the lengthy exchange of letters between Merrill and John Thatcher in the *Western Christian Advocate,* 4/25 to 12/12, 1860.

14. Perhaps the most authoritative sources on the subject were the books on baptism by F. G. Hibbard and Thomas O. Summers. These works were extremely influential on Methodist thought, especially because of their position on the course of study. Hibbard's book was required for study in the northern branch of the church from 1848 to 1876, while Summers's occupied a similar place in the southern church from 1878 to 1902 and was widely read from its publication in 1852. An example from periodical literature was a long series of articles on baptism published in the *Nashville Christian Advocate* in 1850 and 1851 under the pseudonym "The Old Man."

15. See Ralston, *Elements,* pp. 975–92; also long discussions in S. D. Bumpass, *Sermon and Baptism,* (Greensborough, N.C.: Swaim and Sherwood, 1847) and L. Rosser, *Baptism: Its Nature, Obligation, Mode, Subjects and Benefits,* (Richmond: By the author, 1854).

16. For an especially detailed treatment of this analogy, see pamphlet in Duke Divinity School Library entitled "Baptism According to the Holy Scripture," (no title page).

17. In his *The Battle Field Reviewed* (Chicago: 1881), Landon Taylor described his own experiences on the Iowa frontier in the 1840s and recommended a convenient method of immersion in which the candidates were asked "to kneel in the water; this covered most of their person; then all I had to do was to immerse the head and shoulders. But the *best of all* in this form, they are standing on their feet, and spend no *time* in raising

themselves out of the water, and all the pastor has to do is steady them," pp. 93-94.

18. See the series of articles by Lovick Pierce in the *Nashville Christian Advocate,* 10/1857.

19. *Baptismal Demonstrations* (Nashville: Southern Methodist Publishing House, 1859), p. 5.

20. *Sermons on Various Subjects* (Cincinnati: L. Swormstedt and A. Poe, 1852), p. 265.

21. Summers, *Baptism,* pp. 122-23.

22. Ibid., 109n. Similarly ridiculing references to Baptist use of such "contrivances" recurred frequently in Methodist periodicals and books.

23. See "A Strange Snare" in the *Western Christian Advocate,* 11/14/1855.

24. *History of Immersion, as a Religious Rite* (St. Louis: Southwestern Book and Publishing Co., 1852, 1871). The charge of nudity in immersion was repeated frequently by Methodist polemicists.

25. Davis W. Clark, *The Methodist Episcopal Pulpit: A Collection of Original Sermons from Living Ministers of the Methodist Episcopal Church.* Collected and edited by George Peck (New York: Lane and Scott, 1850), pp. 410-36.

26. *Western Christian Advocate,* 11/12/1852, 8/6/1862.

27. An interesting expression of the claims of the Landmark movement was the fictional romance entitled *Theodosia Ernest,* published in two volumes in 1856 and 1857 (Nashville: Southwestern Baptist Publishing House). This simplistic, sentimental polemic went through twenty-six printings in two years.

28. See James A. Clement, *An Exposition of the Pretensions of Baptists to Antiquity* (Nashville: For the author, 1881); Bumpass, *Sermon;* Rosser, *Baptism;* Peter Doub, "Discourses on Christian Communion and Baptism," (Raleigh: William C. Doub-Star Office, 1854); Incognito, *Proselyters Defeated* (Nashville: Southern Methodist Publishing House, 1859).

29. Orceneth Fisher, *The Christian Sacraments* (St. Louis: Southwestern Book and Publishing Co., 1858, 1871), pp. 36-37; Hersey, *Inquiry,* pp. 22-23; Bumpass, *Sermon,* pp. 10-11; Merritt, "Anabaptism Disproved," pp. 14-23.

30. Hersey, *Inquiry,* p. 20; Hibbard, *Christian Baptism,* 2:11-31.

31. William G. Brownlow, *The Great Iron Wheel Examined or, Its False Spokes Extracted, and an Exhibition of Elder Graves, Its Builder* (Nashville: Published for the author, 1856), pp. 231-32; Orceneth Fisher, *The Wilderness of Judea* (St. Louis: Southwestern Book and Publishing Co., 1871).

32. Hiram M. Shaffer, *A Treatise on Baptism, in Two Parts* (Cincinnati: Printed for the author, 1847), pp. 161-68. See similar argument in Hibbard, *Christian Baptism,* 2:11-31.

33. *Zion's Herald,* 8/23/1854.

34. Fisher, *Christian Sacraments,* pp. 183-84.

35. Reports of such occurrences are surprisingly rare throughout the eighteenth and nineteenth centuries.

36. Summers, *Baptism,* p. 74.

37. Ibid., pp. 75, 77.

38. 7/29/1858.

39. Green P. Jackson, *Sunshine and Shade in a Happy Itinerant's Life* (Nashville and Dallas: Publishing House of the Methodist Episcopal Church, South, Smith and Lamar, Agents, 1904), pp. 31-34.

40. See *New York Christian Advocate,* 5/10/1849, 8/26/1858.

41. Ibid., 1858; Rosser, *Baptism,* pp. 378-83.

42. Gilbert Haven in *MQR,* 1/1859.

43. *Arminian Inconsistencies and Errors* (Philadelphia: William S. and Alfred Martien, 1856), p. 260.

44. The *New York Christian Advocate* in 1859 identified several conferences in which only about one-tenth of the children were being baptized–New England, northern and western New York, Michigan, Wisconsin, and Minnesota. In 1864 this paper quoted the *Pittsburgh Advocate* as saying, "Not half of the children of Methodist parents are baptized. This is a shame." No reliable statistics exist by which these figures can be checked, but the problem must have been widespread–the Nashville and North Carolina *Christian Advocates* contained similar criticisms.

45. See sermons on baptism in James W. and Frank L. Reid, *Life, Sermons and Speeches of Rev. Numa F. Reid, DD, Late of the North Carolina Conference* (New York: E. J. Hale and Son, 1874); Samuel Gregg, *Infant Church Membership; or, the Spiritual and Permanent Character of the Abrahamic Covenant.* Edited by D. W. Clark (Cincinnati: Swormstedt and Poe, 1854); Ralston, *Elements,* pp. 963-73; Summers, *Baptism;* Abbey, "Baptismal Demonstrations."

46. These arguments were not always sustained by a great deal of biblical erudition. In his *Autobiography: Chapters from the Life of a Preacher,* J. W. Burke gave a humorous account of a sermon that he heard in Georgia in 1856 in which the preacher repeatedly referred to the apostolic baptisms of "households and straightways," (Macon, Georgia: J. W. Burke and Co., 1884), pp. 44-45.

47. See Clement, *Exposition;* Rosser, *Baptism;* Shaffer, *Treatise;* James L. Chapman, *Baptism* (Nashville: Methodist Episcopal Church, South, 1856) and *Tracts for the Times on Infant Baptism* (Nashville: Methodist Episcopal Church, South, 1855).

48. Henry W. Adams in *Zion's Herald,* 4/29/1846.

49. Fisher, *Christian Sacraments,* pp. 113-14, 131; *Zion's Herald,* 6/10/1846; I. Smith, *Reasons for Becoming a Methodist* (New York: Carlton and Porter, 1850), pp. 76-77; Rosser, *Baptism,* pp. 403-9.

50. *Our Church: A Manual for Members and Probationers of the Methodist Episcopal Church, South* (Nashville: Southern Methodist Publishing House, 1860), pp. 98-99.

51. *1864 Discipline,* pp. 133-34.

52. *New York Christian Advocate,* 8/2/1855.

53. Gregg, pp. 204-8.

54. *MQR,* 1-1859, p. 23.

55. *Western Christian Advocate,* 8/4/1852.

56. Rosser, *Baptism,* pp. 212-25, 386-87.

57. Summers, *Baptism*, pp. 22-23 and *MQR*, 7/1854.

58. *Nashville Christian Advocate*, 8/11/1848.

59. *The Methodist*, 7/1/1865.

60. Brownlow, *Great Iron Wheel Examined*, p. 242.

61. *New York Christian Advocate*, 7/15/1858.

62. *Journal of the 1860 General Conference*, p. 318. Article VII—Of Original or Birth Sin read: "Original sin standeth not in the following of Adam (as the Pelagians do vainly talk), but is the corruption of the nature of every man, that naturally is engendered of the offspring of Adam, whereby man is very far gone from original righteousness, and of his own nature inclined to evil, and that continually."

63. *Nashville Christian Advocate*, 4/16/1847.

64. Volney M. Simons, *Infant Salvation: A Discourse* (St. Albans, Vt.: E. B. Whiting, 1860), pp. 7-9. See also Samuel Gregg's sermon, "Salvation of Infants" in William Hunter, editor, *Original Sermons by Ministers of the Pittsburgh, Erie, and Western Virginia Conferences of the Methodist Episcopal Church* (Pittsburgh: Methodist Book Depository, 1850), pp. 220-35.

65. *Zion's Herald*, 2/9, 1859. See also *Zion's Herald*, 2/2 and 8/28/1859, 1/2/1861 for typical views.

66. Summers, *Baptism*, pp. 184-85.

67. *Nashville Christian Advocate*, 8/3/1849.

68. Graves, *Iron Wheel*, pp. 439-41.

69. See *New York Christian Advocate*, 10/18/1848 and 2/26/1857, *Western Christian Advocate*, 9/12/1860.

70. *New York Christian Advocate*, 7/21/1864. Curry was editor of this publication from 1864 to 1876 and later of the *Ladies' Repository*.

71. *Zion's Herald*, 1/26/1859; *MQRS*, 10/1860. See also *Zion's Herald*, 2/9/1859 and *Nashville Christian Advocate*, 5/4/1847.

72. See *Western Christian Advocate*, 2/26/1847; Shaffer, *Treatise*, pp. 103-5; *New York Christian Advocate*, 10/14/1848; James Porter, *A Compendium of Methodism: Embracing the History and Present Condition of Its Various Branches in All Countries* (Boston: George C. Rand, 1852), pp. 287-88.

73. Gregg, *Infant Church Membership*, p. 196.

74. L. Rosser, *Reply to "Evils of Infant Baptism" by Robert C. Howell, D.D., Pastor of the Second Baptist Church, Richmond, Va.* (Richmond: By the author, 1855), p. 91.

75. Summers, ed. *Pamphlets*, p. 4.

76. (New York: Anson D. F. Randolph, 1858). An earlier book by Mercein, *Natural Goodness: or, Honour to Whom Honour is Due* (New York: Carlton and Phillips, 1855) and his articles in church papers had begun to spur controversy, but widespread debate did not begin to appear until 1858.

77. Mercein, *Childhood and the Church* and "The Relation of Baptized Infants to the Church," *MQR*, 1/1855.

78. For examples, see *Nashville Christian Advocate*, 9/9, 10/28/1858 and 11/29/1860; *Western Christian Advocate*, 10/20/1858, 1/12/1859; *Zion's Herald*, 6/15/1859.

79. Haven was a minister in Massachusetts who would later be editor of *Zion's Herald* (1867-72) and bishop of the Methodist Episcopal Church (1872-80).

80. "Infant Baptism and Church Membership," *MQR*,1/1859.

81. See *Nashville Christian Advocate*, 9/9/1858, 11/29-1858, 11/29/1860; *Western Christian Advocate*, 9/8 and 9/15/1858, 1/19/1859; *New York Christian Advocate*, 7/15, 8/5, 9/16/1858 and 1/13, 6/30/1859; *Zion's Herald*, 8/17/1859; *MQR*, 4/1859. These publications contained numerous other articles and letters on the subject, especially in the period 1858-61.

82. B. H. Nadal in *The Methodist*, 7/8/1865.

83. *MQRS*, 1/1859.

84. For examples, see *Nashville Christian Advocate*, 1847-1853.

85. 7/21/1864.

86. *Zion's Herald*, 8/28/1859; *Western Christian Advocate*, 9/15/1858.

87. *New York Christian Advocate*, 2/16/1865.

88. *Nashville Christian Advocate*, 9/1/1853.

89. See Rosser, *Baptism*, pp. 380-81; *Zion's Herald*, 2/18/1857 and 6/15/1859; *Nashville Christian Advocate*, 3/19/1847.

90. *New York Christian Advocate*, 9/23/1858. See also *Zion's Herald*, 7/13 and 11/30/1859.

91. McClintock (1814-70) was a well known clergyman, writer and educator who served as editor of the *MQR* from 1848 to 1856.

Olin (1797-1851), an outspoken advocate of theological education, served as president of Randolph Macon College and later of Wesleyan University in Connecticut.

92. Stephen Olin, *Works*, 2 vols. (New York: Harper and Brothers, 1852), 1:184 and *Life and Letters*, 2 vols. (New York: Harper and Brothers, 1853), 2:407-8, 392. George R. Crooks, *Life and Letters of the Rev. John M'Clintock, DD, LLD* (New York: Nelson and Phillips, Cincinnati: Hitchcock and Walden, 1876), p. 201.

Congregationalist pastor Horace Bushnell (1802-76) published *Christian Nurture* in 1847. Often cited as among the most influential American books, *Christian Nurture* criticized the reliance on revivalism to convert sinners and urged instead much more stress on Christian education of children.

93. Hibbard (1811-95) was a New York clergyman, best known as an editor and author.

94. *The Religion of Childhood; or, Children in Their Relation to Native Depravity, to the Atonement, to the Family, and to the Church* (Cincinnati: Poe and Hitchcock, 1864).

95. *MQR*, 10/1859.

96. *Christian Baptism*, pp. 6, 296.

97. *Religion of Childhood*, pp. 3-4.

98. Ibid., p. 204.

99. *New York Christian Advocate*, 6/23/1864.

100. See Summers, *Baptism*, pp. 160–1; *MQR*, 1/1861.

101. *MQRS* 1/1861.

102. Mercein in *MQR*, 1/1855.

103. *Nashville Christian Advocate*, 9/30/1852.

104. See *Zion's Herald*, 4/29/1846; *Nashville Christian Advocate*, 8/18/1848, 10/7 and 10/14/1852, 4/5 and 5/17/1855; *New York Christian Advocate*, 8/2 through 9/27/1855; *MQR*, 1/1854 and 1/1855.

105. *Western Christian Advocate*, 8/13/1856.

106. *Journal of the General Conference, 1856*, pp. 133–34.

107. *Journal of the General Conference, 1864*, pp. 202–3.

108. *Discipline*, 1864, pp. 37n., 145–49.

109. *Discipline*, 1856, MEC South, p. 102.

110. *Discipline*, 1858, MEC South, p. 117.

111. *Discipline*, 1866, MEC South, pp. 328–31.

112. The term "confirm" does not appear in a Methodist ritual until 1932.

113. For examples see *North Carolina Christian Advocate*, 5/7/1857; *MQRS*, 1/1861.

114. Bangs (1778–1862) was agent of the Book Concern, founder of the Methodist Missionary Society, editor of the *Methodist Magazine* and the *New York Christian Advocate*, and author of a four volume history of early American Methodism. See Bangs, *An Original Church of Christ* (New York: T. Mason and G. Lane, 1837), p. 322 and *New York Christian Advocate*, 11/7/1834.

115. See *MQRS*, 10/1860, pp. 512–15, which contained this proposal, buttressed by a long, sentimental poem entitled "The Children of the Lord's Supper"—translated by Longfellow from the Swedish author Bishop Tegner.

116. Thomas A. Morris, *Sermons*, p. 246.

117. See Shaffer, *Treatise*, pp. 84–85.

118. *Zion's Herald*, 11/5/1862 and 10/5/1859; Abbey, "Demonstrations," p. 65; *Nashville Christian Advocate*, 7/22/1852, 2/8 and 5/17/1855.

119. *MQR*, 1/1859, pp. 19–20.

120. Rosser, *Baptism*, pp. 388–89. See also *New York Christian Advocate*, 6/30/1859.

121. Summers, *Baptism*, pp. 149–50. See also P. Douglas Gorrie, *Episcopal Methodism, as It Was and Is* (Auburn: Derby and Miller, 1852), p. 171.

122. Morris, *Sermons*, p. 243. See also Gorrie, *Episcopal Methodism*, p. 173; *Nashville Christian Advocate*, 8/5/1852, 2/17/1859, 4/12 and 4/26/1860; Jimeson, *Notes*, p. 272; Moses M. Henkle, *Primary Platform of Methodism; or, Exposition of the General Rules* (Louisville: Southern Methodist Book Concern, 1853), p. 55. An exceptional view was expressed by Boston clergyman James Porter in his *Compendium of Methodism*, p. 426: "Though we occasionally receive one on trial as a *seeker*, we have never known such baptized before being converted. . . ."

123. See Brownlow, *Great Iron Wheel Examined*, pp. 219/21; Fisher, *Christian Sacraments*, pp. 81–84; *Western Christian Advocate*, 1/12/1859; Summers, *Baptism*, p. 213.

124. For examples see *Nashville Christian Advocate*, 9/3/1847 3/3 and 10/6/1848; *North Carolina Christian Advocate*, 11/7/1856.

125. *Nashville Christian Advocate*, 3/24/1848.

126. In John Wesley's "The Rules of the United Societies"—usually referred to as the General Rules—he stated that, "There is one only condition previously required in those who desire admission into these societies—'a desire to flee from the wrath to come, to be saved from their sins.'" The rules went on to specify the "fruits" expected to be evident in the lives of society members. Outler, *Wesley*, pp. 177-80.

127. *Discipline*, MEC, South, p. 329.

128. See *Western Christian Advocate*, 1/28, 3/3 and 11/15/1848 and series of articles throughout 1854.

129. *Discipline*, MEC, p. 84.

130. *Western Christian Advocate*, 4/19, 5/3, 11/15 and 11/29/1848. See also Stephen R. Beggs, *Pages from the Early History of the West and Northwest* (Cincinnati: Methodist Book Concern, 1868), pp. 301-3.

131. *Western Christian Advocate*, 6/28/1848.

132. *Zion's Herald*, 8/18 and 9/22/1847; *MQR*, 10/1864.

133. *New York Christian Advocate*, 1/16/1848, 9/22/1860 and 4/20/1854.

134. *Discipline*, p. 147.

135. Porter, *Compendium*, pp. 290-1; *Zion's Herald*, 9/29/1858.

136. See Ralston, *Elements*, pp. 1005-15 and Doub, "Discourses," pp. 7-76.

137. Fisher, *Christian Sacraments*, p. 112.

138. Hibbard, *Christian Baptism*, pp. 184-89.

139. *MQRS*, 4/1861.

Chapter VI

1. See pp. 80-81.

2. See pp. 47, 61, 84.

3. See p. 82.

4. *Hymnal of the Methodist Episcopal Church, with Tunes* (New York: Phillips and Hunt, 1882).

5. Ibid.

6. Ibid.

7. See pp. 47, 61, 81-82.

8. See pp. 44, 82.

9. *MQRS*, 4/1882.

10. G. W. Hughey, *Baptismal Remission; or, the Design of Christian Baptism* (Cincinnati: Cranston and Stowe, New York: Hunt and Eaton, 1891), p. 2.

11. For examples, see E. P. Buckner, "Baptism Not for Remission of Sins" in R. Hiner, compiler, *Kentucky Conference Pulpit* (Nashville: Publishing House of the Methodist Episcopal Church, South, 1874), pp. 23-59; J. H. Nichols, *Theological Grub-Ax: A Treatise on Infant Baptism* (Nashville: Publish-

ing House of the Methodist Episcopal Church, South, 1908); Z. A. Parker, *The People's Hand-Book* (Nashville: Publishing House of the Methodist Episcopal Church, South, 1893).

12. Representative is Part II of W. B. Godbey, *Baptism: Mode and Design* (Louisville: Kentucky Methodist Publishing Co., 1896).

13. *Nashville Christian Advocate*, 12/19/1889.

14. *New York Christian Advocate*, 5/21/1881; *Christian Neighbor*, 4/10/1873.

15. *Nashville Christian Advocate*, 7/16/1870, 7/5/1873; J. C. Houston, *Sprinkling: Christian Baptism* (New York: Eaton and Mains, 1895), pp. 122-36.

16. *MQR*, 7/1872.

17. *Nashville Christian Advocate*, 2/26/1875.

18. Houston, *Sprinkling*, pp. 235-60; *Nashville Christian Advocate*, various issues in 1896-98. Whitsitt's article on "Baptists" was published in Johnson's, *Universal Cyclopedia*, 1893-97.

19. See *Western Christian Advocate*, 8/25/1869 and *New Orleans Christian Advocate*, 11/1/1877. N. H. Lee devoted an entire book to this subject—*Immersionists against the Bible; or the Babel Builders Confounded*. Edited by Thomas O. Summers (Nashville: Southern Methodist Publishing House, 1881).

20. John Levington, *Scripture Baptism Defended, and Anabaptist Notions Proved to be Anti-Scriptural Novelties* (Chicago: Poe and Hitchcock, 1866); Houston, *Sprinkling*; J. Ditzler, *Baptism* (Nashville: Publishing House of the Methodist Episcopal Church, South, 1898); Godbey, *Baptism*; Parker, *Hand-Book*; J. W. Ellison, "Baptism: The Question Settled" (Nashville: Publishing House of the Methodist Episcopal Church, South, 1889); J. W. Bond, "A Lecture on Infant Baptism and the Mode of Baptism." (Jefferson City: Tribune Printing Co., 1882); William Hewson, "Baptism and Immersion." (Nashville: Publishing House of the Methodist Episcopal Church, South, 1888) are representative.

21. H. M. Ford, "The Baptism of John." (Nashville: Publishing House of the Methodist Episcopal Church, South, 1889), pp. 12-13. See also J. H. Potts, *Pastor and People; or, Methodism in the Field* (New York: Phillips and Hunt, and Cincinnati: Hitchcock and Walden, 1879), pp. 124-25.

22. See Hilary T. Hudson, *The Methodist Armor; or, A Popular Exposition of the Doctrines, Peculiar Usages, and Ecclesiastical Machinery of the Methodist Episcopal Church, South* (Nashville, Dallas, Richmond: Publishing House of the Methodist Episcopal Church, South, 1882), pp. 119ff; Stephen M. Merrill, *Christian Baptism: Its Subjects and Mode* (Cincinnati: Cranston and Stowe, and New York: Phillips and Hunt, 1876), p. 305.

23. See Peter Doub in *North Carolina Christian Advocate*, 12/4/1867; Leonidas L. Hamline, "The Ceremony" in *Works: Sermons* (New York: Carlton and Lanahan, and Cincinnati: Hitchcock and Walden, 1869); Bostwick Hawley, *Manual of Methodism; or, The Doctrines, General Rules, and Usages of the Methodist Episcopal Church, with Scripture Proofs and Explanations* (New York: Carlton and Lanahan, and Cincinnati: Hitchcock and Walden,

1869), pp. 125ff; J. M. Boland, *A Bible View of Baptism* (Nashville: Southern Methodist Publishing House, 1883); D. Stevenson, *Elements of Methodism in a Series of Short Lectures Addressed to One Beginning a Life of Godliness.* Claremont, N. H.: 1879), pp. 82ff.; R. H. Mahon, *The Token of the Covenant, or the Right Use of Baptism* (Nashville: Southern Methodist Publishing House, 1886).

24. Pope's *A Compendium of Christian Theology*, 3 vols. (New York: Phillips and Hunt, and Cincinnati: Walden and Stowe, 1880) replaced the work of Richard Watson on the course of study. It was the standard theological work in the northern church from 1880 through 1896 and in the south from 1882 through 1906. See 3: 322ff. for material on mode of baptism. Miley's *Systematic Theology*, 2 vols. (New York: Hunt and Eaton, 1892–94) was a course requirement from 1892 through 1908. Mode of baptism is discussed in 2:399ff.

25. Miner Raymond, *Systematic Theology*, 3 vols. (Cincinnati: Hitchcock and Walden, 1877–80), 3:305–8. Raymond's work was the first indigenous system of theology to be completed.

26. Buckley, whose influence in ecclesiastical matters was legendary, even upheld the right of trine immersion for those in Dunkard traditions who might request it. See *New York Christian Advocate*, 8/22/1889.

27. *Journal*, 1880, p. 325. This change was made in Chapter 1, Section V of the *Discipline*, which dealt with baptism. The baptismal rituals already spoke of "sprinkle or pour water," or immersion, "if desired." The rituals of the southern church prescribed the same and its *Discipline* contained no comparable section on baptism.

28. See Merrill, *Christian Baptism*, pp. 106ff.

29. This note was first published in the 1872 *Discipline*, p. 39.

30. Alfred Brunson in *New York Christian Advocate*, 5/21/1881.

31. *New York Christian Advocate*, 2/24/1881 and 8/5/1880.

32. Ibid., 10/24/1889 and 8/9/1883. The views of Buckley are of great significance on this issue because his position as editor and his power in the affairs of the church enabled him to wield pervasive influence. The regular section of the *Advocate* which featured questions from readers was rife with inquiries relating to baptism in almost every issue.

33. See Ford, "Baptism of John," pp. 10–13.

34. *New York Christian Advocate*, 6/23/1881.

35. *New York Christian Advocate*, 4/28/1897 and 3/29/1900.

36. Stephen M. Merrill, *A Digest of Methodist Law; or, Helps in the Administration of the Discipline of the Methodist Episcopal Church* (Cincinnati: Cranston and Stowe, and New York: Phillips and Hunt, 1885, revised 1904), p. 281.

37. *Nashville Christian Advocate*, 11/13/1869, 7/29/1871, 12/25/1873.

38. *Christian Neighbor*, 3/28/1878, 10/9/1879, 6/30/1881.

39. *Nashville Christian Advocate*, 10/10/1889.

40. Ibid., 1/2/1869.

41. Ibid., 5/22/1975; *MQRS*, 4/1880 and 7/1880; *New York Christian Advocate*, 8/24/1893; *North Carolina Christian Advocate*, 1/27/1886; N. Doane, *Infant Baptism Briefly Considered* (New York: Nelson and Phillips, and Cincinnati: Hitchcock and Walden, 1875), p. 12.

42. *Nashville Christian Advocate*, 6/5/1875.

43. A cogent presentation of the argument is found in the *North Carolina Christian Advocate*, 7/4/1888.

44. Merrill, *Christian Baptism*, pp. 68–69. See also *North Carolina Christian Advocate*, 4/23 and 10/8/1890; C. W. Miller, *Infant Baptism* (St. Louis: Southwestern Book and Publishing Co., 1872); G. H. Hayes, *Children in Christ; or, the Relation of Children to the Atonement, the Ground of their Right to Christian Baptism* (Cincinnati: Elm Street Publishing Co., 1884).

45. See Doane, *Infant Baptism*, pp. 99–152; *Western Christian Advocate*, 6/30/1897; Boland, *Bible View*, pp. 36–39; Richard J. Cooke, *Christianity and Childhood; or, the Relation of Children to the Church* (Cincinnati: Cranston and Stowe, and New York: Hunt and Eaton, 1891), pp. 1–40.

46. *Zion's Herald*, 11/21/1878. See also R. Abbey, *Christian Cradlehood or, Religion in the Nursery* (Nashville: Southern Methodist Publishing House, 1881). An article in the *North Carolina Christian Advocate*, 8/8/1900, included the advice that even parents who opposed infant baptism should participate in a "Children's Presentation Service" for formal blessing.

47. See *North Carolina Christian Advocate*, 12/10/1890; Mahon, *Token of the Covenant*, pp. 79–86.

48. *New York Christian Advocate*, 12/16/1897.

49. Hudson, *Methodist Armor*, p. 139.

50. Ralston, *Elements*, pp. 149–51; Raymond, *Systematic Theology*, 3:290ff.

51. Miley, *Systematic Theology*, 2:408–9.

52. *Sunday School Magazine*, 1/1883. See also Hawley, *Manual of Methodism*, pp. 135–36.

53. *MQR*, 1/1874; Daniel D. Whedon, *Statements: Theological and Critical.* Collected and edited by J. S. and D. A. Whedon (New York: Phillips and Hunt, and Cincinnati: Cranston and Stowe, 1887), pp. 299–314. See also *Christian Neighbor*, 5/15/1873; John Allen, *Christian Baptism* (Columbia, S.C.: Christian Neighbor Office, 1870), pp. 5–6; Miller, *Infant Baptism*, pp. 76–7; Robert Paine, *Life and Times of McKendree* (Nashville: Publishing House of the Methodist Episcopal Church, South, 1869), pp. 87–88; William Warren, *Introduction* (Cincinnati: Poe and Hitchcock, 1865), pp. 145ff.

54. Doane, *Infant Baptism*, p. 15.

55. *Sunday School Journal*, 2/1895.

56. Merrill, *Christian Baptism*, pp. 23–24. See also Cooke, *Christianity and Childhood*, pp. 101–3; Samuel Regester, *Children and the Church* (Nashville: Southern Methodist Publishing House, 1874), pp. 56–58.

57. See various issues of *Christian Neighbor*, 1869–73; *Baltimore Methodist*, 1888–90, *North Carolina Christian Advocate*, 1878; *Nashville Christian Advocate*, 1870–81.

58. Pp. 88–89 and 66.

59. James Buckley opined that "children that never sinned do not exist except in the imagination, now and then, of a weak or blinded parent." *New York Christian Advocate,* 2/10/1887.

60. *North Carolina Christian Advocate* 9/25 and 10/9/1878, 3/4/1885, 1/3/1900; *Sunday School Teacher,* 5/1867; *New York Christian Advocate,* 5/26/1870. See also George G. Smith, *Childhood and Conversion* (Nashville: Publishing House of the Methodist Episcopal Church, South, Barbee and Smith, Agents, 1891).

61. Cooke, *Christianity and Childhood,* pp. 121–24.

62. *New York Christian Advocate,* 2/13/1873, 7/3/1884, 1/20/1887, 2/18/1897; *Western Christian Advocate,* 2/19/1896; *MQR* 10/1866.

63. *Southern Methodist Recorder,* 4/20/1899.

64. Enoch M. Marvin, *The Doctrinal Integrity of Methodism* (St. Louis: Advocate Publishing House, 1878), pp. 112–17. See also *North Carolina Christian Advocate,* 7/24/1889 and 6/10/1891.

65. *North Carolina Christian Advocate,* 4/8/1868. See also *Sunday School Journal,* 3/1880; *New York Christian Advocate,* 7/28/1887; *Baltimore Methodist,* 11/25/1882.

66. *New Orleans Christian Advocate,* 1/1876 and *MQR,* 7/1900.

67. *Zion's Herald,* 12/28/1898.

68. Regester, *Children and Church,* pp. 68, 111.

69. For examples, see *North Carolina Christian Advocate,* 1886 and 1867; *New Orleans Christian Advocate,* 1880; Hayes, *Children in Christ;* Regester, *Children in Church.*

70. Bond, "A Lecture on Infant Baptism and the Mode of Baptism," pp. 10–11.

71. *New York Christian Advocate,* 12/23/1897 and 10/11/1888.

72. Stevenson, *Elements of Methodism,* pp. 108–9.

73. Matthew Simpson, *Cyclopedia of Methodism* (Philadelphia: Everts and Stewart, 1878), p. 478.

74. 10/28/1869. See also Levington, *Scripture Baptism Defended,* pp. 118–22 and *North Carolina Christian Advocate,* 10/6/1869.

75. *Nashville Christian Advocate,* 6/24 and 7/22/1871. Pierce (1785–1879) was a revered figure in southern Methodism and one of the founders of the Methodist Episcopal Church, South.

76. Ibid., 7/8/1871. McFerrin understood the sacrament to recognize a child's place in the universal church of Christ and not in a particular denomination.

77. Ibid., 8/5/1871.

78. Ibid., 9/9/1871.

79. *New York Christian Advocate,* 11/17/1881, 7/10/1884, 8/19/1886; see also 2/10/1887.

80. *Nashville Christian Advocate,* 7/22/1871 and 9/26/1874; *North Carolina Christian Advocate,* 6/20/1880; *MQRS,* 7/1882.

81. *MQR,* 5/1885.

82. John McClintock and James Strong, eds. *Cyclopedia of Biblical, Theological, and Ecclesiastical Literature,* Volume I (New York: Harper and Brothers, 1869), p. 648.

83. Regester, *Children and Church,* pp. 99–100, 133–47.

84. *MQR* 10/1883. See also Mahon, *Token of the Covenant,* pp. 141–44.

85. *North Carolina Christian Advocate,* 9/5/1883; *Western Christian Advocate,* 4/16/1884.

86. *New York Christian Advocate,* 4/5/1883 and 5/12/1898.

87. See Merrill, *Digest,* p. 42; *New York Christian Advocate,* 7/10/1884.

88. *North Carolina Christian Advocate,* 11/1/1893.

89. Whedon, *Statements,* pp. 316–17. See also *New York Christian Advocate,* 3/29/1866; *North Carolina Christian Advocate,* 3/4/1885; *Western Christian Advocate,* 12/10/1890.

90. 6/14/1879.

91. See *New York Christian Advocate,* 2/2/1866; *Zion's Herald,* 10/17/1872; *Baltimore Methodist,* 11/25/1882 for examples.

92. Regester, *Children and Church,* pp. 148–49.

93. 1866 *Discipline,* Methodist Episcopal Church, South, pp. 147 and 155.

94. *North Carolina Christian Advocate,* 7/24/1878 and *Nashville Christian Advocate,* 1/16/1869. See also *MQRS,* 10/1891 and B. Wistar Morris, *Presbyterian, Baptist and Methodist Testimony to Confirmation* (New York: E. P. Dutton and Co., 1875), pp. 84ff.

95. See *Nashville Christian Advocate,* 4/15/76; *New Orleans Christian Advocate,* 3/18/1880; Cooke, *Christianity and Childhood,* pp. 220–25.

96. *New Orleans Christian Advocate,* 2/26/1880; *Nashville Christian Advocate,* 8/16/1873 and 12/1/1877; *Zion's Herald,* 12/22/1870 and 1/26/1871. There was dispute as to the age at which most children achieved the requisite Christian maturity. Most commentators spoke of a range between the ages of eight and twelve. Abbey, in his influential *Christian Cradlehood,* argued that by the ages of five or six, children comprehended the rite as a way of remembering Jesus; see pp. 249–53.

97. *New York Christian Advocate,* 2/5/1885.

98. *MQR,* 1/1871.

99. *New York Christian Advocate,* 1/26/1873.

100. Pope, *Compendium* 3:321.

101. J. H. Potts in *MQR,* 7/1883. See also Daniel Curry in *New York Christian Advocate,* 1/9/1873 and Merrill, *Digest,* pp. 44–48.

102. *MQR,* 1/1873 and 10/1883; *Statements,* pp. 314–15.

103. *New York Christian Advocate,* 9/9/1880, 7/1/1881, 5/1/1885 are examples. See also S. Olin Garrison, *Probationer's Handbook* (New York: Eaton and Mains, and Cincinnati: Jennings and Pye, 1887), pp. 21–23.

104. *Discipline,* pp. 254–55.

105. Examples can be found throughout the periodical literature; see especially *New Orleans Christian Advocate* in 1874; *Nashville Christian Advocate,* 1877, 1878, 1890, *North Carolina Christian Advocate,* 1885.

106. *New Orleans Christian Advocate*, 1/15, 3/5, 3/12, and 3/19/1874; *Nashville Christian Advocate*, 11/18/1871.

107. *MQRS*, 4/1894. Tillett (1854-1936) was dean of the theological faculty at Vanderbilt.

108. *Nashville Christian Advocate*, 10/17/1874. For similar opinions, see R. L. Abernathy in *North Carolina Christian Advocate*, 4/8/1885 and 8/14/1886.

109. Abbey, *Christian Cradlehood*, pp. 196–203 and *Nashville Christian Advocate*, 5/2/1874. See also Boland, *Bible View of Baptism*, pp. 43–45; *North Carolina Christian Advocate*, 7/18/1877; 1/21, 2/25 and 3/4/1885.

110. *MQRS*, 1/1882 and 1/1884. Record of the practice of the Methodist Episcopal Church, South is found in classbook entries in which persons were designated as "Received into full connexion by baptism." Class members were also classified in terms of "Station in Life"—marital status—and "Station in Grace"—seeker or believer. For examples, see Classbooks of Pleasant Hill, Alabama, Methodist Episcopal Church, South, 1851-79 in Manuscript Collection of Perkins Library, Duke University.

111. Hawley, *Manual of Methodism*, p. 159. See also *North Carolina Christian Advocate*, 11/14/1883 and 3/26/1890.

112. *MQR*, 10/1883.

113. See Raymond, *Systematic Theology*, 3:368–70; Garrison, *Probationer's Handbook*, pp. 21–23; *Nashville Christian Advocate*, 3/11/1876; *New York Christian Advocate*, 5/24/1883 and 10/24/1884.

114. *New Orleans Christian Advocate*, 5/3/1900. In contrast to episcopal Methodism, the Methodist Protestant Church was unequivocal in its position on rebaptism. At approximately the same time as the MEC prohibition which was later revoked, the following rubric was added to the Methodist Protestant baptismal ritual: "This Church disapproves of re-baptism." This statement was retained until the reunion with the MEC and MEC,S in 1939.

Chapter VII

1. George W. Hughey, *The Scriptural Mode of Baptism* (Kansas City: Hudson Press, 1907), p. 9.

2. *Daily Christian Advocate*, 1900, p. 81.

3. Ibid., p. 88.

4. Sermon by J. A. Faulkner of Drew Theological School, in *MQR*, 1/1910, p. 10.

5. R. L. Harford, *An Itinerant's Portfolio: Sermons, Lectures, and Miscellany* (San Francisco: H. G. Parsons and Co., 1885), p. 280.

6. *The Methodist Hymnal* (New York: Eaton and Mains and Cincinnati: Jennings and Graham, 1905).

7. *Daily Christian Advocate*, MEC, South, 1914, p. 82.

8. Harrison, *The Articles of Religion*, p. 200; also *Sunday School Journal for Teachers*, 7/13/1919; DuBose, *The Symbol of Methodism*, pp. 198–99; *MQR,S*, 4/1928, p. 322.

9. See *The Standard Catechism* (New York and Nashville: Abingdon, 1905) and Wheeler, *History of the Exposition of the Twenty-five Articles*, p. 304.

10. See *MQRS*, 10/1911, p. 641 and 10/1921, p. 713. This position is explicated at length in Olin Alfred Curtis, *The Christian Faith Reasonably Given in a System of Doctrine* (New York and Cincinnati: The Methodist Book Concern, 1905); Isaac L. Peebles, *Falling from Grace and Baptism* (Nashville and Dallas: Publishing House of the Methodist Episcopal Church, South, 1905); E. B. Chappell, *The Church and its Sacraments* (Nashville, Dallas, Richmond, San Francisco: Publishing House of the Methodist Episcopal Church, South; Lamar and Whitmore, Agents, 1921).

11. J. C. Carter, *Plain Words for Plain People on the Mode of Baptism* (Nashville: Publishing House of the Methodist Episcopal Church, South, 1907), p. 43; Hughey, *Scriptural Mode*, pp. 284; C. T. Thrift, *Why John the Baptist Sprinkled the Multitudes at the River Jordan* (Clayton, N.C.: C. T. Thrift, 1921), pp. 12–16. By contrast, Francis J. McConnell writing in the *Sunday School Journal for Teachers*, 3/10/1929 stated: "There is something wonderfully stimulating in Paul's reference to being buried with Christ in baptism and rising with him in resurrection. The reference here must be to an immersion." McConnell went on to make clear that he was not contending for immersion as the only acceptable mode.

12. Edmund B. Fairfield, *Letters on Baptism* (Boston and Chicago: The Pilgrim Press, 1893). This kind of argument still tended to expand into anti-Baptist polemic reminiscent of an earlier era. For examples, see John Durrett, *Baptism According to the Scriptures* (Nashville: Publishing House of the Methodist Episcopal Church, South, 1923); J. E. Mahaffey, *The Bible Mode of Baptism* (Columbia, S.C.: The State Co., 1910); W. A. Swift, "Why Baptize by Pouring and Baptize Babies?" (Methodist Publishing House, n.d.).

13. *Sunday School Journal*, 4/1916, pp. 250–51. An interesting sidelight on the discussion about mode of baptism is found in the report of the Standing Committee on Judiciary to the General Conference of the MEC in 1908 (first issued in 1906). The report states that there is no law in the *Discipline* on the subject of trine baptism, "but because of its association with high ritualistic practices, we advise that it not be practiced among us, especially where the form used is immersion." *Journal*, p. 485.

14. Writing in the *Sunday School Journal*, Volume 36, p. 842, in 1904, J. T. McFarland proudly identified himself as the person who had introduced the amendment passed by the 1896 General Conference which eliminated the footnote opposing rebaptism. He argued that, as a result of that action, any person dissatisfied with infant baptism may be "rebaptized" and that pastors were free to do as they chose on the matter,

15. Charles L. Brooks, *All About Infant Baptism* (Nashville: Publishing House of the Methodist Episcopal Church, South, 1923), p. 25. See also Mahaffey, *Bible Mode*, pp. 135ff; Hudson, *Methodist Armor*, pp. 39ff.; *MQRS*, 10/1930, p. 666; and Chappell, *Church and Sacraments*.

16. Harmon, *Rites and Rituals*, p. 163.

17. Curtis, *Christian Faith*, pp. 437-38. A similar position was averred by Albert C. Knudson, *The Doctrine of Redemption*, (Nashville and New York: Abingdon, 1933), pp. 461f.

18. *Sunday School Journal*, 3/10/1929. The extreme of this position is seen in the contention of F. B. McCall that even those who oppose infant baptism should practice a "Children's Presentation Service" for the formal blessing of a child. *North Carolina Christian Advocate*, 8/8/1900.

19. *Sunday School Journal*, 6/1910.

20. DuBose, *Symbol of Methodism*, p. 199.

21. Numerous issues of the *Sunday School Journal* present these ideas; see especially 7/1907, 11/1907, 12/1908, 2/1911. Also see *MQRS*, 1/1924, p. 188. A major influence here was James Atkins who was Sunday School Editor of the MEC,S and later bishop; he was the author of *The Kingdom in the Cradle* (Nashville and Dallas: Publishing House of the Methodist Episcopal Church, South, 1905).

22. Wilbur F. Packard, "Infant Baptism, Reasonable, Scriptural, Ancient and Apostolic." (Houston: 1913), pp. 9-10. This publication was a pamphlet to be given to the mothers of baptized infants; it contained a baptismal certificate for the child.

23. These ideas permeate the church periodicals of the time. For examples, see *North Carolina Christian Advocate*, 1/3/1899; *Western Christian Advocate*, 3/28/1900; *MQR*, 7/1901; *Sunday School Journal*, 1904, p. 842; *MQRS*, 7/1926.

24. *MQRS*, 7/1913, p. 522.

25. *Sunday School Journal*, 8/1912.

26. (New York: Eaton and Mains, Cincinnati: Jennings and Pye, 1903).

27. *MQR*, 3/1901, pp. 17-25. See also William Henry Burns, *Crisis in Methodism* (Chicago and Boston: The Christian Witness Co., 1909), pp. 17-25.

28. See Carl Knudson, "Are Conversions Coming Back?," *MQR*, 7/1924, pp. 511ff.

29. Frank S. Hickman, edited by E. B. Chappell, *Can Religion Be Taught? Evangelical Religion Faces the Question* (Nashville: Cokesbury Press, 1929),pp. 29-34. See also *Sunday School Journal*, 12/1909, p. 881; *MQR*, 7/1900, pp. 524ff. and 5/1901, pp. 465f.

30. Bishop Edwin D. Mouzon quoted in *MQRS*, 7/1929, p. 394.

31. (New York and Cincinnati: Methodist Book Concern, 1921), p. 13.

32. This concern was expressed in almost every issue of the *Sunday School Journal*. It was also a major emphasis of Charles Brooks, *All About Infant Baptism* and E. B. Chappell, *Evangelism in the Sunday School*. Good examples of the contentions were in *MQR*, 7/1901, p. 631ff.; 7/1903, p. 634; 5/1927, pp. 406ff.

33. *Sunday School Journal*, 1905, p. 10.

34. Atkins, *Kingdom in the Cradle*, p. 151.

35. *Sunday School Journal*, 11/1905, p. 806.

36. *Sunday School Journal*, 1/1911, p. 6.

37. *Church School Journal* (formerly *Sunday School Journal*), throughout the period, especially 8/1933, p. 451 and 3/1934, p. 125.

38. Atkins, *Kingdom in the Cradle*, pp. 261f.; Hudson, *Methodist Armor*, pp. 211–219; Eltzholtz, *The Child*, pp. 20f. L. F. Sensabaugh writing in *MQRS* (7/1929, p. 394) even suggested a series of four ceremonies–first at the baptism of an infant, another at the "junior period," a third at middle adolescence, and another at young adulthood.

39. See *Disciplines*, Methodist Episcopal Church, 1900–36, especially rituals and section on Membership.

40. See *Disciplines*, Methodist Episcopal Church, South, 1902–38, especially rituals and sections on Membership.

41. See 1939 *Discipline* of The Methodist Church.

42. See *Disciplines*, MEC 1900–366; MEC,S 1902–38; and MC 1939.

43. See *Disciplines*, MEC, 1900–36.

44. For examples of the wide discussion which this issue engendered see William H. Shipman, *The Doctrinal Test* (New York and Cincinnati: Methodist Book Concern, 1922); Hudson, *Methodist Armor*, pp. 199–210; *MQR*, 1/1912, pp. 81ff: 7/1922, pp. 542ff. and 564f.; 11/1922, pp. 942ff.

45. See various issues of *The Sunday School Journal*, (title changed to *The Church School Journal* in 1926);also, Henry C. Sheldon, *System of Christian Doctrine* (New York: Eaton and Mains and Cincinnati: Jennings and Graham, 1903), pp. 520ff.

46. *Religion in Life*, Vol. 20, p. 255.

47. *The Book of Hymns: Official Hymnal of The United Methodist Church* (Nashville: The United Methodist Publishing House, 1964).

48. *Proposed Revisions of the Book of Worship* (Nashville: The United Methodist Publishing House, 1960), pp. 18f.

49. *Daily Christian Advocate*, 1964, p. 581.

50. Ibid.

51. Robert W. Goodloe, *The Sacraments in Methodism* (Nashville and New York: The Methodist Publishing House, 1953), pp. 105–6.

52. Ibid., p. 113.

53. See Goodloe, p. 101.

54. *New Christian Advocate*, 6/1958, p. 18.

55. Ibid., p. 19.

56. Ibid., pp. 21–22.

57. *Daily Christian Advocate*, April 18, 1960, p. 37.

58. *Adult Student*, 12/1961.

59. *New Christian Advocate*, 6/1958, p. 21.

60. Poem by Lois F. Pasley in *The Christian Home*, 2/1950, p. 64.

61. John M. Moore, *Methodism in Belief and Action* (New York and Nashville: Abingdon-Cokesbury Press, 1946), p. 156.

62. Ibid., p. 170.

63. Harris Franklin Rall, *The Christian Faith and Way* (New York and Nashville: Abingdon-Cokesbury, 1947), pp. 70–72, and L. Harold DeWolf,

A Theology of the Living Church (New York: Harper and Bros., 1953), pp. 337–40.

64. Clinton M. Cherry, *The Beliefs of a Methodist Christian* (Nashville: Tidings, 1952), pp. 67–68.

65. Goodloe, *Sacraments*, p. 122.

66. For examples see "A Hallowed Time . . . ," John W. Cook and "A Sacred Moment—a Focal Point," W. Neill Hart in *The Christian Home*, 10/1957; "For of Such Is the Kingdom," in *Together: The Midmonth Magazine for Methodist Families*, 4/1959; "Infant Baptism: Dedication," Harrison B. Thompson in *Christian Advocate*, 5/24/1962; "The Heresy of Private Baptism," Charles Keysor in *Christian Advocate*, 11/14/1965; "Baptism Is Also Covenantal," David K. Switzer in *Christian Advocate*, 6/16/1966 and "Put Adults Back in Infant Baptism," Robert W. Zeuner in *Christian Advocate*, 6/13/1968.

67. "Each New Creation" in *The Christian Home*, 3/1963.

68. "What Is a Sacrament?," Edward D. Staples in *The Christian Home*, 12/1967, p. 10.

69. Ibid., p. 11.

70. Article XVII.—'Of Baptism'—ends with this sentence: "The baptism of young children is to be retained in the church." The First Restrictive Rule (*Discipline* para. 16) states: "The General Conference shall not revoke, alter, or change our Articles of Religion or establish any new standards or rules of doctrine contrary to our present existing and established standards of doctrine." Paragraph 127 of the *Discipline* stipulates: "We hold that all children, by virtue of the unconditional benefits of the atonement, are members of the family of God, and are therefore graciously entitled to Baptism. It shall be the duty of the pastor of every charge earnestly to exhort parents and guardians within his constituency to dedicate their children to the Lord in Baptism, as early as practicable. . . ."

71. Decision 142 in *Decisions of the Judicial Council of The Methodist Church, Nos. 1–175, 1940–60* (Methodist Publishing House), pp. 329–31.

72. *Discipline*, Evangelical United Brethren Church, 1963, pp. 432–33.

73. *Discipline of the Church of the United Brethren in Christ, 1945–1949* (Dayton, Ohio: The Otterbein Press, 1945), pp. 251–52.

74. T. Leo Brannon, 3/1963, p. 10.

75. *Christian Advocate*, 11/5/1964.

76. *New Christian Advocate*, 6/1958, pp. 20, 22.

77. *Proposed Revisions for the Book of Worship*, 1960, pp. 19–20.

78. *Adult Student*, 5/1963, pp. 12–15.

79. *Methodist Teacher–Nursery*, Spring 1967, p. 91.

80. *Daily Christian Advocate*, 1964, pp. 586–87.

81. *Christian Advocate*, 12/26/1968, pp. 13–14.

82. Goodloe, *Sacraments*, p. 117.

83. Ibid., p. 118.

84. Ibid.

85. Ibid., pp. 124–25.

86. For examples see C. A. Bowen, *Child and Church: A History of Methodist Church-School Curriculum* (New York and Nashville: Abingdon Press, 1960), pp. 243-47; *Child Guidance in Christian Living*, 3/1962, p. 10 and 5/1962, pp. 4-5; *Methodist Teacher*, Summer 1968, pp. 6-7.

87. See Richard L. Ownbey, *Evangelism in Christian Education*, edited by Lucius H. Bugbee and C. A. Bowen (Nashville: Abingdon-Cokesbury Press, 1941), p. 91 and Goodloe, *Sacraments*, p. 115 for examples.

88. *Daily Christian Advocate*, 1964, p. 566.

89. See various issues of *The Christian Home* and *Church School Magazine* for the period, especially *Church School Magazine* 1/1943, p. 7 and 3/1943, p. 132. The latter lists recently published materials available for use in such training.

90. *Church School Magazine*, 3/1942, p. 324; see also 1/1943, pp. 17-18.

91. *Church School Magazine*, 6/1947, p. 29.

92. *New Christian Advocate*, 6/1958, p. 20.

93. *Proposed Revision of the Book of Worship*, 1960, pp. 26-27.

94. *Daily Christian Advocate*, 1964, pp. 581-82.

95. *Daily Christian Advocate*, 1964, pp. 587-88 and *Journal of the 1964 General Conference*, pp. 616-17.

96. *Daily Christian Advocate*, 1964, p. 586.

Chapter VIII

1. Illustrative of this ambiguity was the statement in Article VII "Of the Sacraments" in the United Brethren Confession of Faith: "Also the Baptism of the children shall be left to the judgment of believing parents." This sentence appeared from the nineteenth century until the development of a new Confession of Faith by the Evangelical United Brethren in the early 1960s. The Evangelical Church's Confession of Faith contained no equivalent.

2. William F. Dunkle, Jr. and Joseph D. Quillan, Jr., *Companion to the Book of Worship* (Nashville and New York: Abingdon Press, 1970), p. 50.

3. Ted A. Campbell, "Baptism and New Birth: Evangelical Theology and the United Methodist 'Baptismal Covenant I'," in *Quarterly Review*, Fall 1990, p. 42. See this article for a lucid presentation of some concerns from the evangelical perspective.

4. *Companion to the Book of Worship*, pp. 46-47.

5. William H. Willimon, *Remember Who You Are: Baptism, A Model for Christian Life* (Nashville: The Upper Room, 1980); Laurence Hull Stookey, *Baptism: Christ's Act in the Church* (Nashville: Abingdon, 1982); James F. White, *Sacraments as God's Self Giving* (Nashville: Abingdon, 1983).

6. For examples see *Good News Magazine*, July-August 1989, pp. 19ff; September-October 1989, pp. 21ff; November-December 1989, p. 4.

7. *Journal of the 1972 General Conference*, p. 1665.

8. See *Circuit Rider*, 1/1980, p. 5.

9. Page 5.

10. Nolan B. Harmon, Jr., ed. *The Encyclopedia of World Methodism*, 2 vols. (Nashville: United Methodist Publishing House, 1974), p. 220.

11. *Formal Response of UMC to BEM*, p. 6.

12. *Worship*, 1/1977, p. 45.

13. Retitled *By Water and the Spirit: A Study of Baptism for United Methodists* (Nashville: The United Methodist Publishing House, forthcoming 1993).

Conclusion

1. *Sermons*, p. 172.

2. *Discipline*, 1988, para. 221.

3. One salient illustration of this confusion can be found in the *Invitation* Sunday School series for elementary students for September 9, 1990, in which dedication and baptism are discussed with no distinction being made between them and the sole scriptural reference is the story of Hannah's giving of Samuel to the service of God at Shiloh.

4. See the significant findings of a recent major study in six denominations reported in *Effective Christian Education: A National Study of Protestant Congregations* (Minneapolis: Search Institute, 1990).

INDEX